BYRON'S NEW HOME COOKING

110 RECIPES FOR BUSY COOKS WITH DEMANDING PALETTES

Byron Ayanoglu

VIKING

VIKING

Published by the Penguin Group

Penguin Books Canada Ltd, 10 Alcorn Avenue, Toronto, Ontario, Canada M4V 3B2

Penguin Books Ltd, 27 Wrights Lane, London W8 5TZ, England

Viking Penguin, a division of Penguin Books USA Inc., 375 Hudson Street, New York,
    New York 10014, USA

Penguin Books Australia Ltd, Ringwood, Victoria, Australia

Penguin Books (NZ) Ltd, 182-190 Wairau Road, Auckland 10, New Zealand

Penguin Books Ltd, Registered Offices: Harmondsworth, Middlesex, England

First published 1993

10 9 8 7 6 5 4 3 2 1

Printed and bound in Canada on acid free paper ∞
Text design: Counterpunch/David Vereschagin
Illustrations: Nick Vitacco
Cover calligraphy: Kathryn Adams

Canadian Cataloguing in Publication Data

Ayanoglu, Byron
    Byron's new home cooking

Includes index.
ISBN 0-670-84749-6

1. Cookery. 2. Menus. I. Title

TX714.A93 1993   641.5   C92-095658-0

For my mother,
Despina Ayanoglu,
whose home cooking was
my first taste of greatness;
and for my partner, Algis Kemezys
without whose help and
encouragement this cookbook
would have never been written

A big thank-you to Martha Reilly,
who punched the whole thing into a computer,
so that I wouldn't have to;
and multiple thanks to my friends
who shared their recipes with me:

Aristedes (of Viva, Toronto)
Jack Blum
Kenny Brudner
Sharon Corder
Greg Couillard (of Notorious, Toronto)
Charlotte Dix
Jeff Dueck (of Bistro 990, Toronto)
David Gibbons
Wrenn Goodrum
Tom Hanes
Brian Mathot
Kamala McCarthy
Marion Medad
Meenakshi
Margie and Michael Pagliaro (of Barolo
Ristorante, Toronto)
Judi Roe
Leo Schipani (of Sisi Trattoria, Toronto)
Stephen J. Stafford (of Manoir Hovey, Quebec)
Luis Suarez (of Tapas Bar, Toronto)
Jane Sutherland
Wandee Young (of Young Thailand, Toronto)

Contents

The discovery of a new dish
does more for human happiness
than the discovery of a star

Jean Anthelme Brillat-Savarin

Byron's New Home Cooking

Introduction

Twenty-five years of involvement in the food business has taught me one thing above all else: food tastes and nourishes best when it has been prepared by a happy chef. And chefs, like all of us, are happiest when they're having fun. Fun in the kitchen comes from a love of food and from know-how. We all love food: that is a given. As for the know-how, well, that's what this book is all about.

I address myself to my countless fellow-sufferers who work hard in the marketplace and deserve a good supper, without necessarily having to find it in a restaurant. "Eating in" offers great benefits. Avoiding the cost of a restaurant meal (always a headache) is one consideration. The opportunity to relax at home and unwind with the family is just as important. The value of exercising total control over what goes into one's food – whether "kitchen happiness" or simply healthy ingredients – is by far the best benefit of all.

To achieve kitchen happiness – to have fun cooking to get that knack and know-how – can seem an unscalable mountain at first. There is a huge store of mystique and folklore concerning the perils of the kitchen, most of it ludicrous. It's time to demystify that notion. In fact, cooking

is just like bike-riding: anyone can do it.

One rumour has a grain of truth to it: good cooking takes time. Some dishes, especially those derived from ancient, courtly cultures, can take a day or two to complete. I say, let's enjoy those on special occasions, preferably in restaurants. This book will concentrate on more modern cooking techniques that can be carried out quickly. Happily, these also permit the flavours and textures of the ingredients to shine through.

I learned to improvise and simplify from my very first moment in a kitchen. I was 21, and had just graduated from McGill University. It was the late '60s, a time for alternate lifestyles and educational reform. Six friends and I had secured lots of grant money for an experimental summer college of the arts – an Age-of-Aquarius Oxbridge clone featuring one-on-one contact with professors and tutors, and co-ed communal living.

As an administrator-founder of a 150-student college, with a full arts curriculum and several residences, I was expected to teach a tutorial (I gave a course on Comedy), and also to take charge of one household duty. Eschewing such tedious tasks as accounting, heading clean-up crews, and sweating out public relations with McGill, I opted for the kitchens. I had never cooked much more than eggs, but I had sure eaten a lot, and had the girth to prove it. No one dared question my credentials, and so I assumed a huge budget, along with the daunting responsibility of feeding an army of mini-gourmets (Montrealers of all ages and persuasions like to eat well).

Whip in hand (to tame unwilling kitchen help), I broke all the rules that summer. I had few disasters, and when I had my triumphs, I got resoundingly blissful belches from the collective gullet of my satisfied constituency. I was doing so well that word spread: every night I served 30 or 40 total strangers from the area, and charged them a pretty penny, too.

My secret was a lack of time. It was an endlessly sunny summer that year, and our college was a rollicking, non-stop party (as might be expected from a bunch of young people with money and power). No one, least of all me, wished to spend longer than minimum on chores. As a result, I undercooked everything, and concocted sauces that were ready in half an hour, instead of the traditional two or three hours. I borrowed from the Chinese and the Mediterraneans, stir-frying and sauteing instead of stewing. I sizzled things in a hurry, and for fun, I used *bunches* of herbs: I never sprinkled.

I've cooked in a million different situations since that summer, but for one reason or another, I've rarely had a leisurely gig. I seem condemned always to cook in a hurry, and of necessity I've become an expert at it. During my playwrighting apprenticeship in London and New York, for example, I supported my writing by working as a kitchen temporary. Just like temps in other professions, I got assignments to walk into strange workplaces and get right to work.

By the time I had moved from London to New York in the mid '70s, I had graduated into the position of temporary chef (as opposed to "cook"), which meant walking into famous/rich people's kitchens and creating super-gourmet meals under equally rushed conditions. The stakes were higher, but the time was just as short. Never one to be intimidated, I simply adapted. (As one of my eventual clients and fans, Maureen Stapleton, declared, "Byron has flair.") I compensated for the lack of labour-intensive/time-consuming frills with unusual flavour combinations and intoxicatingly moist textures.

One of the deepest mysteries of food is simply water. Plain old h-two-oh. All foods contain it, and all of them, from a chicken breast to an asparagus, owe their textures to it. The difference between a moist, springy chicken breast and a stringy, chewy one is the amount of water it has managed to retain during cooking. The same is true of a crisp, nutty asparagus spear versus a limp, mushy one.

Heat, the prime element of all cooking, does its job by robbing water from food. A certain amount of this dehydration is desirable. Raw ingredients are "raw" exactly because they contain too much water. The trick is to burn off some of that water without taking all of it. This is just another way of saying "undercook everything."

The masters of undercooking are the Chinese. They have for millennia flash-cooked their foods in red-hot woks, stir-frying for a couple of minutes in boiling oil. It was Chinese food that gave me bouquets of inspiration. It was also Chinese food that persuaded my highest-profile employer.

"Mick Jagger," said my agent (oh yes, in New York, even temporary chefs have agents). She gave me an address and a time. "And he eats Chinese!" she added. (This was in 1977; I hear that he has switched to Japanese since then.) I decided to treat this assignment of cooking for the Most Rolling Stone seriously. I immediately knew that success with this super-real person could turn out to be an important credit for the rest of my life. I invested time in research: I looked for a good cookbook.

The very best Chinese cookery book that I have ever read is *Mrs. Chiang's Szechwan Cookbook*. Armed with its many excellent recipes, most of which I had never tested, and several bags of groceries from Canal Street, I boarded a bus from 8th Avenue for Woodstock, New York. There, in an isolated house-cum-recording-studio, Mick and Jerry Hall were spending the weekend prior to starting rehearsals with the whole band for the tour of *Some Girls*.

Details of breakfasts in bed for rock 'n' roll's royal couple (the time when I was gazing out into the misty Catskills woods, and a voice behind me said "howdy pardner," and I turned to look at Mick Jagger in his bathrobe with his hair all tousled and no shoes on his feet) will have to be reserved for my tell-all autobiography. What I can reveal here is that my Chinese cooking that weekend was "some of the best I've ever eaten, even though you're not Chinese" (Mick Jagger), and that my brief but colourful stint as his chef did indeed prove a passport to a lucrative career.

Once back in Montreal, my Mick Jagger resume-item opened the way to a wealth of opportunities, including Chez Byron, my restaurant, as well as a ten-year stint doing "lunch" catering for the fast-and-furious, "tax-shelter" movie industry of the late '70s and early '80s.

Movie-lunch catering is a specifically defined job. It's meant to provide a proper meal break in the middle of a shooting day to a crew making a movie "on location." This might mean 9 a.m. to 5 p.m., or 9 p.m. to 5 a.m. Location crews can number anywhere from 70 persons to 250, and the "location" can range from a mountaintop to a dusty warehouse in an abandoned part of town. Cinematographic unions demand that a crew, which has no nearby restaurants available, be fed a good, hot meal wherever they are shooting. Meanwhile, producers of the movie demand that the same lunch be served as quickly as possible: in the movie business, like in any business, time is money.

Starting with my first project (Richard Harris's *Your Ticket Is No Longer Valid*), I proved that I could be relied upon to try any crazy thing, and to do it fast. I quickly became known for my daring catering capers, and was hired (at justifiably inflated prices) for the "difficult" projects, i.e. as far away from civilization as possible.

When I cater a movie, I arrive with mobile equipment, which I set up in tents and day-rented halls, and pretend that the whole thing is a big party for gourmet friends. I make the kind of food I like to eat myself, and substitute imagination for whatever ingredient (and/or time) that might be lacking. I strive for home-cooked meals of fine texture and taste. I have catered in a tiny fishing village on Newfoundland's Buena Vista Cape. I nearly killed myself delivering lunch from my kitchen on Mont Tremblant, Quebec to locations deep inside a provincial park in skiing country. And I met my greatest challenge in distant Louiseville, Quebec, where I had to rush (two hours daily each way) to feed the Italian and Canadian crews, as well as the stars, of Sergio Leone's *Once Upon A Time In America*.

The degree of difficulty on that picture was being able to satisfy the high-class cravings of Leone and his world-famous cast, while cooking two completely different sets of lunches: one for the Canadians and a separate one, totally of Italian food, for the Italians, who apparently wither and die unless they can have Italian food every day of their lives. My efforts were rewarded by the ransom-like prices I was charging, and the priceless kudos of the chief star, Robert DeNiro, who declared me "the best movie caterer, bar none."

I worked sixteen to twenty hours a day (seven days a week for six to eight weeks) on those projects, but the actual time I could devote to cooking, amidst all the hullabaloo, never amounted to more than two or three hours per meal. Nevertheless, I never offered less than a ten-item menu, and I made everyone happy with the same old trick of undercooked, texture-rich foods with lovely sauces. In a way, I never really outgrew the frenetic conditions of that original gig from my summer college at McGill. I simply improved on it.

I have never stopped catering ("old caterers don't die; they just train better sous-chefs"), but for the last seven years I've spent most of my food-time at restaurant tables. I have become a professional eater, reviewing restaurants for Toronto's *NOW Magazine.* Fortunately for me and my palate, many of our best chefs have also looked to Asia and to the Mediterranean for inspiration in intense flavours and healthy cooking.

I am happy that the grill and the saute pan have replaced the oven, the deep-frier, and the stew pot as the principal conductors of heat to foodstuffs. This is my kind of modern: it means fresher taste and easier digestion.

These delightful eating thrills can be easily and inexpensively recreated at home with a minimum of fuss and much enjoyment, providing (a) you are not afraid of handling the raw materials for a good meal, (b) you are willing to get organized and stick to a (flexible) schedule, and (c) you are open to the wonderful world of cooking.

In the old days, putting food on the table was a full-time job. Now, it can take less than one hour per supper, as long as you are able to devote three to four hours once every two weekends to prepare freezable/storable essentials. You'll also need to schedule a monthly shopping expedition for restocking the larder with some hard-to-find gourmet ingredients.

The monthly shopping list includes such delicacies as extra-virgin olive oil, sun-dried tomatoes, capers, vinegars, Oriental sauces and condiments, packaged pastas, special, long-life cheeses, multicultural specialties (like Greek filo dough and Japanese wasabe radish), pine nuts, olives, exotic raisins, other dried fruits, tahini, imported chilies, anchovies and aromatic oils, alongside such mundane items as sugars, flours, beans, grains and ordinary spices and condiments.

The bi-weekly cooking sessions vary with the seasons. In the fall, during the profusion of fresh, local produce, you owe it to yourself to preserve and pickle some of your favourites. Be it basil in pesto, jalapeno peppers in brine, or tomatoes concasse, all of us adore opening a Mason jar full of last harvest's bounty during the sterile months of winter.

On the other hand, any time of year will do for a messy, but amusing, hour of cutting butter into flour for a flaky crust that freezes well. It's amazing how easy the decision to bake a dessert pie becomes, when all you have to do for the crust is to defrost it. And there are almost daily uses for frozen home-made chicken broth, rendered from cheap chicken backs and necks weeks in advance, while listening to Saturday-afternoon opera on the radio, live from the Met.

The rewards for establishing a leisurely routine to carry out these chores are immeasurable. With both the larder and the freezer full, supper becomes a much easier and speedier task. But don't get me wrong: it's still a task. Food hasn't yet learned to please us by shopping and cooking itself. Until that happy day arrives, let me offer solace with a system that requires only last-minute shopping for fresh ingredients and then an hour of entertainingly easy kitchen time.

Most of my recipes call for saute pans, grills and woks. However, the oven, which I scoffed at above, does have its uses. There are many worthwhile, all-in-one suppers that can be quickly cooked in the oven. The only novelty here is to use a hot oven (425°–450° F; 220°–230° C), instead of the more common "moderate" (350° F; 180° C) temperature, which takes too long and dries the food.

I pay special attention to vegetables. This book offers many good vegetarian main courses for those taking a respite from meat-eating (or who abstain from meat on principle) as well as splendid side-dishes for a meat-centred dinner.

Seafood occupies much of my thinking, because I love it, and because it's generally (with the exception of lobster) a healthier alternative to meat. Unfortunately, when it comes to fish, which I cannot abide frozen, freshness is a big issue. Even the most expensive shops of our inland cities sell fish that is at least three days old: usable, but far from its best. On the other hand, frozen shellfish (like shrimp, sea scallops and squid), which are seldom available fresh, provide excellent results once thawed. Shellfish, which has higher fat content than fish, is able to retain its quality despite its ordeal in the freezer. Lucky us.

In the case of shrimp and squid, that quality is best retained when the former is frozen with its shell on, and the latter with its innards intact. This is a double-header of obstacles for most of us. Peeling shrimps, or worse, digging clammy goo out of a squid, is not exactly a "lucky" proposition. Fortunately, you can find pre-peeled shrimp and cleaned squid. But there are problems with the ready-to-use seafoods. Pre-peeled shrimp is normally frozen in that state and suffers from frostbite. As for squid, it's typically cleaned and frozen just when its passed its prime. But don't let me deter you: it's preferable to eat slightly frost-bitten shrimp (which may be dry) and squid that's a day older than it should be, than to forego the pleasure of these foods outright.

Salads, soups and desserts, which can be the three joyous elements of a complete and great summer meal (offering welcome consolation in winter, too) occupy a place of honour in my kitchen. A meal that begins with a good soup or salad and ends with an excellent (not necessarily over-sweet) dessert will be celebrated even if its main course is unassuming and inexpensive.

Every cook has his or her favourite quirks regarding techniques, equipment and ingredients. Here's a selective list of my own:

THE SAUTE PAN

Many recipes in this book call for a saute pan (which is a fancy name for a frying pan). It is therefore important to own a good one: one that invites rather than repels. The best ones are those really expensive copper-lined pans that gleam prettily and conduct the heat evenly over the entire cooking surface. They are a joy to use, and last a lifetime.

If, however, you are loath to part with $150 or so, the next best choice is a true restaurant pan (found in restaurant-equipment stores, all of which absolutely welcome home chefs). These are the iron ones that start out a dull metallic colour and turn black as they are tempered and seasoned. My personal least-favourite pans are the stick-free kind, on which one can never use a metal spatula, and which prevent drippings from sticking (their supposed attribute), and therefore hinder proper deglazing and sauce making.

Whatever pan you use, it's important to clean it as soon as possible after use and to dry it right after washing. Leaving a pan dirty for long will make stick-ons harder to scrape off, and that will affect the seasoning of your pan. It takes a long time of proper use to season a pan and it is this seasoning which coddles the food while it's cooking. Soaking a pan with soapy water is even worse for it than serious scrubbing. If there are stubborn stick-ons, then it is best to add a couple of cups of plain water to the pan and place it over high heat until the water boils. The hot water will loosen the stick-ons and they will come off easily when scraped with a wooden spoon or spatula.

Traditionally, sauteing has meant "jump-frying" on a thin surface of fat. The fat used to be a combination of oil and butter. Now that butter is a problem, oil alone does a very creditable job. As for the jumping ("sauter" is French for "to jump"), it's only an expression. It refers to the fact that the process takes a short time, as opposed to actual frying, which takes longer.

BLENDERS/PROCESSORS

I live a life that is like an old Woody Allen comedy routine, in which he used to describe his utter terror of household appliances and machines in general. For example, I refuse even to look under the hood of my car; I've owned a VCR for many years, and yet I still don't know how to record on it (I use it only to watch videos, on a hook-up engineered for me by a mechanical whiz); and I flatly refuse even to acknowledge word processors, let alone work on them, much to the consternation of all editors, who have ever had to edit my antiquated, typewritten copy.

Nevertheless, and only out of sheer necessity, I've had to master the use of two kitchen machines: the blender and the food processor. It's not that I like the idea of either of them. It's just that they are so damned time-saving, not to mention elbow-grease conserving, that they have humbled me. They replace such torturous devices as the mortar and pestle, the food mill and the wire whisk, while producing results that are superior and lightning-fast.

Naturally, both of these machines love to attack human beings. The blades of the food processor are insanely sharp, and extreme care must be taken handling them. As for the blender, it has the annoying habit of boiling over and exploding in one's face if the blending liquid is too hot. This happened to me once just before an important dinner party, as I was trying to finish a bouillabaisse by blending its broth into a veloute. I poured it into the blender directly from the stove, turned on the power, and pow! I served the rest of the meal with a scalded face, and thereafter learned to cool the broth before blending (either by adding some ice cubes to it, or by sitting it in a bowl of ice water).

BOWLS

Throughout these recipes I refer to

"bowls": small ones, big ones, bowls to reserve in, working bowls for mixing large quantities, and smaller working bowls for whisking things like dressings. This fixation on bowls is partly based on my personal cooking habits (or neuroses) which involve preparing as many of the ingredients as possible before I turn on the stove for the "real" cooking.

I therefore do all my chopping, slicing, etc. in advance. In the old days when I was cool and easygoing, and had large restaurant kitchens to work in, I used to prep each ingredient and leave it on the counter wherever it fell until I was ready for it. With advancing age and a shrinking kitchen (in a tiny townhouse), I go berserk unless each ingredient is neatly enshrined in a bowl as soon as I have prepped it. I recommend this tactic because it keeps the counters clean and fills one with a sense of accomplishment, rather than a growing fear of the chaos created by unleashed (i.e. "reserved") ingredients.

"Working" bowls have a place in everyone's kitchen, regardless of your tolerance for disorder. For these, I recommend stainless steel bowls of various sizes. The small ones are particularly useful for whisking. It's impossible to whisk with abandon if you're using porcelain.

FRYING SCREEN

A cheap piece of equipment, this wire-mesh screen is like a squat tennis racket, and can prevent many a painful welt by blocking splattering oil before it hits fragile skin. It sits on the frying pan, protecting while allowing peeks at the ingredients underneath. It's a bit of a hassle to clean, but it stores easily, hanging on a nail by the stove. It falls apart after a while, but as I said, it's cheap. I couldn't do without mine.

GAS VS. ELECTRIC STOVES/OVENS

It's not that I have anything against electric stoves or ovens, it's just that I don't like using them. The electric stove's inability to cool off and heat up in a hurry is legendary. As for the electric oven, it has the nasty habit of using its broiler to preheat, which means that anything placed in it before the oven has completely preheated will get charred on top. Electric users must therefore wait till their ovens have reached the desired heat (and the broiler has turned itself off) before beginning to bake. They must also learn to juggle the stove elements, for example, by shifting a pot to an element on "simmer" once the contents have reached a boil. Better: switch to gas.

MICROWAVE OVENS

I avoid them at all cost. I find anything that comes out of a microwave to be way too hot. I can barely taste it, it burns my mouth, and gives me instant indigestion. All of this is true of food that is either cooked or re-heated in a microwave and meant to be eaten right away. However, whenever there is a period of grace after the nuking, the microwave can be very useful. Pesky little operations like melting chocolate, cooking bacon and defrosting meat or fish become a snap when entrusted to the electronic beam of this brave, new cooking machine.

TIMING

In cooking like in stand-up comedy or race-car driving, timing is of the essence. Not only must each individual operation be timed critically, the timing of the whole show must be correct if dinner is to be a success. Properly judging the timing of individual procedures comes with experience. The recipes in this book indicate exact times that must be followed: stir-fry the garlic for 30 seconds; saute the scallops for *exactly* two minutes on each side, etc. However,

it's hard enough dealing with a hot frying pan, much less simultaneously juggling a stop-watch.

Timing a 30-second operation becomes easier (and almost automatic) as soon as you learn to relax and have fun in the kitchen. It's not the 30 seconds that are important (it could as well take 28 or 32 seconds): it's that the garlic must cook without burning. It is a matter of judgment and know-how. Fortunately, the know-how comes quickly. One need never burn the garlic more than once to understand that it tastes better un-burned. Anyway, whenever in doubt, undercook!

Timing the various elements of the entire menu so that everything is ready more or less at once depends on organization. The overriding point is also the most obvious: do first what takes the longest (cooking potatoes; making rice). Similarly, do in advance what would be frustrating at the last moment: things like chopping parsley for the garnish, or making the salad dressing. Most importantly, do not waste those valuable "free" moments by loafing. If the stew is getting its last ten-minute rest in the oven, spend those minutes finishing the vegetables or prepping the fruit salad for dessert.

Easier said than done, I know. But it's worth the effort. The idea of new home cooking is not only to create lovely food, but also to be able to enjoy it. That enjoyment is a combination of having fun in the kitchen and then sitting down at table when everything is piping hot and at its best.

INGREDIENTS

BROTH

Whether made from chicken, veal or vegetables, broth or stock is a major basic ingredient. It is the base of all soups and most sauces, and the indispensable agent that transforms ordinary foods into glorious, mouthwatering stews. In modern cooking, broth has the additional capability of keeping fancy recipes within one's cholesterol and caloric reach. A quarter-cup of broth is an acceptable substitute for a similar quantity of cream, in whichever sauce calls for it, with only marginal loss of texture (albeit much of the richness).

It is wise always to have broth on hand. In our sinful past, when we were ignorant of the harmful effects of MSG (monosodium glutamate: a salt-like chemical that irritates taste buds, fooling them into a sensation of pleasure), store-bought broth in cans and cubes used to offer an excellent escape-hatch. Now in our enlightenment, we have learned to fear MSG. The alternative is to render broth at home and freeze it ready for use. The

job is a tad messy, but not dauntingly so, and there's no denying the superior quality and taste of the homemade product.

CRUST

Just about anything baked en croute, be it savoury or sweet, is perceived as not only appetizing, but elegant. The crunchy secret of crust's popularity is its hidden fat content, which also gives it its richly browned appearance. The appeal is undeniable, and there are two ways to cater to it.

The easy way is filo dough. These paper-thin sheets of crust come to us courtesy of the eastern Mediterranean basin, and they are widely available in specialty stores as well as most supermarkets. Filo can be stored frozen without loss of quality and is a snap to use, as long as you follow certain ground rules.

Filo must be defrosted thoroughly inside its packaging (to prevent drying), until it comes to room temperature. Then it is laid out, one sheet at a time, on a dry surface. Watery moisture attacks it mercilessly, tearing it and making it useless. Next, each layer of filo must be greased, if the desired crispness is to be achieved. Fat reacts with filo just as it does with the flour of conventional crust, to prevent sogginess, making it airy and light.

Olive oil (and the equally benign and cheaper, though less tasty, vegetable oil) works well with the filo for savoury pies. Melted, unsalted butter (despite its saturated calories) is the only fat suitable for dessert pies. The fat is applied on the filo sparingly and gently with a pastry brush, or even a bunched-up paper towel. The entire surface of each sheet of filo should be greased before the next one is imposed on it.

TOMATO

This wondrous fruit, which is second only to the wondrous bulb (garlic) for culinary popularity, has a thousand and one uses and comes in an equal number of varieties. Nothing will ever beat a fleshy, perfumed tomato fresh from a moist, late-August garden. But as life without tomato would be unbearable during the rest of the year, we must consider the alternatives.

There's nothing wrong with canned tomatoes . . . much. They have little flavour, they're mushy, and they pick up metallic residue from the slightest bump on the can. The ones that are canned in Italy have the best colour, and are acidic enough to evoke the real thing.

I don't have any use for the various grades of tomato "sauce" that line our supermarket shelves. They are loaded with additives and cost too much for what they are: diluted, flavoured tomato paste.

Speaking of which, tomato paste is the one tomato by-product that no amount of bad press can ever suppress. It has taken on its own identity, almost as though it were a separate ingredient from tomato, which it kind of is. It is an indispensable background taste in such heirloom dishes as beef Bourguignon and cassoulet. It is very acidic, and I try to use it sparingly.

The concentrated tomato sensation that I prefer is the sun-dried tomato: a landmark ingredient on the highway of modern cooking. Because it is naturally dried, and not boiled down like tomato paste, it's less acidic, and explosively tasty. Sun-dried tomatoes that are sold rehydrated in oil can be prohibitively expensive. The affordable way is to buy them in the dried state (in which they also last a long time, as long as they are stored airtight in a cool, dark place).

The way to revive them is to take a handful at a time, soak them in some hot water for half an hour, and add an equal measure of olive oil, then store them in the fridge. The oil itself becomes delicious for use as a condiment in salad dressings or on pasta. And by the way, since salt is a prime ingredient of sun-dried tomatoes (being the chemical agent that allows them to dry), the salt content of recipes using sun-dried should be scaled down accordingly.

Still, nothing beats fresh, field-ripened tomatoes. The only kink to cooking with these is that they must be peeled and seeded. The peel curls spikily during cooking and can offend the palate. As for the seeds, they annoyingly find their way into every crevice of the mouth.

The proper way to deal with tomatoes is to make a little slit on their smooth end, immerse them in boiled water for half a minute, and then fish them out with a slotted spoon. The peel slips off like a glove, taking the button-like stem with it. The seeds and juice can then be prodded out of the ventricles either by finger or using a teaspoon. The flesh that remains is what is used for sauces and soups. The seeds can be strained from the juice and discarded. The juice can be reserved for sauces or soups.

Having said all that, let me be honest and admit that there come times when I'm just too rushed (or too frazzled) to deal with peeling and seeding mounds of tomatoes. What I do is wash the tomatoes and chop off their stems (definitely) and then cut them into large chunks. This takes a bit longer to get the sauce going, but the advantage is that as the tomato begins to cook its peel comes off, and since it is in only so many large

pieces, I can fish it out with a spoon and proceed as if nothing has happened. As for the one piece of peel that always escapes and the seeds that inevitably distribute themselves all over the sauce – well, putting up with them becomes the punishment for my short-cut.

OLIVE OIL

I revere and use it at every opportunity. I slather my toast with it, drizzle it over my pasta, salad and fish, and it is my preferred fat for sauteing. And I've felt this way about it even before they discovered that instead of adding cholesterol to the diet, it actually breaks it down and dissolves it. It is quite possibly the only fun food that's good for you.

There is now a dazzling array of olive oils in all our markets. This is the natural consequence of this product's new-found popularity. Concepts such as "extra-virgin" and "cold-pressed" get rattled off at luncheons, usually followed by a long discussion on the relative merits of Luccan (Italian) versus Provençale (French). Those really in the know talk of the clean taste of the Spanish, the distinctive olive flavour of the Portuguese, the upstart but acceptable Californian, and the intensely green colour of the grandparent of them all, the olive oil of Attica, Greece.

The important difference denoted by the various degrees of virginity, aside from the higher price, is the amount of olive flavour in the oil. This extra flavour is the result of the first pressing of the "virgin" olive. The flavour is even more intense if that first pressing was "cold," meaning that no heat was used in the extraction (this process yields less oil and entails more labour). Subsequent pressings (always with the help of heat) from the pulp (or pomace) yield a golden oil, but with less flavour.

This wonderful, expensive flavour can be tasted only when the oil is eaten raw, and disappears once it is heated for cooking. Therefore, a less precious oil (i.e. vegetable) is perfectly suitable for high-heat operations like frying. With sauteing, where the texture of olive oil is an asset, I choose a non-virgin (read, cheaper) variety. On the other hand, when flavour matters, such as on a salad, pasta or fish, I whip out my best and most aromatic oil. Of course, were my extra-virgin olive oil to run out, I get by very nicely with regular olive oil, while saving my money to buy more Luccan.

OTHER OILS

There are occasions, such as with Asian food, when olive oil is either wasted or inappropriate. For frying, I use any vegetable oil that claims to be cholesterol-free. I like safflower oil for its lightness and corn oil for its sweetness. Presently, canola oil is being touted as the healthiest of all of them, and so right now I use it. In general, I find most vegetable oils more or less interchangeable, especially for frying.

Peanut oil, on the other hand, is very distinct, possessing and retaining a peanut flavour that adds a subtle but wonderful element to Asian (particularly Chinese) dishes. It is expensive and not necessary for any other kind of cuisine, so it's a bit of a larder luxury if one cooks only the occasional Chinese meal. I have listed it first (meaning preferred) in all my Oriental-inspired recipes, but I have allowed for its absence by offering vegetable oil as a substitute.

SPICES

The seeds and various other reproductive parts of exotic plants, also known as spices, have a long history in humanity's kitchens. They are strong medicine and should be used judiciously. All spices benefit from a quick fry (30 seconds) to wake up their flavours and tame their volatile oils and gases prior to making a sauce with them. They should never be sprinkled into a finished sauce. Then,

they remain gritty and indigestible. If, on tasting a sauce, you decide it needs more spice, you must fry the additional spice in oil for 30 seconds and then add it to the sauce.

HERBS

I am a true fan of herbs. I like all of them, but I adore parsley, basil, oregano, dill, rosemary (oh, all right, sage and thyme, too). I use them in profusion. And no, I don't expect everyone to do the same. Aside from their delicious flavours and their myriad of vitamins and minerals, herbs are dispensable from just about any recipe. By the same token, they can also be used in excess without any harm.

The notable omission from my quick list of favourite herbs above is fresh coriander. I did not omit because I don't love it (and use it) as extensively as the others, but because it happens to be a singular matter of herbal controversy. Also known as Chinese parsley, coriander (sometimes called by its Spanish name, cilantro) is a staple ingredient of sunbelt cuisine. Many of the people who developed their palates in northern climates find its chalky taste and rather intense perfume hard to take (and even indigestible). Luckily, it can easily be replaced by parsley, or even omitted completely, just like any other herb.

Dried herbs, which are always readily available (and affordable), work nicely in sauces as long as you use enough and add them at the right time. They must cook with the sauce in order to wake up. Otherwise, they can taste rather gritty.

LEMON

I've found so many uses for this delightful fruit that I once came close to owning a New York restaurant and calling it "Lemon." The complicated world of Manhattan lease-holds foiled my bid for the Abingdon Square premises of the proposed Lemon, so I never found out whether New Yorkers would have taken to the name.

The most lemony part of the lemon is its zest. This is the thin, yellow layer of its peel, which contains lemon oil, and adds sparkle to any recipe calling for lemon juice. The zest must be extracted before the lemon has been sliced or cut, and the only way to do it properly is with a lemon zester (wouldn't you know it?). A skinny instrument, invented by the French, it resembles a tiny set of brass knuckles mounted on a handle. It does its job by shaving off only the yellow zest without removing any of the bitter, white pith just underneath.

The zester creates lovely ribbons of fragile lemon essence which are wonderful in sauces. It is best to saute them early in the process (usually along with the garlic), so that their flavour mellows during the rest of the cooking, and caresses rather than shocks the palate with its intensity. Oranges and even grapefruits can be zested by the same nifty instrument. A word about zested citrus fruits: all dehydrate quickly, having lost their outer skin. It is therefore necessary to juice the fruits soon after zesting. Use the juice in the recipe if it calls for it, or store it covered in the fridge or freezer for future use.

VINEGARS

Newly rediscovered, vinegars have become the darlings of our most eclectic chefs. In truth, ounce for ounce, they contain more oomph and taste than most other condiments. And therein lies the pitfall: it's very easy to overdo vinegar. Even the correct amount, when used to sharpen a sauce or a glaze, must be cooked down first to chase out its acidity.

The most common use of vinegar is still, as it always was, in salad dressings. Even here, it's best to use it sparingly, never more than one part vinegar to five parts oil. This is less true of balsamic vinegar (authentically produced only in Modena, Italy), which is sweet. Balsamic vinegar can

even be used solo (if you are dieting, for example). In such cases however I prefer to use lemon: it's gentler.

Berry-flavoured vinegars, like the phenomenally hyped raspberry and the lesser-known cassis (blackcurrant), can be deadly if misproportioned, clouding everything they dress in a mouthwash-like taste. In moderation, they can add an exotic touch to salads.

BOOZE

Cognac, wine and liqueurs have an honourable place in haute cuisine. They are so easy to use that they serve the home cook just as well as the professional chef (as long as they survive the collective household thirst and remain in the larder: never keep kitchen booze in the bar!).

Alcoholic beverages are used in cooking for their concentrated flavours, not their alcohol content. It is always advisable to cook down the booze and drive out the alcohol, which otherwise gets in the way of the taste. If truly loath to watch a lovely spirit going up in steam, you can stand over the saute pan while the alcohol is evaporating and breathe deeply.

ASIAN INGREDIENTS

The magical world of Asian cuisine

has had millennia in which to invent a whole array of condiments and ingredients. These are finding their way into Western home cooking, and there's no looking back. I include a number of Asian-inspired recipes in this book, attempting to reinvent them with easy-to-follow steps. Almost all the ingredients called for in these recipes are widely available in the Asian markets of our major cities, and for the most part they last a long time in the larder or fridge. I list them, according to country of origin:

CHINA

Soya Sauce: The salted, dark, fermented juice of the soya bean is the most-used condiment of Chinese cuisine. There is a great variety of soya or soy-like sauces in Asian markets, from mushroom-flavoured Chinese, to Thai nam pla or fish sauce (see below). Personally, I prefer the clean taste of Japanese soya, and also the lighter, nuttier tamari.

Peanut Oil: A light and flavourful cooking oil, ideal for all Chinese-inspired recipes. With the addition of chilies and a little soya, it makes a fabulous hot sauce.

Sesame Oil: A dark-brown, thick, aromatic oil, used sparingly as a condiment in sauces and marinades. It perks up most dishes that have an Asian accent.

Rice Wine: A salted, clear, alcohol-rich wine, it has a dry taste that beautifully suits Chinese-style recipes. It is distasteful to drink, so a bottle will last a long time.

Black Beans: Preserved, fermented, somewhat musty beans, they are indispensible for many Chinese recipes. They partner other rich tastes, such as garlic and chilies, and transform ordinary ingredients into gourmet specialties. They are very salty and must be rinsed thoroughly, then soaked in water for a few minutes before use. They keep well if wrapped airtight and stored in the fridge.

Chilies: The best (and hottest) chilies for Chinese food are those fresh, small little devils, greenish to red, that are sold in Chinese markets. Failing those, the equally hot, dried, red chilies are a good buy. They last forever and work well in non-Chinese recipes, too. It is essential to wash hands thoroughly after working with fresh chilies. (Dry chilies present less of a problem).

Sesame Sauce: This tahini-like toasted sesame paste is sold in bottles. Its oil has separated from the solids, which are rock-hard and difficult to scoop out. They do eventually yield to prodding. Texturally speaking, it is advisable to use 1 part of the top oil along with 4 parts of the solids. Sesame sauce behaves very well when mixed with twice as much warm water and whisked. It turns a lighter colour and becomes smooth as silk.

Tofu: I left this important item, for last because most of us are acquainted with it after three decades of hippy and post-hippy cooking culture. Chinese markets carry three major kinds of tofu: the white, soft kind that is also available in health food stores; the off-white firmer, pressed tofu, with its more substantial texture, that breaks apart less easily, and the yellow, fried variety, that has many uses, especially in Thai cooking.

THAILAND

Nam Pla: The ubiquitous condiment of Thai food, this is a soy sauce enriched with fish or squid essence and garlic. It has a rank odour on its own, but is irresistibly delicious if used properly and judiciously in cooking. "Squid Brand" fish sauce is the kind most readily available, sold in a tall-necked, wine-style bottle.

Rice Noodles: Also called rice sticks and rice vermicelli, these are opaque, thin, flat rice noodles that come packaged in cellophane, imported from Thailand. They are unlike other noodles in that they soften, not by direct cooking in boiling water, but by being soaked for 2–24 hours in cold water. After that, they

become lustrously al dente in 3–4 minutes of refrying.

Lemon Grass: This fibrous woody weed is a long, thin affair that perfumes many Thai dishes. It is widely available and inexpensive, and is used extensively in soups, sauces and marinades. It is usually chopped up and cooked, and – even though it is inedible – served in the sauce or soup.

Galanga Root: A ginger-like aromatic, this is a major ingredient of Thai soups, lending a perfume and an attractive pink colour. It's difficult to find but worth the effort. In a pinch, it can be replaced by ginger root.

Lime Leaf: A fervently limey ingredient, this leaf is dark green and just as hard to find (and equally worthwhile to search out) as galanga. If unavailable, it can be replaced by lime juice.

Coconut Milk: The pulped, moistened flesh of the coconut is the base of many Thai soups and sauces. In its home country it is obtained from fresh coconuts and used immediately. Elsewhere it is found in cans, and this product is good enough to be used by our best Thai restaurants.

Tamarind Paste: The tart-sweet tamarind is a staple sun-belt ingredient. It's found in commercial Worcestershire sauce and also on Mexico City street corners, where vendors dilute it with water to make a refreshing drink. The Thai product is available as a dry, pressed pulp that is sold widely in Asian markets. It must be soaked, then mashed (best by hand) and strained. This is the secret behind authentic Pad Thai, the stir-fried noodles that are the highest-profile culinary export of that gentle kingdom.

JAPAN

Aji Mirin: A sweet vinegar derived from rice, second in importance only to soya in Japanese cooking. It is the signature flavour of sushi rice and teriyaki sauce. It is widely available and stores well.

Rice Vinegar: A tart version of aji mirin, this is useful in dressings and marinades. It also keeps well. It is available principally in Japanese markets.

Roasted Sesame Seeds: Packaged as beautifully as most other things Japanese, these sesames (which are very tricky to achieve at home from raw sesame seeds) are a crunchy, delicious sprinkle for salads and meats, Japanese-inspired or otherwise.

Wasabe: This fiery, green horse-radish paste, famous from sushi bars, has many interesting uses, in sauces and as a condiment with grilled or poached fish. It is available in Japanese markets as a canned powder. It is meant to be dissolved in equal parts of cold water and then reserved airtight for a few minutes to develop its flavour and heat. Beware when first unwrapping it. It releases a whiff of sinus-shattering steam strong enough to make a grown person cry.

INDIA

Nan Breads: All Indian markets carry these thick, oiled pita-like breads that go so well with curries and even make an excellent crust for home-made pizza. When well wrapped, nans store nicely in the fridge for up to a week, and in the freezer for at least a month or so. They defrost quickly and are a joy to eat, rewarmed in an oven or toaster oven. I always keep some on hand.

Ghee: This is clarified butter, the preferred fat for Indian cuisine. It can be rendered at home by slow-cooking butter to liquefy it and separate its oil from the whey, or it can be purchased ready to use in Indian markets.

Tandoori Paste: This is a collection of spices and aromatics that are packed in oil and make a very delightful (if pungent) marinade for fish or meat. Tandoori spices also come in a powdered form that can be moistened at home with oil. Unfortunately, the powder contains MSG; the paste does not, and is therefore preferable.

Black Mustard Seed: A flavourful spice that adds a subtle heat and perfume to Indian-style chutneys and curries. It's also very useful in salad dressings. It is usually sold cheaply but in large packages in Indian markets. Fortunately, it keeps forever.

Garam Masala: A generic name for "mixed" spice, it can contain as many as 20 different ingredients that hardly anybody bothers to grind at home anymore. All Indian markets carry preground garam masala, and I've never had reason to complain about any of them. It is used both in cooking as well as garnishing almost everything Indian, from curries to raitas.

CHEESE

Gone are the days when we used to melt cheese indiscriminately over everything, from tuna fish to broccoli. Our nutritionists have informed us that an excess of cheese is bad for our health and the waistline too. Nevertheless, there is no denying me a good Romano, Parmesan or Pecorino on my pasta, and bleak indeed would my life be without goat cheese.

Imported or local, the relatively lean cheese of goat's milk is a supreme treat, especially when baked. It complements mushrooms, lettuce and eggplant, it sings under olive oil and freshly ground black pepper, and even makes pizza a fancy dinner. Goat's milk cheese (a.k.a. "chevre," the French word for goat) is as close to a food of the gods as humans can muster. Yes, it is expensive, but a little goes a long way.

Many southern European countries, from Portugal to Italy to Greece, make hard cheeses from goat's milk. Though all of them are wonderful, the ones I adore are the soft goat's milk cheeses that originate in France, and are copied rather successfully in North America. They have a soft, crumbly texture, a stark, deeply dairy flavour and a snow-white colour. The originals from France normally have a tasty covering of mould or ash, whereas the domestic varietes are usually crustless, cost less, and are straightforward. I eat the French chevres on their own and use the North American equivalent for cooking.

LEGUMES

Beans, lentils and peas, in all their many varieties, are tasty storehouses of nutrition in terms of protein, vitamins and important minerals. The cuisines of many sun-belt countries depend on legumes for much of their protein, as they are much easier to digest than meat and just a tad easier to deal with than livestock.

Lentils are the most amenable

legumes for new home cooking, because they can be prepared without lengthy soaking and cooking. Dry lentils can go from the larder to the table in less than an hour and a half (including a quarter hour of rest after cooking to develop the flavour).

On the other hand, dry beans of all persuasions, including the nutty-delicious chick peas, do require a lengthy soak in warm water, prior to a few hours of simmering on the stove. Fortunately for time-harassed modern gourmets, beans do survive the canning process very acceptably. It is important to drain them as soon as the can has been opened, discarding the canning liquid. It doesn't hurt to wash them in running water, gently tossing them in the colander, to remove any leftover odour of their incarceration.

If you do opt for the long process with the dry product, here's a hint from my friend Josée Arsenault: One tablespoon (15 ml) of baking soda (per 1 lb/ 500 g of beans) in the soaking water will remove that pesky, windy consequence of eating beans, and make for a post-prandial conversation without the unavoidably rude punctuations.

FRUITS

The most visible victim of the meteoric rise and fall of the nouvelle cuisine fad has been the fruit garnish. Stupidly over-extended, slices of fruit (cooked and raw) came on every plate of the so-called new cooking, to the point of nausea. Well, it doesn't phase me. The proper use of fruit on the side, or as part of the sauce of meat or fowl has been practiced worldwide for centuries, and there is no reason to give it up.

Cherries or oranges with duck, tart apple with chicken, melon with ham, papaya and mango with shrimp; these are the very taste combinations that inspired the nouvelle-ites, and must not be overlooked just because they were abused. Yes, even the kiwi fruit can be revived.

Well, go on then. Turn the page. Let's cook.

Soups

Inexpensive Chicken Broth

It's useless to bother with home-made soup unless you make your own chicken broth. Except for certain wonderful vegetarian soups (some of which I offer below), chicken broth is where soup begins and ends. Considering the additional uses of chicken broth in sauces, it's a good idea to make more than you need and then freeze the rest. Here's a large recipe that requires a suitably large soup pot to make it in.

INGREDIENTS

7–8 lb. (3–4 kg) chicken backs, necks and carcasses

1 tsp. (5 mL) salt

2 large onions, unpeeled and cut into quarters

3 bay leaves

1 tbsp. (15 mL) whole, black peppercorns

PREPARATION AND COOKING

1   Place the chicken into a soup pot with the other ingredients. Add enough water to cover by an inch or so, if your pot is large enough.

2   Bring to a rolling boil over high heat. At this point a darkish foam will start to rise to the surface. Using a slotted spoon, scoop off this foam and discard. Reduce heat to medium and continue skimming foam until it stops rising (about 10 minutes). Eventually only a clear foam will continue to rise, and you don't have to bother with that.

   Lower heat and simmer uncovered and undisturbed for about an hour and a quarter. Taste the broth. It should be chickeny and grey-yellow in colour with fat floating on top.

3   Take from heat, cover and let sit to develop flavour for 1–2 hours.

4   Place a large working bowl underneath a large strainer. Ladle the broth into the strainer to separate solids from liquid (carefully: this can be very messy if you slip up). Press the solids down somewhat with a heavy spoon to extract as much liquid as possible from them. Discard solids.

5   Allow the broth in the working bowl to cool completely. (Refrig-

erating warm broth causes it to sour.) Cover and refrigerate cooled broth.

After several hours (or overnight), all the fat of the broth will have risen to the top and solidified. Skim this and discard (in another age, this chicken fat would have been used to make some wonderful recipes). Underneath the fat, you'll find the jellied, greyish-yellow broth. If using soup immediately, take what you need and freeze the rest in airtight containers. Otherwise, freeze it all. Another good idea: freeze some of the broth in smaller containers (ice cube trays or plastic baggies work well) for use in sauces.

Total cooking time: 1½ hours. Yields: 14–20 cups (3½–5 L), depending on amount of chicken.

Avgolemono Soup

The very first soup I would urge you to make with your beautiful chicken broth is Greek Avgolemono. This is a chicken-rice soup, velvetized and enriched with egg and lemon juice. It is the soup of my childhood's special occasions, nicknamed "golden soup" by me. What made it golden was not only the colour of the egg, but also the little bit of chicken fat my mother used to leave in the soup to float on the surface like drops of sunshine. But then again, in those days we didn't know just how unhealthy fat is.

INGREDIENTS

3 cups (750 mL) water
⅜ cup (100 mL) cooked rice
8 cups (2L) home-made
   chicken broth

1–2 tbsp. (15–30 mL)
   chicken fat (optional)
2 eggs
1 lemon
parsley

PREPARATION AND COOKING

1 Bring water to a boil in a small pot and add rice. Cook at medium-high heat, stirring once or twice, for 12–15 minutes until the rice is tender (taste a grain). Drain rice and reserve. Discard its cooking water.

2 In a larger pot, bring the chicken broth to a boil. Add cooked rice and chicken fat, if desired. Lower heat to medium-low and let cook 7–8 minutes, stirring occasionally.

3 Meanwhile, wash, dry and chop a few sprigs of parsley. Keep it moist under a wet paper towel.

4 Crack eggs into large working bowl. Whisk until frothy.

5 Squeeze lemon and strain the juice. Measure 2 tbsps. (30 mL) of the juice (reserving the rest, if there is any) and add to the eggs. Whisk the mixture again until frothy.

6 Take the broth off the heat. Using a ladle with one hand and a whisk with the other, dribble hot broth into the egg-lemon in the bowl, whisking actively: the raw egg will scramble if too much hot broth is added at once, or if you don't whisk as soon as you've added it. Add a total of about 2 cups (500 mL) of the broth in this fashion (no doubt wishing all the while that you had a third hand to steady the bowl with the egg, lemon and its slowly increasing quantity of hot broth). After the first 2 cups, the going gets easier. Add another 2 cups (500 mL), but in a slow, steady stream, whisking as you go. By now, half your soup is in the bowl with the egg-lemon and you are ready to reverse the process. Whisking the broth in the pot, add ladlefuls of the egg-lemoned broth in a steady, fast stream, until all the soup is back in the pot. You now have your golden soup (truly golden if you dared to add a bit of chicken fat along with the broth in step #2). Taste. Adjust seasoning and lemon content.

7 The soup now needs a few minutes of reheating, to let the egg thicken and to make it piping hot, which is the only way to enjoy it. Unfortunately, this is a tricky job, because it's all too possible to overheat the soup and curdle the egg, thus reversing your alchemy and ruining all your work. This reheating which is best done just before serving, must be accomplished over a low flame with gentle but continuous whisking. The length of time will depend on how long the soup has had to cool. Once it is warm, whisk a bit more actively, keeping hawk-like watch over it. The soup is ready when it emits steam. Test it. If it's too hot to the touch, it's ready. And if it boils, you've lost it. Just remember to use a low heat and whisk continuously. Do not get distracted. In Greece it's forbidden to disturb the cook who is whisking Avgolemono during its final reheating. Even wars or earthquakes must wait.

8 Ladle into soup bowls, making sure to give everyone some of the rice which has settled to the bottom. Garnish with chopped parsley and serve immediately with crusty bread on the side.

Total prep and cooking time: 45 minutes.
Final reheating: 4—5 minutes.
Serves 4.

BlumCorder Soup

The second most important way to use great chicken broth (after Avgo-lemono) is to concoct a homey soup, thick with compatible vegetables. Spinach, onion and mushrooms (along with some barley for body) are the hearty co-participants in a soup created by Sharon Corder, based on partner Jack Blum's "best-ever" broth. Blum and Corder are two of the finest home cooks on the planet and I had the tasty pleasure of being their next-door neighbour for 7½ years. I dedicate this, their own soup, to them.

INGREDIENTS

½ cup (125 mL) barley
1 bunch spinach
1 onion
1 cup (250 mL) button
   mushrooms
9 cups (2 L) home-made
   chicken broth
1 bay leaf

1 tsp. (5 mL) dried thyme or
   oregano
½ tsp. (2 mL) freshly ground
   pepper
1 tsp. (5 mL) balsamic vinegar
1 tbsp. (15 mL) Worcestershire
   sauce or soya sauce or tamari
1 lemon

PREPARATION

1 Cook barley in plenty of water, over medium-high heat until al dente (about 30 minutes). Drain and reserve.

2 Meanwhile, remove spinach stems, leaving only the leaves (remove even the thick spine of the larger leaves). Wash thoroughly, drain and shred. Bring 1 cup (250 mL) water to boil in a large pot. Add the shredded spinach, cover the pot and cook over a high heat for 3–4 minutes, until the spinach has become deep green and reduced greatly in volume. Take from the heat and immediately drain in a strainer. Run some cold water over the spinach to cool it and then press it with a spoon (or your hand) to extract most of the excess liquid. Reserve in the strainer.

3 Finely chop the onion.

4 Wipe and thinly slice the mushrooms. Collect the slices in a mound and chop them with a chef's knife several times. It is desirable to have unevenly chopped mushrooms, with lots of small bits and some larger ones.

COOKING

5 Bring chicken broth to boil in a soup pot. Add the chopped onion, bay leaf, thyme (or oregano) and freshly ground pepper. Cook over medium heat for 10 minutes to soften the onion.

6 Add the cooked spinach and barley, and also the chopped mushrooms. Raise heat to bring to a boil, then reduce heat to medium-low. Maintain a gentle bubble for 10 minutes, stirring occasionally. Add balsamic vinegar, and Worcestershire sauce (or soya, or tamari) and continue cooking for 8–10 minutes more until the spinach is tender, and the mushrooms are crunchy yet juicy. Test for seasoning. Add some salt if you think it necessary. Take from heat and let rest 5 minutes. Cut a lemon into wedges. Ladle soup into bowls and serve immediately, accompanied by lemon wedges.

Total prep time: 35 minutes.
Total cooking time (including rest time): 40 minutes.
Serves 4–6.

Avocado Soup

Velvety and aromatic, this soup may be eaten hot or cold. The only trouble with serving it cold is that you must make it the night before. The fried tortilla bits are key to its success, and they are added directly from the frying pan, whether you serve it hot or cold. Altogether, between the fried tortillas and oil-rich avocados, this is quite a calorific affair, so it should be followed by a light main course.

INGREDIENTS

1 lime
1 ripe avocado
1 tomato
2 cups (500 mL) home-made
   chicken broth
2 green onions
few sprigs fresh coriander

¼ cup (50 mL) cucumber,
   cubed
2 tortillas
2 tbsp. (30 mL) vegetable oil
hot sauce or salsa (optional)
(see Salsa Cynthia, p. 187)

PREPARATION

1 Squeeze lime, and reserve juice. Cut avocado in half, remove and discard pit, and spoon avocado flesh out of the shell directly into a blender. Add lime juice to the avocado.

2 Blanch tomato in boiling water for 30 seconds, then peel, core and seed it and chop flesh roughly. Add to the avocado. Strain juice from the tomato seeds, discard seeds and add tomato juice to the blender.

3 Over low heat, warm chicken broth just until tepid. Add about half of the broth to the avocado in the blender and blend at high speed for 30 seconds. Add the rest of the chicken broth and blend for 1 minute at high speed.

COOKING

4 Pour contents of the blender into a small pot. Over medium heat, bring soup to a boil, stirring continuously (2–3 minutes). Reduce heat to low and simmer, stirring frequently, for 5 minutes. Meanwhile, mince green onions, and add to soup. Stir. Simmer for 1 more minute and turn off heat. Cover soup pot and let rest for 5–10 minutes. (Or wait to cool down, and then refrigerate if serving this soup cold.)

5 Wash, dry and chop coriander roughly. Chop cucumber into small cubes. Cut tortillas into bits. Heat vegetable oil in a saute pan until it's just about to smoke. Add the tortilla bits and fry, stirring over high heat for 1 minute. The tortillas will become golden and crispy. Scoop them out onto a plate.

6 Ladle the soup into bowls. Immediately garnish with chopped coriander, cubed cucumber and fried tortillas. Drop a dollop of the optional hot sauce or salsa in the middle. Serve immediately.

Total prep time:
less than 10 minutes.
Total cooking time
(including rest): 15 minutes.
Serves 2.

French Vegetable Soup

Despite the high profile of such French soups as onion and vichyssoise, the potage of choice in France (especially on numberless table d'hote menus) is a simple puree of vegetables. Here's a fail-safe recipe of this standard, with a couple of enhancements of my own. I cook the soup entirely free of butter or oil, saving the fat content for the croutons and garlic mayonnaise (aioli), which are added at table by the slurpers themselves. And the best news of all is that this soup does not need chicken broth.

INGREDIENTS

8 cups (500 mL) water
1–2 tsp. (5–10 mL) salt
1¼ lb. (600 g) new potatoes
½ lb. (250 g) young carrots
1 lb. (500 g) leeks
½ lb. (250 g) white onions
1 broccoli (about ½ lb. or 250 g)
¼ lb. (150 g) green beans
2 cups (500 mL) water
melted butter OR extra-virgin olive oil
lemon juice

CROUTONS

4 slices crusty white or brown bread
1 tbsp. (15 mL) olive oil

AIOLI

1 egg
2 cloves of garlic
few sprigs parsley
1 tbsp. (15 mL) lemon juice
1 tbsp. (15 mL) red wine vinegar
½ tsp. (2 mL) white sugar
1 tsp. (5 mL) Dijon mustard
¾–1 cup (175–250 mL) extra-virgin olive oil
salt and pepper to taste

PREPARATION AND COOKING

1   Bring water to a boil in a large soup pot. Add salt to taste.

2   Wash potatoes and carrots and add whole to the soup pot.

3   Trim hairy stems of the leeks and discard. Cut leeks down the middle and wash carefully under running water, making sure to rinse away the grit that hides where the green and white parts meet. Roughly chop the leeks, white and green

parts alike, and add to the soup.

4 Peel and roughly chop white onions. Add to the soup.

5 Trim the bottom 1–2 in. (3–4 cms) of the broccoli and discard. Slice the rest of the stalk up to the florets, and add to the soup, reserving the florets.

6 Bring soup to the boil, reduce heat to medium and cook without stirring for 20 minutes or more, until the potato and carrots are almost tender.

7 Add the broccoli florets, and green beans. Lower heat to medium and continue cooking for another 15–20 minutes, until all the vegetables are tender.

8 Take from the heat and puree the vegetables, using all their cooking broth. The best appliance for this job is a hand blender that purees right in the pot. Otherwise, use a food processor or a blender. (If using blender, you must wait for the soup to cool, or speed the process by draining the vegetables to air them and adding 5–6 ice cubes to the broth to cool it.)

9 Return blended soup to the pot and add 2 cups (500 mL) water to compensate for evaporation during the cooking. Now the soup can wait till you are ready to serve it. Then heat, stirring occasionally, almost to the boil. This soup must be served very hot.

Serve immediately with a little butter or extra-virgin olive oil and drops of lemon juice in each bowl; or better with croutons and aioli, which can be made while the soup cooks.

10 For the croutons, cut 4 thick slices of crusty white or brown bread and cut each slice into 1 in. (2 cm) cubes. Fry bread cubes in the olive oil until browned on all sides. This can also be done in the oven by drizzling the oil over the bread cubes and browning them in a hot oven for 10 minutes or so, then tossing and browning for another 5 or 10 minutes (do not burn). Scatter over the soup.

11 For the aioli: process or blend the egg for 30 seconds, add minced garlic, chopped parsley, lemon juice, vinegar, sugar and Dijon mustard and process for 30 seconds; then slowly add olive oil, processing the while. Add salt and pepper to taste. (For a more comprehensive recipe of aioli, see Garlic Mayonnaise, page 40, steps #1–4). A dollop of the aioli is added to each bowl and stirred in. (Leftover aioli can be thinned with water and used as salad dressing.)

Total prep and cooking time: about 1 hour.
Serves 6–8.

Marion's Squash Chowder

This is a nifty autumn soup from friend and fellow home cook Marion Medad. Fortunately, our markets carry fresh squash all year long, and even corn can always be found, frozen if nothing else. The squash that Marion favours is butternut, but any full-fleshed squash will do — even pumpkin when in season. The bacon is used strictly for its flavour and can be replaced by a tablespoon (15 mL) of butter if you shun pork, but one way or another, this soup needs enrichment. You can scale down this recipe if using only half a butternut squash, but leftovers freeze beautifully.

INGREDIENTS

1 large butternut squash
6 oz. (200 g) new potatoes
6 cups (1.5 L) home-made
    chicken broth
1 leek
2 cloves garlic
1 tsp. (5 mL) ground
    coriander seed
1 tsp. (5 mL) ground cinnamon
½ tsp. (2 mL) grated nutmeg

½ tsp. (2 mL) cayenne
    (optional)
1 tbsp. (15 mL) butter
3 ½ oz. (100 mL) smoked bacon
    (in one chunk)
2 tbsp. (30 mL) brown sugar
2 ears fresh corn OR 1 (300 g)
    package frozen corn kernels
salt
fresh coriander

PREPARATION AND COOKING

1 Bake squash in a hot (375° F; 190° C) oven for 1½ hours. Let cool. Cut in half. Scoop out and discard seeds and the thready pulp from the centre. Scoop flesh out of the skin. Discard skin. Chop flesh into large cubes and transfer to a soup pot.

2 Wash and dice new potatoes into ½ in. (1 cm) cubes. Add to the squash in the soup pot. Also add

chicken broth. Place pot over medium heat and bring to a simmer.

3 Meanwhile, trim leek and slice down the middle. Wash carefully, especially where the green and white parts meet. Dry and chop finely. Reserve.

4 Peel and finely chop garlic. Reserve.

5 In a small bowl, combine coriander, cinnamon, nutmeg and cayenne. Reserve.

6 Melt butter in a saute pan over medium-heat until it begins to foam. Add combined spices from step #5 and stir-fry for 1 minute. Add chopped leek and the chunk of smoked bacon and stir-fry with the spices for 1 minute until the leek wilts. Add chopped garlic and brown sugar and stir-fry for 2 minutes longer, turning the bacon once or twice.

7 Add the contents of the saute pan (scraping off every bit) into the soup pot with the simmering squash. Turn heat up to high to bring the soup to the boil, stirring constantly. Once soup boils, reduce heat to medium and let cook, uncovered and undisturbed, for 20–25 minutes, until the potatoes are tender.

8 While the soup is cooking, slice kernels off the 2 ears of corn (being careful not to take corn silk along with the kernels). Reserve. (If using frozen corn, take the package from the freezer and let it thaw.)

9 When the soup has finished cooking, take from the heat. Fish out the piece of bacon and either discard or reserve it for another use. Puree the rest of the ingredients in a processor or blender. If using a standard blender, the contents must cool first. I hear that the new hand blenders are best for processing soups, as they do the job right in the cooking pot. I have yet to build up my courage to buy one of these. Owning a regular blender is traumatic enough.

10 Put the blended soup back over medium heat and bring to the boil, stirring constantly. Add salt. Add the corn kernels and simmer for 4 minutes, stirring occasionally to prevent sticking.

11 Take from heat, cover and let rest about 10 minutes. Meanwhile, wash, dry and chop some fresh coriander or parsley.

12 Pour soup into individual bowls and garnish with the chopped herb of your choice. Serve immediately.

Squash baking time: 1½ hours.
Total prep and cooking time: 50 minutes.
Serves 5–7. Leftovers freeze beautifully.

TWO THAI SOUPS

Wandee Young, owner-chef of Toronto's Young Thailand Restaurant, is a woman with a mission. She is an ambassador for her native country, furthering the Thai reputation for hospitality and good taste by cooking up daily storms of uncompromisingly authentic feasts. She shares three of her most popular recipes with me: Tom Kha Kai and Tom Yum Goong (the two soups that follow), as well as the noodle dish (Pad Thai) on page 110.

Please note that both these soups contain viciously hot peppers, without which they are incomplete. The peppers in question are the little killers that measure about an inch in length and are indiscriminately red or green. They are always available in Chinese markets, where a visit will yield most of the other ingredients for these soups.

An obstacle is that the equally indispensable galanga root (a ginger root relative) and the delightfully fragrant lime leaves are hard to find. They do exist, but I have had to hunt them down either by going to several Chinese markets or by finding a Southeast Asian (usually Vietnamese) establishment. As indicated below, it is possible to substitute ginger root for galanga and a tablespoon of lime juice for the lime leaves, but it's just not the same.

Finally, there is the matter of inedible substances that get served in the soup, but cannot be eaten. The galanga and lime leaves, as well as the amazing lemon grass (which now seems to be universally available) all have unchewable textures but are traditionally left in the soup, necessitating some fancy spoon-work.

The reward for all these problems is two explosively tasty soups that are relatively inexpensive and always draw raves. Not bad for a concoction of fibrous, hard-to-find, exotic aromatics.

Tom Kha Kai

Chicken-coconut soup

INGREDIENTS

1 16 oz (440 g) can
   unsweetened coconut milk
1 stick lemon grass
1½ in. (3 cm) galanga root
   OR fresh ginger root
2 fresh chilies
4 lime leaves OR 1 tbsp.
   (15 mL) fresh lime juice

4 oz. (150 g) boned, skinned
   chicken breast
juice of 1 lemon
few sprigs fresh coriander
1½ tbsp. (20 mL) Thai fish
   sauce (nam pla)
pinch white sugar

PREPARATION

1 Open can of coconut milk (yes, all our best Thai restaurants use canned coconut milk) and transfer contents to a soup pot. Add ¾ of the can water and stir. Reserve.

2 Chop lemon grass into 1 in. (2 cm) bits by cutting diagonally (to expose more inside surface for a better infusion).

3 Thinly slice unpeeled galanga (or ginger) root.

4 Mince the chilies. (Wash hands right after.) Combine chopped lemon grass, galanga, chilies and lime leaves in a small bowl. Reserve.

5 Slice chicken breast into ½ in. (1 cm) strips. Reserve.

6 Squeeze the lemon. Strain and reserve juice. (If unable to use lime leaves, squeeze the lime, and strain and reserve its juice).

COOKING

7 Place pot with diluted coconut milk over medium heat. Add reserved bowl of lemon grass-galanga-lime leaves-chilies and stir. Heat this broth for 2–3 minutes until it begins to steam but before it comes to a boil, stirring constantly.

8 Reduce heat to medium-low and add the chicken strips. Cook for 5–7 minutes, stirring occasionally until chicken is cooked through.

Make sure the soup doesn't ever actually boil, and don't overcook the chicken.

9 While the soup is cooking, wash, dry and chop several sprigs of fresh coriander. Reserve under a wet paper towel.

10 When the chicken strips have cooked, add 2 tbsp. (30 mL) lemon juice (plus lime juice, if unable to use lime leaves), Thai fish sauce and a pinch of white sugar. Stir and cook for 1–2 minutes. Taste the broth: it should be smooth, spicy and not too acid from the citrus juices.

11 Transfer to a serving bowl. Garnish with plenty of fresh coriander and serve immediately.

Total prep time: less than 15 minutes.
Total cooking time: 10 minutes.
Serves 3–4.

Tom Yum Goong

Shrimp-Lemon Grass Soup

INGREDIENTS

4 cups (1 L) home-made chicken broth, skimmed of all fat
16 medium shrimp
3½ oz. (100 g) button mushrooms
juice of 2 or 3 limes
1 stick lemon grass
1½ in. (3 cm) galanga root OR ginger root
2 fresh chilies
1½ tbsp. (20 mL) Thai fish sauce (nam pla)
pinch white sugar
4 lime leaves OR 1 tbsp. (15 mL) lime juice
few sprigs fresh coriander

PREPARATION

1 Put the chicken broth into a soup pot and place over medium-low heat.

2 Meanwhile, shell the shrimps, reserving the shells. Wash shells and add them to the simmering broth (where they should simmer for 10–15 minutes while you

continue with the preparations). Returning to the shelled shrimps, scrape off their back veins, wash and lay out on a paper towel to dry.

3 Wipe mushrooms and chop into quarters. Reserve.

4 Squeeze 2 limes. Strain juice and reserve. You should have 3–4 tbsps. (45–60 mL) of juice: if not, then squeeze another lime.

5 Chop lemon grass into 1 in. (2 cm) bits, cutting diagonally (to expose more inside surface for a better infusion).

6 Thinly slice unpeeled galanga (or ginger) root. Combine chopped lemon grass, galanga and lime leaves in a small bowl. Reserve.

7 Mince chilies (wash hands right after) and transfer to yet another small bowl. Add Thai fish sauce, sugar and lime juice (adding an extra tablespoon if you were unable to find lime leaves). Stir and reserve.

COOKING

8 Strain chicken broth to extract the boiled shrimp shells. Discard shells. Transfer strained broth back to the soup pot and raise heat to medium to bring it to a boil.

9 Add quartered mushrooms and reserved mixture of lemon grass, galanga and lime leaves. Cook for 10 minutes at less than a boil yet more than a simmer: a gentle bubble.

10 While the soup cooks, wash, dry and chop several sprigs of fresh coriander. Reserve under a wet paper towel.

11 At the end of the 10 minutes, add the reserved mixture of chilies, sugar, Thai fish sauce and lime juice to the soup. Stir. Raise the heat a notch (to medium-high) and cook for 2 minutes.

12 Add the shrimps and cook for 1–2 minutes until shrimps are pink and are firm to the touch. Do not overcook.

13 Immediately transfer to a serving bowl, garnish with plenty of fresh, chopped coriander and serve.

Total prep time: 15–20 minutes.
Total cooking time: 15 minutes.
Serves 3–4.

Salads & Cold Appetizers

It's hard to imagine, but the original salad that was served in Roman times was nothing more than greens and a little salt. The very word "salad" derives from the Latin "sal," meaning salt. Nowadays a salad can be composed of anything from seafood all the way back to those original greens. As for salad dressing, its only apparent constant is salt itself, in that all salad dressings are improved by it. Otherwise, the field is wide open: oil, yoghurt, vinegars, aromatics, spices, fish extract, anything goes. The only limitation is your regard for your waistline. After all, salad — like pasta — is indeed lean food, were it not for the sauce.

I offer a number of unusual salad ideas below, yet it seems most fitting to start the list with some dressings for greens, now and forever the common denominator of all salads.

Vinaigrette Dressing

INGREDIENTS

1 tbsp. (15 mL) whole-grain or smooth French mustard

1 tbsp. (15 mL) white wine vinegar

2 tbsp. (30 mL) red onion, minced

few leaves fresh tarragon OR sprigs parsley

¼ cup (50 mL) extra-virgin olive oil

salt and black pepper

PREPARATION

The French like to make their vinaigrette in the bottom of their salad bowl, then pile all the greens on top. They don't toss the salad till it's time to serve, but they're assured of having the bottom leaves totally soaked in the dressing. This way once the whole salad is tossed, the few over-dressed leaves are distributed throughout to provide extra zesty bites here and there. The other way, obviously, is to make your dressing in a separate bowl, and let the diners add as much (or as little) as they like.

1. In either case, the method begins with the whole-grain (or smooth) French mustard at the bottom of a working bowl. Add the white wine vinegar and beat with a whisk or, if you're good at it, a fork until the mustard is dissolved in the vinegar.

2. Finely mince the red onion and add to the dressing.

3. Wash, dry and stem fresh tarragon leaves from a few sprigs and mince enough to have 2 tbsp. (30 mL) (Failing availability of tarragon, use parsley.) Add to dressing. Add salt and freshly ground pepper.

4. Beat all ingredients while adding olive oil in a steady stream. A light emulsion will emerge. Taste for seasoning and adjust. Reserve till ready to use. If presenting your dressing on the side, give it a good whisking just before serving.

Total prep time: about 10 minutes. Serves 3–4.

Garlic Mayonnaise

The advent of food processors and blenders has obviated the need for store-bought mayonnaise. What used to take an eternity of elbow grease in the days of whisks can now be achieved in almost no time (if we don't count washing up). This dressing is particularly wonderful on salads of slightly bitter greens like watercress, endive and escarole. On the other hand, it works very well on soft greens like Boston and butter lettuce.

INGREDIENTS

2–3 cloves garlic
few sprigs parsley
1 lemon
1 egg
1 tbsp. (15 mL) red wine
    vinegar

1 tsp. (5 mL) Dijon mustard
½ tsp. (2 mL) sugar
¾–1 cup (175–250 mL) extra-
    virgin olive oil
3–4 tbsp. (45–60 mL) cold
    water
salt and pepper

PREPARATION

1 Mince 2–3 cloves garlic (depending on your love of the bulb). Even better, press garlic in a garlic press. Reserve the minced garlic in a small bowl.

2 Wash, dry and chop parsley. Add to the garlic. Add salt and freshly ground black pepper to the mixture and reserve.

3 Squeeze lemon, strain juice and reserve.

4 Break egg into bowl of processor or blender. Process at high speed for 30 seconds and stop. Add the garlic-parsley mixture as well as 1 tbsp. (15 mL) lemon juice, red wine vinegar, Dijon mustard and sugar. Process at high speed for 1 minute, till everything is frothy.

5 Still processing at high speed, add olive oil by droplets at first, then in a thin stream. At about ¾ cup, a blender clogs and the mayonnaise is thick and ready. The food processor (which makes a slightly softer mayonnaise) can take a full cup.

6 Transfer the mayonnaise to a working bowl. If using as a sauce for things like French Vegetable soup (page 30), then it's ready. If using as a salad dressing, take a whisk in hand and add cold water 1 tbsp. (15 mL) at a time, whisking vigorously for 15 seconds after each addition. The water thins the sauce and makes it suitably runny for the salad.

Total prep time: no more than 15 minutes. Serves 4–6. It's impossible to make less, but leftovers if covered, and refrigerated, will keep to dress a salad the next day.

Sesame Dressing

A light and aromatic salad dressing, it's made with Chinese sesame sauce, the brown sesame-seed paste that is available in all Asian markets. This tahini-like bottled substance is usually quite dense, with an inch or so of oil separated and risen to the top. In this recipe it is crucial to use some of the oil along with the solids (a ratio of 1 part oil to 4 parts solids is about right). This dressing can be used on a green salad, but is most effective with blanched and/or raw vegetables like broccoli, carrot, snow peas and bean sprouts.

INGREDIENTS

3 tbsp. (45 mL) Chinese
   sesame sauce
½ cup (125 mL) warm water
1 in. ginger root (2 cm)

2 green onions
2 tbsp. (30 mL) Japanese rice
   vinegar OR lime juice
1 tsp. (5 mL) soya sauce or
   tamari

PREPARATION

1 Scoop out sesame sauce including a bit of the oil and transfer to a working bowl. Prod it with a fork to loosen it a little, then add warm water, a little at a time, whisking with a small wire whisk. It will appear hopelessly lumpy at first, but gives up resistance after 2–3 minutes of whisking and becomes very smooth.

2 Peel and mince ginger root. Add to the sesame. Trim and finely chop green onions, white and green parts alike. Add to the sesame.

3 Add rice vinegar (or lime juice) and soya or tamari to the sesame.

4 Whisk the sauce until everything is integrated (1 minute). Serve alongside salad. This dressing works best if used at the table and mixed in just before eating. It tends to dry on the surface of the vegetables if pre-tossed.

*Total prep time:
under 15 minutes.
Serves 4–5.*

GREEK SALADS

There are two generic Greek salads: one for the cold months when tomatoes are out of season, and one for the summer when they are in season. For most people, especially if they have vacationed in Greece in summertime, a Greek salad means nothing without its tomatoes, and so wherever there are Greek restaurants (and there are Greek restaurants everywhere), a salad will always have tomatoes, whatever the season. In Greek, the word for "lettuce" means salad (literally), and so it's with us for most of the year. The only constant is the feta cheese, which appears on salads throughout the year.

Greek Winter Salad

INGREDIENTS

1 lettuce (preferably romaine)
several sprigs of fresh dill or
   parsley
3 green onions

DRESSING

¼ cup (50 mL) olive oil
1 tbsp. (15 mL) red wine vinegar
salt-pepper

TOPPING

3½ oz. (100 g) feta cheese
pinch of oregano
8 Calamata olives

PREPARATION AND ASSEMBLY

1 Separate the lettuce leaves, wash thoroughly and dry. Laying the lettuce leaves on top of each other, slice across them to obtain ribbons of ¼ in. (½ cm) thickness. Transfer to a working bowl.

2 Wash, dry and finely chop several sprigs of fresh dill (if you can't find dill, you can use parsley, but it won't be the same). Sprinkle the chopped dill on the lettuce.

3 Trim and chop green onions in ¼ in. (½ cm) bits. Sprinkle on salad, white and green parts alike.

4 Make the dressing: In a bowl or

bottle, combine olive oil, vinegar, salt and pepper. Mix well and sprinkle on the salad. Toss the salad to distribute dressing. Transfer dressed salad to a serving bowl or platter.

5   Handling it with authority, wash feta cheese in cold water to remove some of its salt. Drain or pat dry with a paper towel. Break it up into several large chunks and scatter it decoratively on the salad. Sprinkle a pinch of oregano (dried or fresh) on the chunks of feta. Finish by placing 8 black olives (preferably Calamata) wherever they'll best contrast with the white feta. Serve soon, if not immediately (before the dressed lettuce wilts too much).

Total prep and assembly time: about 15 minutes.
Serves 4–6.

Greek Summer Salad

Here's the salad everyone talks about. All the ingredients are widely available and can certainly be found in Greek or Middle Eastern establishments. The ripeness and flavour of the tomatoes is essential here, making this dish an expensive proposition out of season, when good tomatoes come from far away and cost a fortune.

INGREDIENTS

½ red onion
¼ cup (50 mL) pickled green peppers (pepperoncini)
1 lemon
4 oz. (150 g) feta cheese
fresh oregano leaves OR dried oregano

1 small English cucumber
1½ lb. (700 g) tomatoes
salt and pepper
¼ cup (50 mL) extra-virgin olive oil
8 Calamata olives

PREPARATION

1 Slice ½ red onion into thin slivers. Reserve.

2 Drain pickled peppers and refresh with cold water. Drain again.

3 Squeeze lemon and strain juice. Reserve.

4 Wash feta cheese in cold water to remove some of its salt. Drain or pat dry with a paper towel and transfer the cheese to a cutting board. Cut into slices of ¼ in. (½ cm) thickness. There will be some crumbling: that's fine. Reserve.

5 If using fresh oregano, wash, dry and chop it. Reserve.

6 Peel (or wipe off and use un-peeled) a small English cucumber. Cut into rounds ¼ in. (½ cm) thick.

7 Wash tomatoes and cut away their stems. Place tomatoes on cutting board and slice into 1 in. (2 cm) wedges by cutting first in half, then in quarters and even in eighths, depending on the size of the tomato (use a sharp, serrated knife for a clean slice).

ASSEMBLY

8 Scatter tomato wedges on a flat platter. Scatter cucumber rounds in between tomatoes, trying to avoid pile-ups. Both cucumber and tomato should be touching bottom. Scatter onion slices all over. Arrange pepperoncini and olives alternately around the perimeter of the plate. Salt and pepper the salad lightly. Drizzle lemon juice over the tomatoes and cucumbers: 2–3 tsp. (10–15 mL) should do it. Drizzle olive oil evenly all over the salad.

9 Arrange the feta slices (including the crumbles) decoratively down the spine of the salad. Lightly sprinkle fresh or dry oregano over everything, especially the feta. Decorate with Calamata olives. This salad can wait 5–10 minutes as is, but should be served soon after that.

Total prep time: about 20 minutes. Total assembly time: less than 10 minutes. Serves 4–6.

Greek Bean Salad

Here is a Greek salad that hardly anyone knows. It was a popular item in my mother Despina's party buffets and tasted even better when any was left over the next day. It can be whipped up in no time, if you don't mind using canned beans.

INGREDIENTS

2 eggs

1 19 oz. (540 mL) can white
  kidney beans

1 medium onion

1 small tomato

¼ cup (50 mL) olive oil

1 tbsp. (15 mL) red wine
  vinegar

salt and pepper

¼ cup (50 mL) pickled green
  peppers (pepperoncini)

1 small cucumber

8 Calamata olives

6 anchovy fillets (optional)

few sprigs of parsley

PREPARATION

1 Boil eggs until hard. Shell and reserve.

2 Meanwhile, drain white kidney beans in a strainer and refresh with cold water, tossing to remove all residue of canning liquid. Transfer to a working bowl.

3 Slice the onion into very thin slivers. Add to beans.

4 Wash tomato and cut away the stem. Dice into ½ in. (1 cm) cubes and add to the beans, including, if possible, the tomato juice that resulted from the dicing.

5 In a small bowl or bottle, combine the olive oil, wine vinegar, salt and pepper. Mix to integrate

and drizzle over the bean mixture in the bowl. Toss the salad (folding gently so as not to break up the beans) until all the ingredients are evenly distributed. Transfer the dressed salad in a low mound onto an oval presentation platter.

ASSEMBLY

6 Drain and refresh pepperoncini. Drain.

7 Slice cucumber (peeled or unpeeled) into ¼ in. (½ cm) rounds.

8 Quarter the hard-boiled eggs. Decorate the rim of the platter with alternating pepperoncini, cucumber rounds and egg wedges and 8 Calamata olives. If desired, place 6 anchovy fillets down the middle of the mound of beans.

9 This salad can be served immediately or can wait several hours, as long as it is covered tightly with food wrap and refrigerated. Half an hour before serving, take it out of the fridge to temper it. Just before serving, wash, dry and chop several sprigs of parsley and scatter it over everything.

Total prep time:
about 20 minutes.
Total assembly time:
about 10 minutes.
Serves 4–6.

Roasted Peppers Antipasto

A taste and texture sensation like no other, the flesh of a bell pepper bathed in olive oil has only one drawback: the pesky chore of peeling and coring it after roasting or grilling. Contemplating a blackened vegetable with its messy, wet innards is enough to drive most people to the nearest Italian restaurant to pay $6 or $7 for an appetizer of the same. At least, this is what happens when the process involves the correct use of entire peppers. I've devised a method that eliminates most of the problem: I core and cut my peppers in half before roasting or grilling. This tends to dehydrate and shrink the flesh a little, making it fragile, but it's a heck of an easier job.

INGREDIENTS

2 bell peppers, preferably of
    different colours (green,
    yellow or red)
1 tsp. (5 mL) vegetable oil
shaved Parmesan cheese
red onion

few sprigs of parsley
1 tbsp. (15 mL) balsamic
    vinegar
¼ cup (50 mL) extra-virgin
    olive oil
salt and pepper

PREPARATION

1 Preheat oven to 425° F (220° C). Cut peppers in half and core, discarding seeds and inner white pulp. Oil the outside skin with the vegetable oil. Arrange peppers, without crowding, in an oven pan, skin side up. Bake for 20–25 minutes, just until the skin has crinkled but before it has blackened (if you wait till the skin turns black, then the flesh of these halved peppers will totally disintegrate). Take out of the oven and let cool 5–10 minutes.

While the peppers are cooking, shave some Parmesan using a vegetable peeler or paring knife. Sliver the red onion and chop the parsley. Reserve.

2 Using a spatula, pry the cooled peppers off the pan. Transfer them to a plate and pull at the skin. It should come off easily and more or less in one piece. Handling the fragile flesh carefully, transfer peppers to a serving plate. Cut each half-pepper into 5 or 6 strips right on the plate.

ASSEMBLY

3 Moisten the pepper strips with balsamic vinegar. Then douse them with the olive oil. Add salt and peppers to taste. Decorate with the Parmesan, onion and parsley just prior to serving. The oiled peppers will wait (and improve) up to an hour after preparation. If covered and refrigerated, they can wait up to two days.

Total prep time: 25 minutes.
Cooling-off time: 10 minutes.
Assembly time: 5–10 minutes.

Serves 4 as an appetizer to pasta, but 2 can easily make short work of this quantity. For more, increase proportionately, except for the oil, which can increase by half at a time.

Served on a larger platter, the peppers can be bolstered with various ingredients to become a party antipasto. Black olives, marinated sun-dried tomatoes, sliced Italian salami, sliced ripe tomatoes and slices of bocconcini (or other kinds of fresh mozzarella) are favourites.

Insalata Caprese

This one works only in real tomato season, when the aroma and sweetness of the world's most famous fruit-vegetable matches its crimson ripeness. Bocconcini are fresh, golf-ball sized mozzarella curds that must be kept in water until they are needed. They are widely available. In supermarkets, they usually sit in plastic tubs right by the ricotta and other Italian dairy products.

INGREDIENTS

1 lb. (500 g) ripe tomatoes
½ red onion
½ green pepper
2 tbsp. (30 mL) balsamic
    vinegar

¼ cup (50 mL) olive oil
salt and freshly grated black
    pepper
6 oz. (200 g) bocconcini
fresh basil leaves and black
    olives

PREPARATION

1 Wash tomatoes and dry. Cut away and discard the stems. Slice tomatoes into rounds ½ in. (1 cm) thick, arriving at the last slice just before the bottom layer of skin, which you discard. Arrange tomato slices on a flat platter (cut them in half if large tomatoes are used). Just about the entire surface of the platter should be lined with tomato slices.

2 Slice onion and green pepper thinly. Reserve.

3 Wash, dry and chop basil roughly. Reserve under a wet paper towel.

4 Combine balsamic vinegar and olive oil in a small sauce bottle or bowl. Mix vigorously for 30 seconds until an emulsion forms.

ASSEMBLY

5 Pour the oil-vinegar emulsion evenly over the tomatoes. Sprinkle salt and freshly cracked pepper to taste.

6 Scatter the sliced red onion and green peppers over the tomatoes.

7 Fish the bocconcini out of their water, dry with a paper towel and slice into rounds ¼ in. (½ cm) thick. Dot the cheese rounds over the entire salad, making sure that each morsel of tomato gets at least one.

8 Scatter the basil over everything, and place black olives decoratively here and there.

9 This salad can be served immediately, but it can also wait up to 20 minutes while other parts of the meal are being prepared. There will probably be dressing left over after the salad is eaten (unless it has been sopped up with bread). It can be scraped into a bowl and reserved for use in another salad the next day.

Total prep time:
about 10 minutes.
Total assembly time:
about 5 minutes.
Serves 4 as an appetizer,
accompanied by crusty bread.

Eggplant with Mint

All Mediterranean cultures roast or grill their eggplant, transforming an otherwise spongy vegetable into a creamy vessel for olive oil and garlic. Baba-ganoush and Greek eggplant puree (without tahini) are labour-intensive preparations that are more akin to dips than salads. This Sicilian recipe is just as tasty, but much more sparing of the elbow grease.

INGREDIENTS

1 medium eggplant
1 lemon
3 cloves garlic
1 fresh chili (optional)

few sprigs fresh mint OR
   1 tsp. (5 mL) dried mint
¼ cup (50 mL) olive oil
salt
tomato wedges and black olives
   (to garnish)

PREPARATION

1 Preheat oven to 450° F (230° C). Place the eggplant just as is in an oven pan and let it roast undisturbed for 45 minutes.

2 Meanwhile, prepare the dressing: Squeeze lemon, strain juice and transfer to a bowl. Peel and pulp garlic (preferably in a garlic press). Core and seed the optional hot chili (leaving some of the seeds for extra heat). Slice very thinly and then chop a few times (wash hands right after). Wash, dry and chop fresh mint finely. Add garlic chilies and mint to lemon juice. Add olive oil, and salt to taste.

   You have now combined all the saucing ingredients. Mix well and reserve dressing.

ASSEMBLY

3 Remove eggplant from the oven. It'll be a dark brown colour, but not quite charred. Transfer it to a large working plate. Cut off 2 in. (4 cms) at the stem end and discard (this part never quite cooks through). The skin of the eggplant peels off very easily. Pick at an edge from the cut end, pull upward and discard. It'll come off in strips. When the top side is done, carefully roll the eggplant over and peel the bottom side. Now cut the eggplant in half and flip over, in effect butterflying it, so that the entire interior is facing you. You'll see tongues of seed-pods, much like a tomato's. Scoop them out with a spoon and discard, leaving as much flesh as possible. There are some additional seed-pods hiding inside. Slice each cleaned half in half again and you'll see them. Deal with these seed pods as above and discard. Now all that is left on your plate is the usable flesh of the eggplant. Slice it so that you get strips that are 2 in. (4–5 cm) long and half again as wide. Transfer these strips into a presentation bowl.

4 Whisk the dressing from step #2 to form a light emulsion and add to the eggplant. Fold gently, without breaking the eggplant pieces, until everything is well mixed. The salad is now ready to eat. It'll be even better if it waits. Refrigerate any leftovers tightly sealed. It'll be explosively delicious the next day.

Total prep time: 45 minutes.
Total assembly time: 10 minutes.
Serves 3–4 as an appetizer or side course to grilled meat or fish. If an appetizer, garnish with tomato wedges and black olives.

Marinated Mushrooms

This is a refreshing and meaningful appetizer or side vegetable that requires next to no cooking and can sit nicely in the fridge (for up to 2 days) waiting to be needed, improving its flavour the while.

INGREDIENTS

½ lb. (500 g) button
   mushrooms
¼ red onion
3 cloves garlic
1 tsp. (5 mL) olive oil
¼ cup (50 mL) walnut pieces
fresh basil or parsley

2 tbsp. (30 mL) white wine
   vinegar
6 tbsp. (90 mL) extra-virgin
   olive oil
1 tbsp. (15 mL) soya sauce
pinch cayenne (optional)
salt and pepper

PREPARATION AND ASSEMBLY

1 Wipe the mushrooms. Trim stems to within ½ in. (1 cm) of the cap and reserve for another use. Cut caps in half and transfer to a working bowl.

2 Slice red onion into thin slivers. Add to the mushrooms. Mince garlic in a garlic press and add to the mushrooms.

3 In a small saute pan over medium heat, warm olive oil for 30 seconds. Add walnut pieces and stir-fry for 1–2 minutes until they have browned (do not overcook). Add to the mushrooms.

4 In small bowl combine white wine vinegar, olive oil, soya, cayenne, salt and pepper. Mix and fold into the mushrooms.

5 Leave uncovered. Stir gently every 15 minutes or so, for an hour. The mushrooms can be served after this hour of marination, or covered and refrigerated for up to 2 days.

6 Half an hour before serving, take mushrooms out of the fridge to temper them and stir them gently to wake them up. Just before serving, wash, dry and chop several sprigs of fresh basil or parsley (or both). Transfer the mushrooms and their marinade to a serving dish, garnish liberally with the herbs and serve.

Total prep and assembly time: about 20 minutes.
Marination time: 1 hour minimum.
Serves 4–6.

Marinated Salmon

Of all the ways to treat salmon (smoking, pickling, etc.), marinating in the Italian style is easiest and quickest. Nevertheless, it offers a taste and texture sensation that rivals all other techniques. Unfortunately, it's not entirely carefree in the preparation. Marinating involves the slightly unpleasant task of slicing raw fish. And then there is the wait: though far less onerous than the 3-day curing period for gravlax, this marinated version does require a minimum of 90 minutes, and is at its best 4–5 hours, (even 24 hours) after it's assembled.

INGREDIENTS

1 or 2 lemons
¼ red onion
few sprigs parsley
¼ cup (50 mL) extra-virgin
  olive oil

salt and pepper
½ -¾ lb. (300 g) fillet of fresh
  salmon, bone off, skin on
1 tsp. (5 mL) capers, drained
parsley

PREPARATION

1 Juice 1 lemon, strain and reserve. You should have 2–3 tbsp. (30–45 mL) of juice. If not, squeeze ½ a lemon more.

2 Slice the red onion into thin slivers. Wash, dry and chop the parsley roughly.

3 Choose a flat dish with a bit of a border (a ceramic pie dish works well). Moisten the bottom of the dish with a little olive oil and lemon juice and scatter some onion slivers and parsley in it. Add salt and freshly ground black pepper.

4 Address your chunk of salmon. Run your fingers along its surface and expose any lateral bones that might be lurking. Pull them out, using small pliers if necessary. Wipe the surface of the fish with a paper towel. Take a sharp, longish knife in hand and cut ¼ in. (½ cm) slices across the

width of the salmon from the head towards the tail (the thinner the slices, the better). Make a diagonal start, so that subsequent slices will get wider, yet be elegant and thin. The knife will stop against the skin at the bottom. Remove your slice from the skin by sliding the knife forward. As each slice is liberated, lay it on the seasoned bottom of your dish, until the whole surface of the dish is covered. Then sprinkle lemon juice and olive oil on the salmon layer, add some salt, freshly ground pepper, slivers of onion and parsley. Cut more salmon and keep layering in this fashion until all the fish and condiments are used up. (You'll probably have 2 or 3 layers of salmon, depending on the width of the dish and the thinness of your slices.)

5 Cover the dish tightly and refrigerate for at least 1½ hours, if not overnight.

ASSEMBLY

6 When ready to serve, transfer the salmon onto a platter, arranging it attractively in a single layer. Moisten with some of the sauce, and add capers and few sprigs of parsley. Serve with brown bread.

Total prep time:
less than 30 minutes.
Marination time: 1½ hours
minimum and up to 24 hours.
Serves 2–3.

Italian Squid Salad

Were it not for the ubiquitous Greek fried squid with tzatziki sauce, far too many of us would have remained sadly unintroduced to this delicate, flavourful seafood. Here's a recipe for a refreshing, light salad that works as an appetizer or as a summer main course. The only problem with it is cleaning the squid. Like much else in life, however, this task too can be enjoyable. Just make sure the squid are not ice cold, and then get into it as if it were a bizarre sexual practice.

INGREDIENTS

½-¾ lb. (300 g) fresh squid
1 bay leaf
pinch dried basil
½ lemon
½ tsp. (2 mL) balsamic vinegar
3 tbsp. (45 mL) olive oil

½ red onion
¼ red bell pepper
few sprigs parsley
pinch oregano
lettuce leaves, washed and
   drained

PREPARATION

1 Prepare squid by cutting tentacles at the point where they meet the eye-like ink sac, then by scooping out all the innards. These are joined to the ink sac, and cleaning them out is possible only by getting your fingers into it. Shove a finger inside the squid as deeply as it will go, and then prod the soft material out. It should come out more or less in one piece. Grope inside once more to make sure that everything has been removed, then wash the cavity with cold running water. Protruding from the edge of the body

on the cavity side you will see a small plastic see-through-like substance. Grab the edge of this quill and pull. It comes out in one clean piece. Discard it and the rest of the innards. Reserve the cleaned body and the tentacles. Repeat with the rest of the squid.

2 Over high heat, bring water to a boil with the bay leaf and a pinch of basil. Reduce heat and wait until the water simmers. Add all the squid and tentacles at once. Stir to settle. Simmer for 4–5 minutes (test by fishing one out and tasting a small bit: it should be tender, yet crunchy). Drain and run cold water over the squid. Drain and transfer to a chopping block.

ASSEMBLY

3 Slice the squid into rings about ½ in. (¾ cm) thick. Cut the ten-

tacles into 2 pieces, discarding the hard, ball-like beak. Transfer everything into a mixing bowl. Squeeze half a lemon: it should yield about 3 tbsp. (45 mL) of juice. Drizzle it on the squid along with the balsamic vinegar and olive oil. Mix well, tossing gently.

4 Finely chop the red onion and bell pepper. Add to the squid.

5 Wash, dry and chop parsley. Add to the squid. Add a pinch of oregano. Mix well, tossing gently. Let rest 15 minutes.

6 Arrange a whole lettuce leaf on each plate and pile the salad on the lettuce. Serve with Italian bread slices that have been brushed with olive oil and toasted.

Variation: This salad also works as a shrimp-and-squid combination. Simply substitute 5 oz. (150 g) of shrimp for half the squid, and cook the shrimp (shells on) along with the squid in the same water. Then shell the shrimp, quarter each and add to the squid, proceeding with the recipe as above.

Total prep time:
15 minutes.
Total assembly and
rest time: 25 minutes.
Serves 4 as an appetizer.

A▼ocado Salad

No other fruit, not even the tomato, is as suitable for the role of centrepiece of an appetizer salad as the avocado. Its subtle and refreshing taste can be enhanced in a variety of ways and its oil content (considerable to say the least) satisfies the early pangs of hunger, making the wait for the main course much less agonizing. I offer two recipes for this magic ingredient, starting with this uncomplicated, colourful salad.

INGREDIENTS

1 lime
1 ripe avocado
¼ red bell pepper
¼ red onion

2 tbsp. (30 mL) extra-virgin
   olive oil
salt (to taste)
few sprigs fresh coriander

PREPARATION AND ASSEMBLY

1 Squeeze lime, strain juice and transfer to a working bowl.

2 Now take the avocado in hand. It goes without saying that you were lucky enough to find an avocado that is perfectly ripe, without any brown spots and flesh that is parrot-green near the peel and canary-yellow around the seed in the middle. There are several ways to deal with your perfect avocado. Either slice it in half, discard the pit, and scoop the flesh out with a spoon; or, peel the fruit, cut it in half, separating flesh from pit, and then slice the flesh into long strips ½ in. (1 cm) wide. In either case, add the liberated avocado morsels to the lime juice and gently fold to moisten evenly: this prevents discoloration. (Note: If, like most of us who don't live in California, you find it difficult to locate a ripe, unblemished avocado, buy an unripe one and store it in a brown paper bag at room temperature. Monitor it and in a day or two you'll find it has ripened.)

3 Slice red bell pepper and red onion into thin slivers. Add to the avocado. Sprinkle olive oil evenly over all. Fold ingredients gently, so as not to break up the avocado, several times until thoroughly mixed. Transfer to a serving plate and spread out attractively.

4 Wash, dry and chop several sprigs

of fresh coriander. Scatter the chopped coriander all over the salad, season with a little salt, and serve with Salsa Cynthia (page 187) on the side. The hot stuff is optional, but altogether welcome. Avocado loves its hot sauce.

Total prep and assembly time: about 20 minutes.
Serves 2 as an appetizer, accompanied by corn chips.

Jane's Chicken Salad

My salad days in London of the late '60s, and early '70s, were an exhila-rating mixture of playwrighting, cooking and poverty. I often found refuge in south-of-the-river Barnes, in the cheerful company of Jane and Michael Sutherland. Lovers of food, all three of us, we used to spend hours on end cooking and eating. My fondest food memory from those days is Jane's chick-en salad, which I have recreated often over the years in my restaurant and for my movie catering. Whenever I make it I'm once again 25 and eternally smiling as the English springtime sun shimmers on the Thames and I travel on the upper deck of the number 9 bus.

INGREDIENTS

1 lemon
½ green apple
1 stick celery
¼ red onion
handful of seedless grapes
    (about 20, preferably red)
few sprigs fresh tarragon or
    parsley
1 small tomato
1 tbsp. (15 mL) olive oil
½ lb. (500 g) chicken breasts,
    skinned and boned
¼ cup (50 mL) walnut pieces

salt and pepper
sliced cucumber and black
    olives (to garnish)

MAYONNAISE

1 egg
1 tbsp. (15 mL) white wine
    vinegar (preferably tarragon-
    flavoured)
1 tsp. (5 mL) Dijon mustard
pinch salt
¾-1 cup (175–250 mL) extra-
    virgin olive oil

PREPARATION

1 Squeeze lemon; strain and reserve the juice.

2 Pour 1 tbsp. (15 mL) of your lemon juice into the bottom of a large working bowl (reserve the rest of the lemon juice for later). Slice the green apple (peeled or unpeeled) thinly. Immediately add apple slices to the lemon juice in the bowl. Turn them in the lemon juice to coat them and prevent discolouration.

3 Chop celery stick into ¼ in. (½ cm) bits. Add to the apples.

4 Chop red onion into thin slivers. Add to the apple and celery.

5 Cut grapes in half with a serrated knife. Add to the bowl.

6 Wash, dry, stem and chop a few sprigs of tarragon (or parsley, or both) and add to the bowl. Turn once to start mixing the ingredients.

7 Dice tomato into ½ in. (1 cm) cubes and add to the bowl with whatever juice the tomato has shed.

COOKING AND ASSEMBLY

8 Heat olive oil in a saute pan over high heat for 1 minute. Add chicken breasts and sear one side for 90 seconds. Turn and sear the other side for 90 seconds. Reduce heat to medium-high and continue cooking the second side for another 2 minutes. Turn and recook the first side for 1–2 minutes. At this point, cut into the meat. If only the very slightest pinkness has remained, it is done. Remove the chicken onto a cutting board, leaving the pan on the heat. Add the reserved lemon juice from step #2, scrape the pan to deglaze the stick-ons and cook for less than 2 minutes.

Take from heat and add contents to the bowl, scraping every drop with a rubber spatula. Mix into the salad ingredients.

9 Slice the cooked chicken breasts lengthwise into ¼ in. (½ cm) strips. Try not to break them as you cut so that you end up with long, elegant strips. Transfer them into the bowl with the vegetables, adding whatever chicken juice has emerged during the cutting. Add the walnut pieces to the bowl, as well as some salt and freshly ground pepper.

10 Toss and fold the salad gently but firmly. Cover and let rest a few minutes while you make the mayonnaise.

11 The easiest way to make mayonnaise is in the blender or the food processor, and the least amount you can make uses 1 egg. This makes about a cup (which also means about 1 cup of oil). If you're really extravagant with calories, fold in the whole amount with the other ingredients for a lush, smooth salad. However, you can use less by serving the salad as is with the mayo on the side for each guest to take what he or she will. (Leftover mayo may be covered and refrigerated, but must be stirred before reuse.) If you are seriously avoiding extra fat, you can serve the salad as is or enhance it with drops of white wine vinegar and a scant drizzle of oil.

Back to the mayo: Process an egg in a blender or food processor at high speed for 30 seconds. Add wine vinegar, Dijon mustard and salt to the egg, and process at high speed for 1 minute. Add olive oil by droplets at first, then in a steady stream, while the machine processes at high speed. (Blenders clog after ¾ cup, but processors can take a full cup.) Transfer mayo to bowl.

12 Uncover salad and fold once more. If dressing with mayo, combine now, folding until integrated. Otherwise, transfer salad to a serving bowl, and serve with mayo on the side.

Total prep time:
about 15 minutes.
Total cooking and
assembly time: 20 minutes.
Total rest and mayonnaise
time: 10 minutes.
Serves 4–6 as an appetizer;
or 3–4 for a summery main
course, along with other salads
and bread.

Yam and Pecan Salad

This is a spectacular salad. The pecans are a slight extravagance. This works as an appetizer, and also as one course of an exotic summer dinner.

INGREDIENTS

2 large yams

½ sweet red pepper

1 or 2 limes

½ red onion

fresh coriander

1 tbsp. peanut or other
   vegetable oil

¼ cup (50 mL) peanut or other
   vegetable oil

1 tsp. (5 mL) mustard seed

pinch each ground cumin,
   cinnamon and cayenne

⅓ cup (75 mL) pecan halves

1 tsp. (5 mL) sesame oil

½ tsp. (2 mL) salt

PREPARATION

1 Preheat oven to 450° F (230° C). Boil yams in a pot of water for 7 minutes over medium heat. Drain. Cut in rounds ½ in. (1 cm) thick.

2 While the yams are boiling, slice the red pepper in ½ in. (1 cm) strips.

3 Juice the limes: strain and reserve the juice. You should have about 3 tbsp. (45 mL).

4 Thinly slice the red onion.

5 Wash, dry and chop the coriander. Reserve, covered with a wet paper towel.

6 Grease the bottom of an oven pan with 1 tbsp. oil. Add the sliced yams and red pepper strips, so that everything touches the oil. Bake in the preheated oven for 10 minutes (or until the yams are easily pierced).

7 Meanwhile, over high heat, heat the ¼ cup oil in a saute pan until it's just about to smoke. Quickly add the spices (mustard seed, cumin, cinnamon and cayenne), and stir-fry for 30 seconds. Add the pecans and lower heat to medium. Stir-fry for 2 minutes, until the pecans have browned a little on both sides (do not burn).

ASSEMBLY

8 Remove the baked yams and red peppers from the oven. Using a spatula, carefully transfer yams and peppers onto a serving plate. Do not overlap.

9 Drizzle lime juice, sesame oil and salt evenly over the yams. Scatter sliced red onions over the yams. Using a spoon and a rubber spatula, scrape off the contents of the saute pan – oil, spices, pecans – and as much as possible, distribute evenly over the yams.

10 Let rest 10–15 minutes. Then garnish with the chopped coriander and serve.

*Total prep time:
about 20 minutes.
Assembly time: 5 minutes.
Rest time: 10–15 minutes.
Serves 4–6 people, either as a
starter or a salad.*

Asian Seafood Salad

My ever-continuing quest to find yet more ways to serve seafood (a certifiable crowd pleaser) has led me to this pan-Asian recipe for a salad of multicultural overtones. Thai nam pla (fish sauce), Japanese wasabe (horseradish), and fresh ginger combine with fruits, vegetables and seafood to become a truly North American appetizer. Sliced poached squid has a definite right to be included here, but I've left it out to make things easier, considering the already tricky chores of dealing with shrimp and scallops. If you want to bother with squid, then use half as many shrimp and poach ½ lb. (250 g) squid for 3–4 minutes over medium heat. A description of how to clean and chop squid can be found in the recipe for Italian Squid Salad (page 56).

INGREDIENTS

1 lb. (500 g) small shrimp, fresh or frozen	1½ in. (3 cm) fresh ginger root
¼ lb. (125 g) sea scallops, fresh or frozen	1 ripe mango OR 2 peaches
2 tbsp. (30 mL) peanut or other vegetable oil	½ red onion
1 tsp. (5 mL) wasabe powder	½ red bell pepper
2 oz. (50 g) snow peas	1 tbsp. (15 mL) Thai fish sauce OR soya sauce
2 limes	2 tbsp. (30 mL) peanut or other vegetable oil
	fresh coriander or chives

PREPARATION AND ASSEMBLY

1   Defrost shrimp and scallops, if using frozen. Shell the shrimp. If absolutely fastidious, you can also devein them (by scraping the coloured matter from their backs), but this is unnecessary for shrimp this size. Wash and let rest in strainer.

2   Over high heat, bring some salted water to a boil. Add the shelled shrimp and cook for 1–2 minutes, just until they have turned pink all over and are firm to the touch. Strain immediately and refresh with cold water. Drip-dry them by tossing them a few times in the strainer. Then transfer them into a large working bowl.

3   Transfer defrosted sea scallops into a strainer and refresh them

with some cold water. Toss them in the strainer, and let them relax to drain their liquid.

4   Meanwhile, heat 2 tbsp. peanut oil in a saute pan over high heat until it's just about to smoke. Add the scallops and stir-fry them for 2 minutes, turning with tongs or spatula to cook them all over. They are done when they turn white, having lost their opaque gloss. Add the scallops and all the oil from the pan to the shrimp and mix.

5   Mix wasabe powder with 1 tsp. (5 mL) cold water in a small bowl. A light green paste will emerge. Cover the bowl to activate the wasabe and reserve.

6   Pull the hard stems of the snow peas, removing as well the attendant string that runs down one side. Heat some water in a small pan to the boiling point, and add the snow peas. Cook for exactly 90 seconds and immediately drain and refresh with cold water. Strain well and add to the bowl with the seafood.

7   Squeeze 2 limes, strain the juice and sprinkle all over the emerging salad. Peel and finely dice the fresh ginger root. Scatter all over the salad.

8   Peel 1 ripe mango (or 2 ripe peaches) and cut flesh into large chunks. Add to the salad.

9   Finely slice red onion and bell peppers. Scatter on the salad. Toss salad by gently folding to mix all ingredients.

10 Uncover the wasabe. Add Thai fish sauce (or soya) and stir to dissolve. Add 2 tbsp. (30 mL) peanut oil. Mix. Sprinkle dressing on the salad and toss-fold a few times to distribute it. Transfer salad to a serving bowl. It can wait like this for up to 20 minutes, or even longer if covered and refrigerated. Ten minutes before serving, take from fridge and mix a few times to redistribute the dressing.

11 Wash, dry and finely chop several sprigs of fresh coriander (or chives). Garnish the salad with the herb and serve with a slotted spoon as an appetizer or as part of a party buffet.

Total prep and assembly time: 45 minutes
Serves 4–6 as an appetizer.

Don Don Noodles

This cold noodle specialty is one of the inexpensive street-foods of China's Szechwan province. It's sweet and spicy, and hits the spot perfectly as the curtain-raiser to a high-voltage meal. Do not serve these if the rest of the meal has subtle tastes. The sesame sauce used here is actually just ground-up sesame seeds, a kind of Chinese tahini, brown in colour because it is made of toasted sesames. It is sold bottled in Chinese markets. The oil will have separated from the solids, which will be hard and dense. When using it for this recipe try to scoop out some of the oil along with the solids. The rest will keep well and can be used instead of tahini in other recipes. (Tahini is unsuitable for this sauce: it's too sweet and not nutty enough.)

INGREDIENTS

½ lb. (250 g) dry Chinese
  noodles
1 tbsp. (15 mL) sesame oil
2 tbsp. (30 mL) peanut oil
½ tsp. (2 mL) dried red chili,
  crushed
1 tsp. (5 mL) soya sauce
3 tbsp. (45 mL) Chinese
  sesame sauce

½ cup (125 mL) warm water
2 cloves garlic
1 in. (2 cm) fresh ginger root
1 tbsp. (15 mL) soya sauce OR
  tamari
1 tsp. (5 mL) white sugar
½ tsp. (2 mL) black pepper
3 green onions
1½ in. (3 cm) cucumber

PREPARATION

1 Boil noodles in salted water according to package directions till cooked but not too soft. Drain and refresh with cold water. Drain again and transfer to a bowl. Sprinkle sesame oil on the noodles and toss to coat. Let rest.

2 Make the hot oil: Heat peanut oil in a small pan over high heat until it's just about to smoke (1–2 minutes). Take from heat. Add chili, seeds and flakes alike. The chili will sizzle in the oil and turn darker. (If it turns black then your oil is too hot: start again.) Add soya to the oil and take cover. It'll react violently for 5–10 seconds, and could splatter. When it has subsided, stir once

and transfer to a small bowl. Reserve.

3 Make the don don sauce: Spoon Chinese sesame sauce into a working bowl. Chop it with a fork to loosen it a bit and add warm water, a little at a time, whisking with a small wire whisk. The lumps will disappear after 2–3 minutes of whisking and it will become very smooth. Mince garlic and add to the sauce. Peel and finely chop ginger root and add to the sauce. Add soya (or tamari), white sugar and black pepper. Whisk to blend all ingredients.

The 3 components of this meal (boiled noodles, hot oil and don don sauce) are now ready. They can wait up to several hours before serving (cover and refrigerate the noodles; cover the other two and let stand).

ASSEMBLY

4 When ready to serve, take noodles out of the fridge. Finely chop the green onions. Dice cucumber (either peeled or not) into ¼ in. (½ cm) cubes. Divide the noodles into 4–6 appetizer bowls. Top with equal amounts of don don sauce (do not mix in: that happens at table). Garnish with chopped green onions and diced cucumber. Serve, accompanied by hot oil, drops of which are added at table.

Total prep time:
30 minutes.
Assembly time: 10 minutes.
Serves 4–6 as an appetizer.

Hot Appetizers

Baked Goat Cheese Appetizer

A favourite item from my former New York-based catering company La Grande Soiree, this recipe comes from my friend and partner, Wrenn Goodrum. She used to insist on the bitter radicchio leaves, but I find it just as wonderful on other lettuces, whether bitter like endive or escaroles or sweet like the inner leaves of romaine or Boston. This is an easy party dish because it can be prepared in advance, stored in the fridge, and baked at the last minute, to be passed as a stand-up hors d'oeuvre.

INGREDIENTS

3½ oz. (100 g) soft goat cheese
1 tbsp. (15 mL) olive oil
¼ cup (50 mL) pine nuts
1 tbsp. (15 mL) green
   peppercorns, drained

small lettuce leaves (radicchio,
   Belgian endive or inner leaves
   of Boston or romaine lettuce)

PREPARATION

1 Let cheese stand in a mixing bowl to soften (15 minutes).

2 Heat the olive oil in a small frying pan over medium heat. Add the pine nuts and saute, tossing often to brown them evenly (2 minutes). Be careful; they burn easily.

3 Add the sauteed pine nuts and drained green peppercorns to the softened cheese. Mix gently but thoroughly. Using your hands, roll small dollops of the mixture to form balls about ¾ in. (1½ cm) in diameter. Set balls on a plate as they're rolled, without crowding them. You should have 12–14 balls by the time you're done.

Cover loosely with waxed paper and refrigerate for 45 minutes to an hour to set. (If you're in a hurry, the freezer does the job in about 10 minutes. But don't forget them for longer than that, this could ruin the cheese.)

COOKING

4 Preheat oven to 425° F (220° C). Spread leaves of lettuce on a serving tray. Remove cheese balls from the fridge or freezer and transfer, without crowding, to a greased oven pan. Bake for 4–5 minutes, until cheese is bubbling

and begins to spread. Remove
from oven.

5   Using a small spatula, scrape each
    baked cheese ball and carefully
    transfer to the middle of a lettuce
    leaf (the leaf acts as a picker-
    upper for the cheese, and is eaten
    with it). Serve immediately.

Cheese softening time: 15 minutes.
Total prep time:
about 10 minutes.
Refrigeration time: 45 minutes
(or 10 minutes in the freezer).
Baking and transferring time:
8 minutes.
Serves 2 as an appetizer, along
with crusty French bread and red
wine, or 4–6 as a passed hors
d'oeuvre without bread, for
cocktails.

Chicken Yakitori

With its pin-point exactness in frying, cutting and decorating, Japanese cooking can be rather daunting for the home cook. But even here there are some easy recipes whose only challenge is a leisurely visit to a Japanese grocery store for the right ingredients. This chicken is a signature dish of its home country and can be recreated at home very successfully.

INGREDIENTS

1 whole (double) chicken breast, skinned and boned
½ green or red bell pepper
2 green onions
1 tbsp. (15 mL) peanut or other vegetable oil
1 ½ in. (3 cm) fresh ginger root

2 tbsp. (30 mL) soya sauce or tamari
¼ cup (50 mL) aji mirin
¼ cup (50 mL) chicken broth
1 tsp. (5 mL) cornstarch
1 tbsp. (15 mL) cold water
roasted sesame seeds
orange slices

PREPARATION

1 Cut chicken breast into strips, each ¾ in. (1½–2 cm) wide. Slice the strips into 3 pieces, each of which will be 1½ in. (2–3 cm) long. Each half-breast will thus yield 12 nuggets (24 nuggets from the two sides).

2 Cut the bell pepper into 1 in. (2 cm) squares, for a total of 8 pieces.

3 Trim away most of the green ends of the green onions and reserve for another use. Halve the white parts (with a bit of green remaining), then slice each half twice again to obtain a total of 8 pieces about 1½ in. (3 cm) in length.

4 You will need 8 bamboo or other skewers. Each skewer will hold 3 chicken nuggets, one square of pepper and one green onion, thus: skewer first a chicken nugget, then a green onion, then another chicken nugget, then a bell pepper and finally, the third piece of chicken. Using a pastry brush, brush the skewers lightly with oil. Reserve, covered with waxed paper (in the fridge, if the wait is to be longer than 30 minutes).

without crowding, on a broiling sheet. Broil, turning once, 3 minutes on each side for a total of 6 minutes (or grill them on a barbecue for the same time, turning once).

9 Holding the hot skewers with an oven mitt or kitchen towel, dip them one at a time into the warm sauce (using a spoon in the latter stages), making sure that all the skewered ingredients are thoroughly covered with sauce. Lay the yakitori skewers on a serving platter. Sprinkle generously with roasted sesame seeds and decorate with orange slices. Pour remaining sauce into a small bowl and fit that onto the platter (for whimsical dipping at table). Serve immediately.

Total prep time:
about 15 minutes.
Total cooking time:
(sauce, broiling, assembly)
15–16 minutes.
Serves 4 as an appetizer or
2 as a main course.

♣ **SUGGESTED MENU IF THIS IS A MAIN COURSE**
Starter: Asian Seafood Salad (page 64)
Side dishes: rice; Caraway Carrots (page 214)
Dessert: Baked Apple (page 219)

5 Peel the piece of ginger. Slice horizontally into 3 disks, then vertically 6 or 7 times, creating a bunch of matchstick-sized strips. Holding these strips together, cut against the grain, creating tiny specks of ginger (don't cut your fingers!).

COOKING

6 Over medium heat, combine soya, aji mirin and chicken broth in a sauce pan. Add minced ginger and bring to a boil. Lower heat to medium-low and cook gently for 3–4 minutes (until the broth is aromatic with ginger).

7 Dissolve cornstarch in cold water. Add to the sauce in the sauce pan and stir to mix. Continue cooking and stirring until the sauce bubbles and thickens to a light syrupy consistency (2–3 minutes). Turn heat off and let stand uncovered.

8 Lay out the chicken skewers

Chicken Sate

The traditional way to skewer chicken for sate is to cut it into long, thin strips and weave it onto a bamboo skewer. I use an easier method, skewering nuggets of chicken as in souvlakis. The difference in taste is negligible, and the benefit of larger chunks is better, moister texture. The sate sauce that gives this dish its name is a high-profile peanut concoction native to several South-East Asian countries (principally Indonesia) and therefore comes in several versions. This one is my own variation. I like it because it's easy and fairly fool proof.

INGREDIENTS

1 whole (double) chicken breast, skinned and boned

1 tsp. (5 mL) peanut or other vegetable oil

2 tbsp. (30 mL) shredded coconut

¼ cup (50 mL) hot water

1 onion

1 lime

½ cup (125 mL) chicken broth or water

2 tbsp. (30 mL) peanut or other vegetable oil

½-1 tsp. (2–5 mL) chili flakes (optional)

1 tbsp. (15 mL) brown sugar

3 tbsp. (45 mL) peanut butter

1 tbsp. (15 mL) soya sauce or tamari

fresh coriander

1 mango

PREPARATION

1 Cut chicken breast into strips, each ¾–1 in. (1 ½–2 cm) wide. Slice the strips into 3 pieces, each of which will be 1½ in. (3 cm) long. Each half-breast will thus yield 12 nuggets (24 nuggets from the two sides).

2 You will need 8 bamboo or other skewers. Skewer 3 chicken nuggets per each. Using a pastry brush, brush skewers lightly with oil. Reserve, covered with waxed paper (in the fridge if the wait is to be longer than 30 minutes).

3 Combine shredded coconut with hot water in a small sauce pan and cook over medium-low heat for 5–6 minutes.

4 Dice onion and reserve. Squeeze lime and reserve.

5 Heat chicken broth (or water) and keep handy.

COOKING

6 Heat peanut or other vegetable oil in a small saute pan or sauce pan over high heat for 30 seconds. Add onion and chili flakes and fry, stirring constantly, for 2 minutes, until the onion is wilted but not yet brown. Add brown sugar and stir into frying onions for 1 minute. Add peanut butter and the simmering coconut with its water to the sauce pan and stir steadily for 1 minute. Add lime juice and tamari and stir for 30 seconds.

7 The contents of the pan should be a thick, richly brown paste. Add half the hot chicken broth (reserving the rest) and stir. The paste will loosen and turn a milk-chocolate colour. Lower heat to low and cook, stirring, for 2–3 minutes. The oil of the peanut sauce will separate: don't panic. This is normal and will be remedied below in step #10. Turn off heat and cover sauce. This recipe can wait at this point. When ready to proceed:

8 Wash, dry and chop fresh coriander. Reserve. Peel and slice a ripe mango. Reserve.

9 Lay out the chicken skewers, without crowding on a broiling sheet. Broil, turning once, 3 minutes on each side for a total of 6 minutes (or grill them on a barbecue for the same time, turning once).

10 When the skewers are just about ready, return the peanut sauce to low heat and bring the reserved ¼ cup (50 mL) chicken broth to a boil. Add the chicken broth to the peanut sauce and stir. It will immediately re-emulsify to the consistency of thick syrup and look smooth and beautiful. Remove from heat immediately and transfer to a bowl – this

will stop cooking and prevent separation of the oil. If this should happen, a tablespoon of hot water, stirred into the sauce with alacrity, will restore the emulsion.

11 Holding onto them with an oven mitt or kitchen towel, dip the hot skewers one at a time into the peanut sauce (using a spoon in the latter stages), making sure that the chicken is heavily covered with sauce. Arrange the sate skewers on a serving platter. Sprinkle generously with chopped coriander. Decorate with mango slices. Pour remaining sauce into a small bowl and fit it onto the platter for dipping at table. Serve immediately.

Total prep time:
about 15 minutes.
Total cooking time:
about 20 minutes.
Serves 4 as an appetizer or
2 as a main course.

❖ **SUGGESTED MENU IF THIS IS A MAIN COURSE**
Starter: Tom Yum Goong
(page 36)
Accompaniments: rice; Jalapeno
Broccoli (page 205)
Dessert: Tiremisu (page 231)

BYZZA

Pizza for me is a last-resource food. It's what I order at 3 a.m. during a lingering poker game, or might eat a slice of while strolling downtown streets looking to get mugged. However, I'm in a minority. Not only do most folks love (even occasionally crave) pizza: they have created a demand for culinary innovation on the subject. Now designer (read: expensive) pizza is readily available in most upscale restaurants, which even offer it as the main course of chic dinners. So, I've buckled under the pressure and invented this recipe (named half-way after me). Quick and entertaining, it works for snacks as well as the main course of a casual dinner. It employs a convenient crust: a ready made "nan," which can be purchased wherever East Indian foods are sold. Nan can be stored frozen, ready to use whenever that pizza urge hits (at a pinch, these recipes also work with regular pita bread, which is more widely available). Byzza's only half-way difficult step is the tomato sauce, and even that is a snap once you've mastered the blanching-peeling-seeding of fresh tomatoes. The very first Byzzas were served to the 1,000 guests of NOW Magazine's eighth birthday party at Toronto's RPM club in 1989.

Goat Cheese Byzza

INGREDIENTS

3 nan breads or pitas
2 tbsp. (30 mL) olive oil
3½ oz. (100 g) soft goat cheese
3½ oz. (100 g) mozzarella
  cheese
½ red onion
½ green pepper
1 zucchini

TOMATO SAUCE
2 ripe tomatoes
1–2 cloves garlic
4 sun-dried tomatoes
2 tbsp. (30 mL) olive oil
pinch each oregano and basil
  (dried or fresh)
dash balsamic vinegar
black pepper

PREPARATION

1 Defrost nans or pitas.

2 Make tomato sauce: Blanch the tomatoes in boiling water for 30 seconds, then peel, core and seed them. Cut the flesh into small pieces. Mince the garlic. Chop the sun-dried tomatoes coarsely. Heat the olive oil in a pan, add the garlic and fry for 30 seconds. Add the tomato pieces, sun-dried tomatoes, oregano, basil, balsamic vinegar and black pepper to taste. Cook sauce for 10–12 minutes over medium heat, mashing the ingredients with a potato masher. Turn off heat and let rest.

3 While the sauce is cooking, prep the rest of the ingredients: Mash the goat cheese and shred the mozzarella, then mix the two cheeses together in a bowl; reserve. Thinly slice the red onion and green pepper; reserve. Slice the zucchini lengthwise into ¼ in. (½ cm) strips; reserve. Wash, dry and chop the parsley. Reserve, covered with a wet paper towel.

ASSEMBLY AND BAKING

4 Preheat oven to 425° F (220° C). Brush all the nans on both sides with olive oil and arrange in an oven pan.

5 Divide the sauce evenly among the 3 nans, spreading to cover the surfaces.

6 Divide the mixed cheeses evenly among the 3 nans, and sprinkling over the tomato sauce.

7 Top with the sliced onions, green peppers and zucchini, arranging the vegetables attractively on top of the cheese.

8 Bake the assembled Byzzas in the preheated oven for 15–20 minutes, until the cheeses are bubbling, the vegetables have charred a little, and the bottoms of the nans have crusted.

9 Remove from the oven, transfer to a cutting surface and cut each Byzza into quarters with a pizza cutter or a heavy chef's knife. Garnish with chopped parsley. Serve immediately.

Total prep time: 15–20 minutes.
Total assembly and baking time: 25 minutes.
Serves 2 as a main course and up to 6 as a starter. If a starter, serve it on its own. If a main course, serve it along with marinated mushrooms and at least one salad. And for dessert, some fruit.

Byzza Putanesca

Having committed myself to Byzza, I proceeded to invent three more varieties. I share them all with you, starting with this perky little number that highlights the buttery smoothness of fried eggplant with tasty things like feta cheese, anchovies and garlic.

INGREDIENTS

3 nan breads or pitas

5–6 cups (1½ L) cold water

1 tbsp. (15 mL) salt

1 medium eggplant

2 tbsp. (30 mL) fresh mint OR
   1 tsp. (5 mL) dried, crumbled

few sprigs parsley

2 green onions

6 black olives (Calamata or
   Gaeta)

3 large cloves garlic

2 tbsp. (30 mL) olive oil

pinch oregano

¼ cup plus 2 tbsp. (50 mL +
   30 mL) vegetable oil

1 cup (250 mL) all-purpose
   flour

⅓ cup (75 mL) feta cheese

3 anchovy fillets OR 1 tsp.
   (5 mL) capers, drained

PREPARATION

1 Defrost nans or pitas.

2 Combine cold water and salt in a large bowl. Mix to dissolve salt. Trim ½ in. (1 cm) from the head of the eggplant and discard. Cut round slices just less than ½ in. (1 cm) thick until you have 12 slices. Immediately dunk slices into the salted water and put a small plate on them to keep them submerged. Let rest at least 10 minutes.

3 Meanwhile, prep the other ingredients: Wash, dry and chop the mint and the parsley. Chop the green onions finely and mix with the mint and the parsley. Pit the olives and chop the flesh into large bits. Reserve. Peel the garlic and cut lengthwise into thin, oval slices. Reserve.

ASSEMBLY AND BAKING

4 Preheat oven to 425° F (220° C). Brush all the nans on both sides with olive oil and arrange on an oven pan. Sprinkle a little oregano over the nans.

5 Heat vegetable oil in a large saute

pan over high heat, until it's just about to smoke. Meanwhile, pour flour onto a plate. Fish out 6 of the eggplant rounds and dredge on both sides with the flour. Carefully slip eggplant into the hot oil (it tends to splutter) and cover pan with a frying screen. Fry on this first side for 2–3 minutes till golden brown. Turn the eggplant to fry the other side for 2 minutes. When slices are done on both sides, take from the pan and lay on a paper towel to absorb excess oil. Immediately add 2 more tablespoons oil (30 mL) to the pan. Working as fast as you can, dredge the remaining 6 slices of eggplant in the flour and repeat the frying process.

6   While the eggplant is frying, crumble feta cheese into a dish. Divide evenly on the nans, covering as much of the surface as possible. Sprinkle the chopped mint, parsley and green onion mixture over the feta.

7   When all the eggplant has finished frying, lay it on top of the herbs, using 4 slices per nan. The eggplant will cover the entire surface, with some overlapping. Shred anchovy fillets, and scatter them evenly over the eggplant layer (or, scatter a few drained capers). Proceed by scattering the

olive bits and finally the garlic slices.

8   Bake assembled Byzzas in the preheated oven for 12–15 minutes, until the garlic has turned yellow and the bottoms of the nans have crusted.

9   Remove from oven, transfer to a cutting surface and cut each Byzza into quarters with a pizza cutter or a heavy chef's knife. Serve immediately.

Total prep time: 25 minutes.
Total assembly and baking time: 25 minutes.
Serves 2 as a main course and up to 6 as a starter. If a starter, serve it on its own. If a main course, serve it along with a tomato-cucumber salad and blanched greens. For dessert: fruit.

Sausage Byzza

Here's one for the meat-eaters in the family. I don't use pepperoni, though this could easily be used instead. The Italian sausage I favour has all the spice of pepperoni but much less salt, and will be less greasy once cooked. A seriously tasty cheese is a must for this one — if not Asiago, then a Pecorino, or at the very least an aged Cheddar must be used.

INGREDIENTS

3 nan breads or pitas
1 tsp. (5 mL) vegetable oil
3 Italian sausages (sweet or hot)
3½ oz. (100 g) Asiago or
    Pecorino cheese
½ red onion
few sprigs parsley
2 tbsp. (30 mL) olive oil

TOMATO SAUCE

2 ripe tomatoes
1–2 cloves garlic
4 sun-dried tomatoes
2 tbsp. (30 mL) olive oil
pinch each oregano and basil
    (dried or fresh)
dash balsamic vinegar
black pepper

PREPARATION

1 Defrost nans or pitas.

2 Make tomato sauce: Blanch the tomatoes in boiling water for 30 seconds, then peel, core and seed them. Cut the flesh into small pieces. Mince the garlic. Chop sun-dried tomatoes coarsely. Heat the olive oil in a pan, add the garlic and fry for 30 seconds. Add the tomato pieces, sun-dried tomatoes, oregano, basil, balsamic vinegar and black pepper to taste. Cook sauce for 10–12 minutes over medium heat, mashing the ingredients with a potato masher. Turn off heat and let rest.

3 While the sauce is cooking, take a small frying pan and heat vegetable oil over medium heat. Add Italian sausages and fry, turning occasionally, for 8–10 minutes until golden brown all over and firm to the touch (use a frying screen to avoid oil splutters).

4 While both sauce and sausages are cooking, you have time to slice the cheese thinly (it'll crumble a little, but that's okay). Also thinly slice the red onion.

7 Divide the sauce evenly among the 3 nans and spread to cover the surfaces.

8 Divide the sausage slices evenly among the 3 nans and arrange them on top of the tomato sauce. Similarly, divide the cheese evenly and top the sausage with it. Lastly, do the same with the red onion.

9 Bake the assembled Byzzas in the preheated oven for 15–20 minutes until the cheese has melted, the onions have charred a little and the bottoms of the nans have crusted.

10 Remove from the oven, transfer to a cutting surface and cut each Byzza into quarters with a pizza cutter or a heavy chef's knife. Garnish with the chopped parsley. Serve immediately.

Total prep time: 25 minutes.
Total assembly and baking time: 25 minutes.
Serves 2 as a main course and up to 6 as a starter. If a starter, serve it on its own. If a main course, serve it along with Insalata Caprese (page 49) and black olives. Fruit makes a good dessert.

Reserve these items separately. Wash, dry and chop the parsley. Reserve under a wet paper towel.

5 When the sausages are cooked through, slice them into round or oval slices ¾ in. (1½ cm) thick. Reserve. At about this time, the tomato sauce will be ready. Take from the heat for its brief rest.

ASSEMBLY AND BAKING

6 Preheat oven to 425° F (220° C). Brush all the nans on both sides with olive oil and arrange in an oven pan.

Shrimp Mushroom Byzza

A mild-tasting Byzza, the better to feature the crunchy and delicate shrimp, this one is for those occasions when you want something soothing, yet interesting. Fancy mushrooms (portobello, oyster or shiitaki) add some of that interest, but button mushrooms also work well (and are cheaper). Do not overcook this Byzza. The idea is to retain as much as possible of the shrimps' juicy texture.

INGREDIENTS

½ lb. (250 g) small shrimp, fresh or frozen

3 nan breads or pitas

½ lb. (250 g) mozzarella cheese

4 black olives (Calamata or Gaeta)

1 tomato

½ lb. (250 g) fancy or button mushrooms

3 green onions

3 tbsp. plus 2 tbsp. (45 mL + 30 mL) olive oil

salt and pepper

parsley and capers

PREPARATION

1 Defrost shrimp, if using frozen. Shell the shrimp. You can also devein them (by scraping the coloured matter from their backs), but this is unnecessary for small shrimp. Wash and lay them out on a paper towel to dry.

2 Shred mozzarella cheese on the coarsest side of a grater. Reserve. Pit olives and chop the flesh into bits. Reserve.

3 Blanch tomato in boiled water for 30 seconds, then peel, core and seed it. Cut flesh into small pieces. Reserve.

4 Chop mushrooms and green onions into ½ in. (1 cm) pieces. Reserve separately.

5 Heat 3 tbsp. (45 mL) olive oil in a large saute pan over high heat for 30 seconds. Add salt, pepper and all the mushrooms. Cook, tossing for 1 minute. Add green onions and continue stir-frying for 1–2 minutes till the mushrooms have darkened and the green onions have wilted. Transfer to a working bowl and reserve.

ASSEMBLY AND BAKING

6 Preheat oven to 425° F (220° C). Brush the nans on both sides with remaining 2 tbsp. (30 mL) olive oil and arrange in an oven pan.

7 Divide the tomato pieces and scatter over the nans. Divide the shrimp and arrange on the tomatoes. Divide the mushroom-green-onion mixture evenly and pile on top of the shrimp layer. Top with equal amounts of shredded cheese, and dot the olives on top of the cheese.

8 Bake the assembled Byzzas in the preheated oven for 14–17 minutes until the cheese is melted and the bottoms of the nans have crusted. While the Byzzas are baking, wash, dry and chop some parsley and drain some capers. Reserve.

9 Remove Byzzas from oven. Transfer to a cutting surface and cut each into quarters with a pizza cutter or a heavy chef's knife. Garnish with chopped parsley and capers. Serve immediately.

Total prep time:
about 25 minutes.
Total assembly and baking time:
25 minutes.
Serves 2 as a main course and up to 6 as a starter. If a starter, serve on its own. If a main course, serve it along with a green salad, with fruit for dessert.

Baked Main Courses

Further to my comments regarding crust in the Introduction of this book (page 11), I offer the following five recipes for individual pies that work equally well as appetizers or as main courses. Though these pies could be made with a flour-and-butter crust, I personally prefer using filo. It is easier to work with, it is fail-safe, and it is also less fattening because it is enriched with oil rather than butter.

Filo dough, which stores well in the freezer, must be thoroughly thawed in the fridge and then left out for an hour or so (inside its packaging) to reach room temperature before being used. Once out of its package, it'll dry with prolonged exposure, but will survive nicely for 10–15 minutes while you work steadily to wrap the pies. It's unnecessary to expose filos that are not meant for immediate use. Therefore, when you're ready to start wrapping, take out the amount of filos that you need and wrap the rest properly to store (in the fridge if you're using them soon, or back in the freezer for future use).

The filo must be laid out on a clean, dry surface, and it must be brushed lightly with oil if it is to bake fluffy and crisp. Lightly is the operative word here. I suggest ½ cup (125 mL) of oil for 8 sheets of filo (enough for 4 pies), but I'm hoping you'll have some oil left over at the end. If you brush too liberally, ½ cup will run out by the fifth or sixth filo, and you will have a greasy pie at the end of it.

Most of these pies are accompanied by a sauce or a chutney, which makes them more fun to eat. However, if you are watching calories, the sauce can be omitted, as all the pies are eminently enjoyable on their own.

Basic Method for Filo Pies

This is the basic method for the 5 pie recipes that follow. It requires 8 sheets of filo in order to make 4 pies.

1 Prepare pie filling according to instructions for the recipe of your choice.
2 Pour ½ cup (125 mL) olive oil into a small bowl. With a pastry brush (or crunched-up paper towel), grease the bottom of an oven pan with the olive oil.
3 Preheat oven to 450° F (230° C).
4 Spread out a sheet of filo dough

on a clean, dry surface. With the same pastry brush, lightly oil the entire surface of the filo. Spread another filo on top of the first and oil this one similarly.

5 Now you are facing a square canvas of oiled filo. It's time to indulge in some geometry, a.k.a. rolling the filo pie. Basically, you'll be enveloping the filling in filo, to end up with a plump, rectangular pie about 4 in. x 2 in. (10 cm x 5 cm). To begin, transfer ¼ of the filling onto the upper-middle portion of the filo — about 2 in. (5 cm) from the top — in a neat, rectangular pile (use a slotted spoon and allow the excess liquid to sieve through before transferring the filling onto the filo). Now, fold the top flap over the filling and brush oil on it. Then fold the two sides over each other, oiling them as you go. The canvas is now only ⅓ as wide as it used to be, with the filling folded into the top of the long skirt of layered filo. Using both hands, take hold of the filled part and roll it onto itself, to use up the whole length and form the rectangular pie. Oil the top of the pie, and place it on the waiting oven pan.

6 Wipe off the working surface with a paper towel and continue until you have rolled all 4 pies.

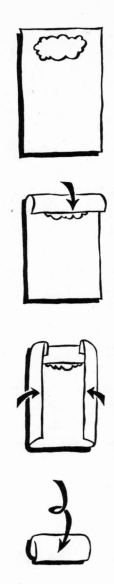

There should be some liquid left over in the bottom of the filling bowl. You can discard this. The pies in the oven pan should be spaced so that they don't touch each other. The pies are now ready to bake in the preheated oven.

Salmon Leek Pie

Chunks of fresh salmon surrounded by lively leek are featured in this simple recipe that is suitable for the most elegant occasions.

INGREDIENTS

1 leek
½ lb. (250 g) skinned, boned
    salmon fillet
1 lemon
salt and pepper
1 tsp. (5 mL) capers
1 egg
1 tsp. (5 mL) cornstarch
few sprigs fresh parsley

few sprigs fresh dill OR 2 tsp.
    (10 mL) dried
8 sheets filo dough
½ cup (125 mL) olive oil

SAUCE

½ tsp. (2 mL) olive oil
½ cup (125 mL) plain yoghurt

PREPARATION

1 Trim and discard the hairy end of the leek. Remove any outside leaves that look bruised or tired. Trim and discard the bottom 1½ in. (3–4 cm) of the green part. Cut remaining leek in half lengthwise. Wash carefully, especially in the inside skirts where the white and green parts meet and grit usually hides. Dry the leek and finely chop the green and white parts alike. Mix the two colours, and transfer into a mixing bowl

2 Examine the salmon for hidden bones: pull out any you find. Wipe salmon with a paper towel, then cut into cubes of about 1½ in. (3 cm). Add the salmon cubes to the leeks in the bowl and mix.

3 Squeeze lemon and add half the juice (about 1 tsp. or 5 mL) to leek-salmon mixture. (Reserve the rest of the lemon juice.) Add a little salt and freshly cracked pepper. Add capers. Mix.

4 Beat egg in a small bowl and add to the other ingredients. Mix. Add cornstarch and mix well (all this mixing should be gentle, so as not to injure the fish).

5 Wash, dry and chop parsley. Add to bowl. Wash, dry and chop a few sprigs of dill. Add half the dill to the bowl and reserve the other half. (If you are using dried dill, add 1 tsp. to the bowl now.) Mix everything one final time.

Now follow Basic Method for Filo Pies (pages 85–86), steps #1–6. To continue:

BAKING

6 Place the pies in the hot oven and bake for 10 minutes until the filo has turned golden.

7 Meanwhile, make the sauce: Add ½ tsp. (2 mL) olive oil and the remainder of the dill from step #5 (or use 1 tsp. dried dill). Place in a sauce pan over medium heat. Cook, stirring, for 30 seconds. Add yoghurt and cook, stirring, for 2–3 minutes, just until the sauce begins to bubble. Take from the heat and add 1 tsp. (5 mL) of the lemon juice from step #3. Stir, cover, and let rest until the pies are baked.

8 Remove pies from oven. Some yellow, eggy fluff may have leaked from them. Scrape that off with the edge of spatula, then lift the pies onto two warm plates. Spoon some sauce decoratively alongside. Serve immediately, with the rest of the sauce in a gravy boat, and a salad on a separate plate.

Total prep time: about 50 minutes.
Total baking time: 10 minutes.
Serves 2. These pies can also be served one per person as appetizers for 4.

❖ **SUGGESTED MENU IF THIS IS A MAIN COURSE:**
Starter: Yam and Pecan Salad (page 62)
Accompaniments: just the sauce and a green salad
Dessert: Baked Apple (page 219)

Chicken Rosemary Pie

Certain things (like caviar and champagne or baseball and hot dogs) go so well together that enjoying one without the other would be almost unthinkable. Chicken breast and bitter, earthy rosemary are not quite so famous a marriage as the couples mentioned above, but if the recipe for this pie takes off, they soon will be.

INGREDIENTS

¼ lb. (125 g) green beans
1 whole (double) chicken
    breast, skinned and boned
1 onion
3 cloves garlic
1 tbsp. (15 mL) fresh rosemary,
    minced OR 1 tsp. (5 mL)
    dried
2 tbsp. (30 mL) olive oil
salt and pepper
1 tbsp. (15 mL) whole-grain
    mustard
1 lemon

few sprigs parsley
1 egg
1 tsp. (5 mL) cornstarch
8 sheets filo dough
½ cup (125 mL) olive oil

CHUTNEY

1 pear OR 1 apple
1 tbsp. (15 mL) butter
1 tsp. (5 mL) whole-grain
    mustard
black pepper

PREPARATION

1 Pinch the woody ends off the green beans and then cut into 1 in. (2 cm) pieces. Bring some salted water to a boil in a small pot and add the green beans. Boil for exactly 3 minutes. Immediately drain and refresh with ice-cold water. Drain again and reserve.

2 Cut the chicken breast into 1½ in. (3 cm) cubes by cutting each half in 2 pieces then chopping each half into 3 pieces. You'll have 12 pieces in all.

3 Thinly dice 1 onion. Reserve. Mince garlic. Chop fresh (or crumble dried) rosemary and add to garlic. Reserve.

4 Heat 2 tbsp. (30 mL) olive oil in a saute pan over high heat. Add diced onion, salt and freshly cracked pepper and cook, stirring, for 2 minutes. Add the garlic-rosemary combination and stir-fry for 30 seconds. Add chicken cubes and fry, stirring often, for 2 minutes. All sides of the chicken must hit the oil and turn whitish, but they must not cook through; 2 minutes is maximum.

5 Transfer contents of the saute pan into a working bowl. Add whole-grain mustard and toss gently. Squeeze lemon, strain the juice and sprinkle half of it (about 1 tsp. or 5 mL) on the chicken (reserve the rest for use in the sauce of step #8). Wash, dry and chop a couple of sprigs of parsley. Add to chicken. Add the reserved green beans. Fold to mix.

6 Beat egg in a small bowl. Add to chicken and mix. Add cornstarch and fold-mix a final time, gently but thoroughly.

Now follow Basic Method for Filo Pies (pages 85–86), steps #1–6. To continue:

BAKING

7 Place the pies in the hot oven and bake for 10 minutes until the filo has turned golden.

8 Meanwhile, make the chutney: Peel and core the pear or apple. Slice into ¼ in. (½ cm) wedges. Over medium heat, melt butter in

a small saute pan for 30 seconds. Add fruit slices and the whole-grain mustard and cook, stirring, for 1 minute. Add 1 tsp. (5 mL) of your reserved lemon juice, and also some freshly cracked pepper. Cook, stirring, for 5 minutes until the fruit has broken down somewhat and a chutney-like sauce has emerged. Take from the heat.

9 Remove pies from oven. Some yellow, eggy fluff may have leaked from them. Scrape that off with the edge of a spatula. Then lift the pies onto two warm plates. Spoon some chutney decoratively alongside. Serve immediately, with the rest of the chutney in a bowl, and a salad on a separate plate.

Total prep time:
about 50 minutes.
Total baking time: 10 minutes.
Serves 2. These pies can also be served one per person as appetizers for 4.

❖ **SUGGESTED MENU IF THIS IS A MAIN COURSE:**
Starter: Insalata Caprese
(page 49)
Accompaniments: just the chutney and a green salad
Dessert: Wrenn's Ricotta Pie
(page 229)

Oriental Shrimp Pie

The more I experiment with the endless possibilities of filo pies, the more inventive I get. Basically, any delicious concoction, providing it's not too juicy, can be wrapped in oiled filo. One egg and 1 tsp. (5 mL) of cornstarch provides a bit of a binder, and the alchemy of the filo does the rest. This shrimp pie combines a Mediterranean notion with Asian flavours — an unlikely marriage that somehow works. The pie is flavourful yet mild. I highly recommend a hot oil on the side for dipping. However, the spicy condiment can be omitted if you are averse to chilies.

INGREDIENTS

½ lb. (250 g) small shrimp
(fresh or frozen)

½ lb. (250 g) button or
other mushrooms

3 green onions

2 in. (4 cm) fresh ginger root

⅓ cup (75 g) snow peas

⅓ cup (75 mL) water chestnuts
(canned or fresh)

3 tbsp. (45 mL) peanut or
other vegetable oil

1 tbsp. (15 mL) soya sauce or
tamari

1 tbsp. (15 mL) Chinese
rice wine

1 egg

1 tsp. (5 mL) cornstarch

8 sheets filo dough

½ cup (125 mL) peanut or
other vegetable oil

HOT OIL SAUCE

2 tbsp. (30 mL) peanut or
other vegetable oil

½ tsp. (2 mL) dried chili,
crushed

1 tsp. (5 mL) soya sauce or
tamari

PREPARATION

1 Make the hot oil, so that it's out of the way:

Heat peanut oil in a small pan over high heat until it's just about to smoke (1–2 minutes). Take from heat. Add chili, seeds and flakes alike. The chili will sizzle in the oil and turn darker. (If it turns black then your oil is too hot: start again.) Add soya to the oil and stand back. It'll react violently for 5–10 seconds, and could splatter. When it has sub-sided, stir once and transfer to a small bowl. Reserve.

2 If using frozen shrimp, defrost. Shell the shrimp. You can also devein them (by scraping the coloured matter from their backs), but this is unnecessary for small shrimp. Wash and lay them out on a paper towel to dry.

3 Slice mushrooms and green onions into 1½ in. (1 cm) pieces. Reserve each separately.

4 Peel and chop ginger root, then dice finely. Reserve.

5 Wash snow peas. Pull off the hard stem from each, including the string that runs down one side of the pea. Bunch them up on your cutting surface, and using your chef's knife, give them several cuts horizontally as well as diagonally, chopping them roughly (the idea is to end up with unevenly chopped bits).

6 Deal with the water chestnuts: If you're using fresh, then peel them (3½ oz./100 gm of fresh, unpeeled chestnuts will yield ⅓ cup /75 gm of usable product). If using canned, wash them (you'll need about ¼ of a medium can of water chestnuts). Refrigerate the rest, in a sealed glass jar, topped up with fresh

water. Chop enough water chestnuts ¼ in. (½ cm) thick to make
⅓ cup (75 mL). Reserve.

7 Heat 3 tbsp. peanut oil in a saute
pan over high heat till it's just
about to smoke. Add ginger and
stir-fry for 30 seconds. Add the
mushrooms and fry, turning
often, for 2–3 minutes, until they
darken. Add soya and rice wine
and stir-fry for 30 seconds. Add
the snow peas and green onion
and fold in, stirring and frying for
1–2 minutes, until some of the
liquid has evaporated and everything seems well oiled and has
warmed through. Take from the
heat and immediately fold water
chestnuts into the other ingredients, mixing and tossing. Then
transfer the whole mixture into a
working bowl. Let rest 3–4 minutes to cool.

8 Gently fold the shrimp into the
mixture. Beat egg in a small bowl,
and add to the mixture. Add
cornstarch. Mix thoroughly, but
gently, so as not to injure the
shrimp.

Now follow Basic Method for
Filo Pies (pages 85–86), steps
#1–6. (In this recipe, you'll be
substituting peanut or another
vegetable oil for the ½ cup olive
oil.) To continue:

BAKING

9 Place the pies in the hot oven and
bake for 10 minutes until the filo
has turned golden.

10 Remove pies from oven. Trim
away any yellow, eggy fluff that
may have leaked from them. Lift
the pies onto two warm plates.
Serve a small dish of the hot oil
on the side, and other accompaniments on a separate plate.

Total prep time:
about 50 minutes.
Total baking time: 10 minutes.
Serves 2. These pies can also be
served one per person as appetizers
for 4.

♣ **SUGGESTED MENU IF**
THIS IS A MAIN COURSE:
Starter: a clear soup
Accompaniments: stir-fried broccoli
and wilted bean sprouts
Dessert: Fried Pineapple
(page 233)

Mushroom Pie

The resurgence of home cooking has brought with it a serious demand for many rare ingredients that have suddenly become available in all our stores — even supermarkets, the barometer of popular consumption. Among the most welcome of these delicacies are exotic mushrooms such as portobello, oyster and shiitaki. Any of them, or a combination of all three, makes this humble pie a real treat, but also really expensive. If money is an object, button mushrooms (at a quarter of the price) work just fine. I don't recommend any sauce with this one. It is plenty moist, and should be enjoyed on its own.

INGREDIENTS

5 large dried Chinese mushrooms

1 large clove garlic

3 green onions

3 sprigs parsley

½ lb. (250 g) mushrooms (fancy or button)

3 tbsp. (45 mL) olive oil

black pepper

3½ oz. (100 g) goat cheese

1 egg

1 tsp. (5 mL) cornstarch

½ cup (125 mL) olive oil

8 sheets filo dough

PREPARATION

1 Bring 1½ cups (375 mL) water to a boil in a small sauce pan and add Chinese mushrooms. Lower the heat to medium and cook 20–25 minutes till soft.

2 Meanwhile: Mince garlic and reserve. Chop green onions into ½ in. (1 cm) pieces and reserve. Wash, dry and chop parsley. Reserve under a wet paper towel. Wipe mushrooms and chop into ½ in. (1 cm) pieces.

3 Heat 3 tbsp. (45 mL) olive oil in a large saute pan over high heat for 1 minute. Add salt and freshly cracked pepper and all the mushrooms. Cook, tossing for 2–3 minutes, until the mushrooms have all been somewhat fried and have darkened. Add the garlic and stir-fry for 1 minute. Take pan from heat and transfer contents into a working bowl.

4 Add chopped green onions and parsley to the mushrooms. Mix. Crumble goat cheese over the

mushrooms. Mix. Beat one egg in a small bowl and add to the mushrooms. Mix. Add cornstarch. Mix well. The mixture should be homogeneous.

5 By now, the Chinese mushrooms should be soft and fully reconstituted. Take from the heat and drain. Chop them into small bits ½ in. (1 cm) square and transfer them to a strainer. Press them with your fingers (not too forcefully) to extract some of their water. Fold into the mixture.

Now follow Basic Method for Filo Pies (page 85), steps #1–6.

BAKING

6 Place the pies in the hot oven and bake for 10 minutes until the filo has turned golden.

7 Remove pies from oven. Lift them onto a platter. Serve at leisure (they are better after a cooling-off period of 10 minutes or so). Serve alongside a green salad, and perhaps a potato salad too if this is a main course.

Total prep time: 50 minutes.
Total cooking time: 10 minutes.
Rest time: 10–15 minutes.
Serves 4 as a starter on its own or 2 as a main course with salads and a light dessert.

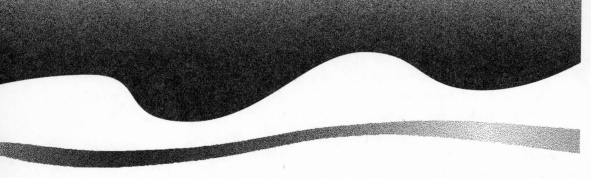

Spinach Feta Pie

Unarguably the most famous filo pie on earth, spinach pie (or Spanoko-tyropita) can now be eaten in Greek restaurants from Hong Kong to Athens and beyond. This recipe is different because it uses raw spinach and leeks in its filling, making for a crunchier, more fresh-tasting pie. I offer no sauce because traditionally these are eaten on their own as appetizers or light lunches.

INGREDIENTS

1 lb. (500 g) fresh spinach
1 large leek
3½ oz. (100 g) feta cheese
2–3 oz. (75 g) grated
   mozzarella cheese
few sprigs parsley
few sprigs fresh dill OR
   1 tsp. (5 mL) dried

2 tbsp. (30 mL) currants or
   raisins
black pepper
1 egg
1 tsp. (5 mL) cornstarch
8 sheets filo dough
½ cup (125 mL) olive oil

PREPARATION

1 Wash the spinach thoroughly and dry. Pick out all the stalks and discard. Also remove the large vein that runs into the leaves; so that only the soft leaves of the spinach are used). On a chopping block, finely shred the spinach. Give the pile a couple of horizontal cuts to chop them even more finely. Transfer to a working bowl.

2 Trim and discard the hairy end of the leek, along with any outer leaves that are brown. Trim and discard the bottom 1½ in. (3–4 cm) of green. Cut remaining leek in half lengthwise. Wash carefully, especially where the white and green parts meet and grit usually hides. Dry the leek, and then finely chop green and white parts alike. Mix the two colours and add to spinach.

3 Crumble feta cheese; grate mozzarella and add both to spinach.

4 Wash, dry and finely chop several sprigs of parsley and also of dill. Add to spinach.

5 Add currants (or raisins) and freshly cracked black pepper to spinach. Mix.

6 Beat egg in a small bowl. Add to spinach and mix. Add cornstarch and mix thoroughly. You will notice that the volume of the mixture is half what it used to be before the wet ingredients were added.

Now follow Basic Method for Filo Pies (pages 85–86), steps #1–6. To continue:

BAKING

7 Place the pies in the hot oven and bake for 10 minutes until the filo has turned golden.

8 Remove pies from oven. Scrape off any yellow, eggy fluff that may have leaked from them. Lift the pies onto a platter. Serve at leisure (they are better after a cooling-off period of 10 minutes or so) alongside a Greek salad.

Total prep time:
about 50 minutes.
Total baking time: 10 minutes.
Serves 4 as a starter on its own, or 2 as a vegetarian main course with salads and a light dessert.

Pasta

Two thousand years after the fall of the Roman Empire, the residents of the Italian peninsula have finally found a way to conquer the planet: through their pasta cookery. It's impossible to go anywhere in the world and not be able to find at least one restaurant that serves a good bowl of Italian pasta; and who would want it any other way?

Possibly the most famous of all pastas (and indeed, a synonym for the very concept) is spaghetti with tomato sauce. My list of pasta recipes therefore begins with this quick-to-make tomato sauce for spaghetti.

Tomato Sauce

This is a generic tomato-basil sauce that works with spaghetti, as well as dishes like veal or eggplant parmigiana (breaded, fried veal or eggplant, topped with tomato sauce, slices of mozzarella and grated Parmesan cheese, and baked in the oven).

INGREDIENTS

2 lb. (1 kg) ripe tomatoes
1 large onion
3 large cloves garlic
several sprigs fresh basil OR
   1 tbsp. (15 mL) dried
¼ cup (50 mL) olive oil

salt and black pepper
1 tsp. (5 mL) chili flakes
   (optional)
1 tsp. (5 mL) balsamic vinegar
2 tbsp. (30 mL) olive oil
fresh parsley

PREPARATION

1 Blanch tomatoes in boiling water for 30 seconds, then peel, core and seed them. Cut the flesh into large pieces. Strain the seeds and discard, reserving the tomato juice.

2 Dice the onion. Mince the garlic. Reserve each separately.

3 If using fresh basil, wash, dry and chop finely. Reserve.

COOKING

4 Heat ¼ cup (50 mL) olive oil in a deep saute pan over high heat. Add salt, pepper and the onions and saute, stirring frequently for 2 minutes.

5 Add the garlic and the chili flakes. Stir-fry continuously for 30 seconds. Then immediately add 2 tbsp. (30 mL) of the reserved tomato juice from step #1.

6 Keeping the heat high, add all the tomato pieces at once and carefully stir to blend. This operation takes 4–5 minutes and can be messy in terms of spills. Bear with it. As soon as the tomato begins to break apart, mash it down with a large spoon or better, with a potato masher, until most of it has been pulped (some pieces will remain in lumps: this is just fine).

7 If using the dried basil, add it now. Also add the balsamic vinegar. Stir well. Reduce heat to medium-low and cook, uncovered, for 20 minutes, stirring occasionally (the sauce should neither boil, nor simmer, but something in between).

8 If using fresh basil, add it now. Cook for an additional 5 minutes. The sauce is now ready, but needs 10–15 minutes (or longer) to rest. This is a good time to cook your pasta. When ready to use sauce, bring it to a quick boil; turn off heat; mix 2 tbsp. (30 mL) olive oil into it; and sprinkle with chopped fresh basil (or chopped fresh parsley, if using dried basil).

Sun-dried tomato note:
If making the sauce when tomatoes are out of season, add ¼ cup (50 mL) of chopped sun-dried tomatoes (for additional flavour) in step #7. Use less salt, accordingly.

Meat note: Fried or grilled Italian sausage (hot or sweet), cut up into ½ in. (1 cm) slices, can be added in step #8 for a lusty, Tuscan country-style pasta sauce.

Prep time: 5 minutes.
Cooking time: 35 minutes.
Rest time: 10–15 minutes.
This sauce will serve up to 4; leftovers are even better the next day. Leftovers of sauce can be turned into nice tomato-rice soup: Stir 1 cup (250 mL) sauce into 2 cups (500 mL) chicken broth or veal stock; add ¾ cup (175 mL) cooked rice; bring all to the boil. Serves two.

Linguine **Pagliaro**

This palate-dazzler comes from Margie and Michael Pagliaro, owner-chefs of Barolo, one of Toronto's mega-temples to gastronomy. It's very simple and relatively inexpensive, considering its elegance. It's also ideal for parties because the linguine can be cooked in advance; making the sauce and reheating the pasta then takes less than 10 minutes, and can thus comfortably be done at the last moment, after the guests have finished their antipasto.

INGREDIENTS

½ lb. (250 g) linguine noodles
2 tbsp. (30 mL) olive oil
1 stalk broccoli
¼ cup (50 mL) pine nuts
1 tsp. (5 mL) olive oil
fresh parsley

4–5 sun-dried tomatoes
¾ cup (175 mL) 10% cream OR
  ¾ cup (175 mL) chicken
  broth with 2 tbsp. (30 mL)
  olive oil
2 oz. (50 g) Gorgonzola cheese

PREPARATION

1 Cook the noodles to the desired tenderness and drain in a colander. Immediately add 2 tbsp. (30 mL) olive oil and toss the noodles until all are somewhat coated with the oil. Reserve (if the wait is long, transfer to a bowl and cover tightly to avoid drying out).

2 While the noodles are cooking: Cut away the tough part of the broccoli and reserve for another use. Separate the little florets into individual pieces. You will need 10–12 florets in total. Blanch them in boiling water for 2 min-utes. Drain and cool with ice water. Drain again and reserve.

3 Saute the pine nuts in 1 tsp. (5 mL) olive oil over medium heat for 1–2 minutes, tossing often to avoid burning. Reserve.

4 Wash, dry and chop some parsley. Reserve under a wet paper towel.

5 Chop the sun-dried tomatoes into ½ in. (1 cm) strips.

COOKING

6 Heat the cream (or the oiled chicken broth) in a skillet over medium heat until it begins to steam. Break up the Gorgonzola and add to the liquid, stirring to dissolve it (about 1 minute). While the cheese dissolves, add the sun-dried tomatoes and the broccoli florets. Lower heat and cook, stirring, for about 5 minutes, until the sauce is smooth and piping hot.

7 Add the reserved linguine and raise the heat to medium. Cook for 2–3 minutes, tossing continuously, making sure that all the noodles are well sauced and have heated through (taste one).

8 Transfer to pasta bowls. Top with the browned pine nuts and chopped parsley. Additional cheese is unnecessary. Serve immediately.

*Total prep time:
about 15 minutes.
Total cooking time: less than
10 minutes.
Serves 2 for main course and 4 as
pasta course.*

Fusilli with *Leeks*

A smooth, pink sauce studded with green-and-white leeks, served with colourful, ridged fusilli noodles, this recipe is a sure-fire pleaser, even for fickle appetites. The cream content, though essential, need not be the 35% variety (which is optimal); even 10% cream will do. The cream can be omitted completely, but at significant loss of smoothness and richness.

INGREDIENTS

1 small leek
1 large or 2 small ripe tomatoes
few leaves of fresh sage OR
    a pinch of dried
salt and black pepper
1 tsp. plus 2 tbsp. (5 mL +
    15 mL) olive oil

½ lb. (250 g) 3-colour fusilli
pinch oregano
2–3 tbsp. (30–45 mL) 10% or
    35% cream
½ cup (125 mL) chicken broth
grated Parmesan cheese

PREPARATION

1 Trim and discard the hairy nib of the leek. Then trim the leek so that you have an equal length of white and green (about 5 in./ 12 cm in all). Slice lengthwise and wash carefully to remove hidden grit. Chop crosswise in ¼ in. (½ cm) pieces. Reserve.

2 Blanch tomatoes in boiling water for 30 seconds, and then peel, core and seed them. Chop flesh into pieces. Strain seeds and discard, reserving tomato juice.

3 If using fresh sage (which I highly recommend), chop finely.

COOKING

4 Heat enough water in a pot: add salt and 1 tsp. olive oil. Wait for it to boil and add the noodles. Stir once and let boil, uncovered, for desired tenderness (6–8 minutes).

5 Meanwhile: Heat 2 tbsp. (30 mL) olive oil in a skillet over high heat for 30 seconds. Add chopped leeks, salt and freshly cracked pepper. Stir-fry for 2 minutes. Add oregano and sage and stir for 10 seconds. Add tomato pieces

and stir-fry for 1 minute. Add cream and stir for 1 minute. Add chicken broth. Cook at high heat for 3–4 minutes, stirring. The sauce will become the consistency of light cream (a little lighter, if no actual cream was used). If by chance you have allowed it to become too thick, then thin it now with a tablespoon or two of the reserved tomato juice.

6 By now the noodles will have cooked. Lower heat under sauce to medium. Strain noodles, and toss in colander to extract all water. Add to the sauce. Cook, stirring and tossing to ensure that all of them are well coated (1–2 minutes).

7 Transfer to pasta bowls. Top generously with freshly grated fine Parmesan and serve immediately.

Total prep time: 3–4 minutes.
Total cooking time:
less than 10 minutes.
Serves 2 for main course and 4 as a pasta course with salad.

Spaghettini with Anchovies

A sparely sauced pasta, this dish combines the basic ingredients of pesto (basil, pine nuts, garlic) with anchovies and capers on the long, thin noodles. It has a pleasant bouquet (and taste) that works beautifully either as a pasta course or the main course of a light dinner.

INGREDIENTS

1 tsp. (5 mL) plus ¼ cup
   (50 mL) olive oil
2 cloves garlic
salt and pepper
1 dried red chili
several sprigs each of fresh basil
   and parsley

½ lb. (250 g) spaghettini
   noodles
1 tbsp. (25 mL) pine nuts
3 anchovy fillets
½ tsp. (2 mL) capers, drained
½ tsp. (2 mL) grated Parmesan
   or Pecorino cheese

PREPARATION

1 For the noodles: Heat water with some salt and 1 tsp. (5 mL) olive oil in a large pot.

2 Peel garlic and cut into large chunks.

3 Heat ¼ cup (50 mL) olive oil in a skillet over medium-high heat. Add a little salt, freshly ground pepper, the chopped garlic and the whole dried chili. Stir occasionally, cooking until the garlic turns brown (3–4 minutes). Mash the garlic pieces once to release their oil. Then take pan off the heat, scoop out cooked garlic and chili and discard, reserving the flavoured oil, ready for its next step.

4 Wash, dry and finely chop fresh basil and fresh parsley. Reserve under a wet paper towel.

COOKING

5 When the pasta water boils, add spaghettini so that they can begin to cook (5–7 minutes). Meanwhile, return the saute pan with the flavoured oil to medium heat and add the pine nuts, stirring often to brown them evenly (1–2 minutes). When they begin to show colour, reduce heat to low and add anchovy fillets. Cook, stirring for 1 minute, mashing the anchovies with a wooden spoon. When they have disintegrated, turn off heat and immediately add chopped basil and parsley, stirring to blend.

6 When the spaghettini has cooked to the desired tenderness, drain. Immediately add to the pan with the flavoured oil. Toss well to coat all the noodles. Add capers.

7 Transfer into individual bowls, making sure they all get their share of pine nuts. Serve immediately with grated cheese (Parmesan or Pecorino) on the side.

Total prep time: 5 minutes.
Total cooking time: 7 minutes.
Serves 2 as a main course and
4 as a pasta course. For more,
increase all ingredients proportionately except for the oil, which
increases only by half.

Pasta "Fazul"

*Michael Pagliaro serves this old Calabrian favourite in his restaurant Barolo.
I have adapted his recipe for home cooking but couldn't find a substitute for
the prosciutto. The prosciutto bone of Pagliaro's original recipe is indeed
hard to find, but locating a prosciutto "end" shouldn't be a problem in delis
and fine food stores that sell this Italian ham. The thin end of the prosciutto
cannot be sliced properly and is therefore sold as a piece at a discount.*

*I use canned beans for expedience but never settle for less than the best
home-made chicken broth (page 23). Country cookery such as this is pre-
dicated on the excellence of each individual ingredient.*

INGREDIENTS

5 cups (1¼ L) home-made
   chicken broth
1 lb. (500 g) tomatoes plus 1
   tbsp. (15 mL) tomato paste, if
   tomatoes are not in season
black pepper
4–5 oz. (150 g) prosciutto end
3 cloves garlic

3 tbsp. (45 mL) olive oil
3½ oz. (100 g) small pasta
   (mini-shells, bow ties, elbows)
1 19 oz. (540 mL) can red
   Romano beans
fresh parsley
Romano cheese
extra-virgin olive oil

PREPARATION AND COOKING

1 Bring chicken broth to a simmer.
2 Meanwhile blanch tomatoes in
   boiling water for 30 seconds,
   then peel, core and seed them.
   Chop flesh roughly and strain,
   discarding the seeds and reserving
   the juice. Add tomato pieces and

juice to the simmering chicken
broth (along with tomato paste, if
tomatoes are out of season).
Increase heat to medium-high
and bring to a rolling boil.
3 Add freshly ground black pepper
   and the entire prosciutto end.

Reduce heat to medium-low. Wash, dry and chop several sprigs of parsley. Add to cooking broth.

4 Mince garlic. Heat 3 tbsp. (45 mL) olive oil in a small pan over high heat until it's just about to smoke. Add the garlic and stir-fry for 1 minute or so until garlic begins to darken. Add this oil and garlic to the cooking broth. Cook enhanced broth over medium-low heat for 30 minutes total from the beginning of step, maintaining a bubbly but not vigorous pace.

5 At the end of the 30 minutes, fish out the piece of prosciutto. Handling it gingerly (it's hot), cut off the rind and discard. Then chop the meaty parts finely and return them to the broth.

6 Increase heat to medium-high and add pasta. Cook for 4–5 minutes, stirring occasionally, until pasta is not quite al dente.

7 Transfer Romano beans from their can into a strainer. Run cold water through them to remove all canning residue. Drain well and add to the soup. Let it reach a bubble and reduce heat to medium-low. Stirring occasionally, cook for 5–6 minutes, until the broth has thickened somewhat and the pasta is cooked to your liking.

8 Take from heat, cover and let rest only as long as it takes you to organize your garnishes: wash, dry and chop some parsley; grate some Romano cheese.

9 Transfer to bowls, making sure everyone gets solids as well as broth. Garnish with drizzles of extra-virgin olive oil as well as the grated Romano cheese and chopped parsley. Serve immediately with crusty bread for a hearty lunch or a simple supper. Follow it with a salad, and fruit for dessert.

Total cooking time: 1 hour.
Serves 3–4.

Stir-Fried Rice Noodles

Rice noodles are as different from wheat noodles as rice-growing countries are from producers of wheat. Rice makes a noodle that is airy and yet substantial, and cooks quickly. Rice noodles love to be stir-fried in oil and flavoured with soya. This makes them a natural and welcome alternative to rice in Far Eastern-inspired meals.

The most attractive rice noodles come from Thailand, and are called alternatively "rice sticks" or "rice vermicelli." Under any name they are snow-white, brittle and thin, with a thickness hovering around $\frac{1}{4}$ in. ($\frac{1}{2}$ cm). One user-friendly task is required before cooking them: They must soak in cold water from 2–24 hours (in the fridge, if for the longer period). This prolonged dunking softens them and lets them absorb heat and oil very quickly once drained and cooked.

The most famous venue for rice noodles is Pad Thai (see next recipe), but if you're not in the mood for such a complex job, this recipe will provide very wholesome noodles in next to no time.

INGREDIENTS

½ lb. (250 g) dried Thai rice noodles

2–3 tbsp. (30–45 mL) peanut or other vegetable oil

2 tbsp. (30 mL) Thai fish sauce (nam pla) OR soya sauce OR tamari

3 green onions

PREPARATION

1 Place noodles in a large bowl with cold water to cover and soak.

2 When ready to cook, trim green onions and chop into 3 cm pieces, white and green parts alike.

COOKING

3 Drain the noodles well, tossing them in a colander.

4 Heat oil in a large saute pan (or wok) over medium-high heat until it's just about to smoke. Add the drained noodles and the chopped green onions. Stir-fry, tossing the noodles briskly with 2 spatulas or spoons to expose all of them to the hot oil quickly. They will very soon (in about 90 seconds) become supple and warm.

Add Thai fish sauce (or soya or tamari) and continue to stir-fry for 2—3 minutes till the noodles are heated through and are uniformly brown, and the green onions are limp and shiny. Taste a noodle to test for temperature and toothsomeness. Serve immediately.

Total soaking time: 2—24 hours.
Total prep and cooking time:
under 10 minutes.
Serves 3—4 as a side course.

Pad Thai – Thai Noodles

The undisputed sovereign among the world's pasta dishes, at least in terms of complexity, is Pad Thai (or Thai noodles). This dish is composed of 16 ingredients, including 6 that require special shopping expeditions. Four of these, namely the rice noodles, the fried tofu, the tamarind paste and the nam pla (a.k.a. Thai "Squid Brand" Fish Sauce) are usually available in major Chinese markets. Of the remaining 2 ingredients, the crushed roasted peanuts can be processed at home either from raw, skinned peanuts (by roasting them first: a tricky proposition) or from already roasted, unsalted peanuts, available in health food stores. The final problem is the roasted chili flakes (which are normally offered as an additional hot condiment for sprinkling at table). This is an elusive ingredient. A home-made version involves slow baking the volatile little monsters. I have replaced this ingredient with another of Thailand's favourite hot sauces, which is very easy to make, and pleases just as well.

This noodle recipe comes to me courtesy of Wandee Young, a native of Phuket, Thailand, the personable owner-chef of Toronto's Young Thailand Restaurant. I dedicate my version of Young's recipe to Meg Masters, the very excellent editor of this book.

INGREDIENTS

½ lb. (250 g) dried Thai rice
  noodles
¼ cup (50 mL) tamarind paste
¼ cup (50 mL) warm water
2 cloves garlic
3½ oz. (100 g) fried tofu
3½ oz. (100 g) skinless,
  boneless chicken breast
8 medium shrimp, fresh or
  frozen
1 lemon
2 tbsp. (30 mL) Thai fish sauce
  (nam pla)

1 tbsp. (15 mL) brown sugar
3 green onions
⅓ cup (75 mL) roasted,
  unsalted peanuts
few sprigs fresh coriander
3 tbsp. (45 mL) Thai fish sauce
  OR soya sauce OR tamari
2 fresh hot chilies
¼ cup (50 mL) vegetable oil
1 egg
6–7 oz. (200 g) bean sprouts
1 lime

PREPARATION

1 Place noodles in a large bowl with cold water to cover and soak for at least 2 hours (and up to 24 hours). (The ideal schedule is to initiate this procedure in the morning, and let the noodles soak in the fridge all day.)

2 Make tamarind sauce from tamarind paste: Soak paste in warm water for 15 minutes. Then mash the softened paste with your fingers or a spoon, until a light brown, mud-like mixture forms. Transfer to a strainer held over a bowl and mash the solids, forcing as much liquid as possible through the strainer. 1–2 tbsp. (15–30 mL) of smooth, thick sauce will emerge (most of it will cling to the underside of the strainer: scrape this off into the bowl). The leftover solids in the strainer can be discarded.

3 Mince the garlic. Reserve.

4 Taking care not to mash it, slice fried tofu into ¾ in. (1½ cm) cubes. Reserve.

5 Slice chicken breast into strips ½ in. (1 cm) wide. Reserve.

6 If using frozen shrimp, defrost them. Peel and devein shrimp. Wash and lay out on a paper towel to dry.

7 Juice lemon. Strain juice to obtain 1–1 ½ tbsp. (20 mL) and add to it the tamarind sauce from step #2. Add 2 tbsp. (30 mL) Thai fish sauce and the brown sugar. Mix to dissolve sugar. Reserve.

8 Chop green onions into 1½ in. (3 cm) pieces, white and green parts alike.

9 Process peanuts until they resemble coarse meal. Reserve.

10 Wash, dry and chop several sprigs of fresh coriander. Reserve under a wet paper towel.

11 Pour 3 tbsp. (45 mL) Thai fish sauce (or soya, or tamari if you are averse to the flavour of raw fish sauce) into a nifty little bowl. Mince chilies and add to the fish sauce (wash hands right after). Reserve sauce.

COOKING

12 Heat vegetable oil in a large saute pan (or wok), over medium-high heat until it's just about to smoke. Add garlic and stir-fry for 30 seconds.

13 Add tofu and chicken, and stir-fry for 1 minute.

14 Add shrimp and stir-fry for 1 minute (both chicken and shrimp will be barely cooked by now: do not overcook).

15 Beat one egg in a small bowl and

add to the pan. Stir-fry for 30–40 seconds, until the egg begins to set. (Note: after all this stirring, the tofu will break down. This is normal.)

16 Strain the soaked noodles and add to pan. Turn a couple of times to wake them up (30 seconds) and immediately sprinkle all over the noodles the reserved tamarind mixture from step #7. Working steadily with 2 spatulas or spoons, stir-fry the noodles for 3–4 minutes. This process involves continuous folding and mixing so that all the condiments are evenly distributed and all the noodles get somewhat fried. At the end of this step, the noodles will take up half their previous volume and will be al dente and glistening with a slightly pink glaze.

17 Immediately reduce heat to medium and add half the bean sprouts, all of the chopped green onions and half of the crushed peanuts. Stir-fry into the noodles, tossing continuously, for 2 minutes.

18 Transfer the finished noodles onto a serving plate. Garnish with the remaining sprouts, peanuts and a whole lot of chopped coriander. Quarter a lime and fit the wedges around the plate. Serve immediately with the hot sauce from step #11 on the side.

Total prep time (not including noodle-soaking time): about 40 minutes.
Total cooking time: 14 minutes.
Note: A perfectly delicious, meatless version of this recipe is prepared and cooked in exactly the same way, simply by omitting chicken and shrimp, and doubling the quantity of tofu. (If you prefer, substitute unfried tofu for the prefried variety.) The tofu is added in step #13 and fried for 2 minutes prior to adding the egg of step #15. In this case omit step #14 altogether.
Serves 2.

❖ **SUGGESTED MENU FOR THIS MAIN COURSE:**
Starter: a Thai soup, either Tom Kha Khai (page 35) or Tom Yum Goong (page 36)
Accompaniments: Asian Seafood Salad; page 64 and a green vegetable
Dessert: fruit or sherbet

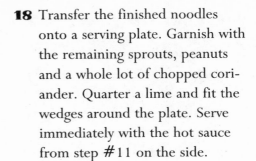

Main Courses

Fillet of Sole with Hazelnuts

Sole is the most benign and non-fishy of all the foods of the sea. Indeed it has next to no flavour of its own, which is an asset, in that it lends itself to any number of innovations. As well, sole is singularly able to withstand freezing. It ranks second only to shrimp for acceptable texture once defrosted (as long as the defrosting is gentle: leave it in the fridge to thaw gradually over 24 hours). Sole's only drawback stems from its best asset — its fragility. It is rather difficult to turn in the pan. The spatula must be slid under it deftly and the turning must be accomplished by a smooth flick of the wrist (dealing blackjack is very good practice for turning sole).

Here's a simple yet elegant recipe that echoes the more famous version with almonds. This variation uses hazelnuts (or filberts, as they're also known in health-food stores), which taste far nuttier.

INGREDIENTS

¼ cup (50 mL) raw hazelnuts
   (a.k.a. filberts)
3 green onions
few sprigs parsley
1 lemon

½ cup (125 mL) all-purpose
   flour
4 fillets of sole, fresh or frozen
2 tbsp. (30 mL) vegetable oil
salt and white pepper
1–2 tbsp. (15–30 mL) unsalted
   butter

PREPARATION

1 Lay the hazelnuts on a flat surface. Using a mallet or the flat side of a chef's knife, crack them a couple of times to smash them into irregularly sized bits (they will jump around and try to escape when hit: do the deed slowly).

2 Chop green onions in ¼ in. (½ cm) bits. Reserve. Wash, dry and finely chop parsley. Reserve under a wet paper towel. Slice a lemon into quarters. Reserve.

3 Spread flour on a plate and thoroughly dredge both sides of the fillets in it.

COOKING

4 Heat vegetable oil in a large saute pan over medium-high heat until it's just about to smoke. Add

salt and white pepper and the dredged sole, spacing the fillets to avoid overlapping.

5   Reduce heat to medium and fry the fish for just about 90 seconds. Turn and fry the flip-side for another 90 seconds. The fillets should not brown, but turn snow-white and lustrous.

6   Transfer fillets to a warm serving plate and return the pan with its drippings back to the heat. Add butter more or less (depending on caloric restrictions) and melt it, casually scraping the pan to deglaze the stick-ons. Add the smashed hazelnuts and the chopped green onion. Stir-fry for 2–3 minutes until the onions have wilted and the nuts are brown. Take from the heat and spoon this sauce evenly over the fillets of sole. Garnish with chopped parsley and fit the lemon quarters around the plate. Serve immediately.

Total prep time: 7–8 minutes.
Total cooking time: 7–8 minutes.
Serves 2.

❖ **SUGGESTED MENU FOR THIS MAIN COURSE**
Starter: Mushrooms Provençale (page 213)
Accompaniments: parsleyed potatoes; steamed broccoli
Dessert: Apple Betty (page 220)

Fillet of Sole Florentine

I borrowed the idea for this recipe from a popular brunch item: eggs Florentine, which counterpoints poached eggs with spinach and cheese. I simply substituted fillet of sole for eggs and came up with a silky-smooth item that even non-fish eaters seem to enjoy. It's heavy on dairy products, but the leanness of the sole compensates.

INGREDIENTS

½ bunch fresh spinach
fresh tarragon or parsley
3 green onions
½ tsp. (2 mL) capers
¼ cup (50 mL) freshly grated
    Parmesan
½ lemon
unsalted butter

3 fillets of sole
salt and white or black pepper
1 cup (250 mL) water
1 tbsp. (15 mL) unsalted butter
pinch black mustard seed
1 tbsp. (15 mL) all-purpose
    flour
2 tbsp. (30 mL) 10% cream OR
    chicken broth

PREPARATION

1   Preheat oven to 425° F (220° C). Wash and dry spinach thoroughly. Cut off and discard the tough stalks. Chop the leaves very finely (either by hand or in a processor). Reserve in a bowl.

2   Wash and dry the tarragon (or parsley). Chop fine (you should have about ¼ cup /50 mL) and add to reserved spinach. Chop the green onions into ¼ in. (½ cm) pieces. Add to spinach-herb mixture.

3   Chop the drained capers. Reserve. Grate the Parmesan on the coarsest side of the grater. Reserve. Squeeze half a lemon.

Strain the juice and reserve.

COOKING

4   Lightly butter the bottom of a small, ovenproof dish (or 3 individual ramekins). Place the three fillets of sole so that half of each lies on the bottom, and the other half overhangs the lip of the dish. Salt and pepper the fish. Spoon the reserved spinach-herb-green onion mixture over them, so that there is an even amount on each fillet. Fold in the loose end of the fillets. You now have 3 bundles of sole folded over the spinach mix-

ture. Smear more butter on the top surface of the fish. Pour the cup of water into the pan so that it comes about ⅔ of the way up the sides of the fish. Cover loosely with a piece of foil or waxed paper, and bake in the preheated oven for 12 minutes.

5 Have 2 saucepans ready on the stove. As soon as you have removed the sole from the oven, carefully pour out its cooking juices (a thin broth) into one of the pans and boil at high heat until it's reduced to about half its volume (5 minutes).

6 Meanwhile, over low heat, melt 1 tbsp. (15 mL) of butter in the second pan. Add the black mustard seed. As soon as the butter begins to foam, add 1 tbsp. (15 mL) of flour and cook, stirring continuously, for 2 minutes. It'll look like a juicy paste, bubbling slightly and turning light brown (this is a roux, the first step to making bechamel). Keep stirring.

7 At this point, the roux is ready for its liquid. Turn to the vigorously boiling first saucepan (the fish-cooking liquid should have reduced by half by now), and add all the liquid at once to the roux. Beat with a wire whisk. The sauce will thicken instantly. Whisk a couple more times and turn off the heat. Add the Parmesan,

capers, cream and lemon juice. Stir to mix well.

8 Spoon the sauce equally over the stuffed fillets of sole. (A little liquid will have accumulated in the bottom of the pan. This is all right; it'll become part of the final sauce.) Place the pan under a hot broiler for up to 5 minutes, until the sauce has browned and is happily bubbling.

9 Transfer to individual serving bowls, making sure that each portion is served browned side up and is surrounded by a pool of sauce, along with whatever spinach has spilled out. (If using ramekins, serve intact, direct from the oven — on a plate, to avoid burns.) Serve immediately.

Total prep time: 5–7 minutes.
Total baking and saucing time: 15–20 minutes (at this point the recipe can wait for as long as 30 minutes).
Final broiling: 5 minutes.
Serves 2–3.

❧ **SUGGESTED MENU FOR THIS MAIN COURSE**
Starter: a light soup
Accompaniment to the sole: Herbed Potatoes (page 215), Mushrooms Provençale (page 213) and a green salad
Dessert: Tom and Gerry's New Orleans Bread Pudding (page 236)

Poached Fish with Black Butter

Charlotte Dix, my wonderful friend and frequent collaborator, turned me on to black butter sauce, and my waistline took years to recover. Currently, I restrict myself to enjoying it once every 3 weeks or so, and it sure is a lovely way to beat the winter blues. A dose of delicate fish doused with a sinfully rich sauce makes my heart sing with pleasure, whatever the season.

INGREDIENTS

1 lb. (500 g) firm white fish
  fillet (cod, haddock or
  halibut)
1 small onion
few sprigs parsley
1 lemon
½ cup (125 mL) water
½ cup (125 mL) white wine

1 bay leaf
pinch thyme
1 tsp. (5 mL) white wine vinegar
salt and pepper
2–4 tbsp. (30–50 mL) unsalted
  butter
1 tsp. (5 mL) black or white
  sesame seeds

PREPARATION

1 Wipe fish with a paper towel. Cut into 4 equal pieces.

2 Chop onion, skin on, into quarters. Reserve. Wash parsley. Reserve. Slice off ⅓ of the lemon (reserving the rest for serving at table with the fish).

COOKING

3 In a deep skillet, combine water, white wine, the chopped onion, parsley, ⅓ lemon, bay leaf, thyme, white wine vinegar, salt and pepper and bring to a boil. Reduce heat to low and add fish.

Liquid should cover fish. If not, add more hot water. Simmer, uncovered, for 5–8 minutes. The contents must never boil. Test the fish by pressing it with your finger: if it has firmed, it's either close to done or done.

4 During the last 3–4 minutes of poaching, place a small frying pan over medium-low heat and add butter (more rather than less, if you can afford the calories). Cook the butter, stirring, for 3–4 minutes, until it has turned chocolate-brown. (Despite its name, the butter in this dish must not

be allowed actually to burn and turn black.) Immediately turn off heat and add black or white sesame seeds. They'll sizzle.

5 When the fish has poached, scoop it out of the liquid. (Reserve the strained liquid for another use if desired.) Arrange 2 pieces of fish on each of 2 warm plates. Spoon the black butter and its sesames equally over all. Serve immediately with lemon wedges on the side.

Total prep time: about 10 minutes. Total cooking time: less than 10 minutes. Serves 2.

❧ **SUGGESTED MENU FOR THIS MAIN COURSE**
Starter: Eggplant with Mint (page 51)
Accompaniments: steamed potatoes; fried zucchini
Dessert: Baked Apple (page 219)

Swordfish Schipani

My very good friend, chef Leo Schipani, serves a grilled swordfish with a loaded dressing featuring balsamic vinegar (a.k.a. Schipani juice) and sun-dried tomatoes. For someone like me, who enjoys that succulent fish with a simple enhancement of bay leaf, lemon and olive oil, this seems a heresy. Yet, I quickly learned to love the Schipani way, and have returned to his restaurant often for another dose. Here's an adapted recipe for home cooking.

INGREDIENTS

1 lb. swordfish steak 1 in. (2 cm) thick, cut into 4 pieces
1 tbsp. (15 mL) olive oil
1–2 bay leaves
3–4 Italian black olives
2–3 sun-dried tomatoes
¼ red onion
1 tbsp. (15 mL) balsamic vinegar
2 tbsp. (30 mL) extra-virgin olive oil
salt and white or black pepper
few sprigs parsley

PREPARATION

1 Wipe fish with a paper towel. Sprinkle 1 tbsp. (15 mL) olive oil onto the fish and rub in, covering both sides. Crumble bay leaf and scatter over the fish, patting the bits into the surface to ensure that they stick.

2 Prepare the dressing: Pit the olives and chop roughly. Reserve. Pour ¼ cup (50 mL) boiling water over the sun-dried tomatoes and let soak 2–3 minutes. Sliver red onion. Reserve. In a bowl, combine balsamic vinegar, extra-virgin olive oil and salt and pepper. Beat to form a light emulsion.

3 Drain the sun-dried tomatoes and chop into thirds. Add chopped sun-dried tomatoes, olives and onion to the bowl with the oil and vinegar. Stir to combine all the ingredients.

4 Wash, dry and chop parsley. Reserve under a wet paper towel.

COOKING

5 Grill or broil the swordfish (either in an outdoor barbecue or indoor oven) for 3 minutes on the bay leaf side and 2 minutes on the other side. This is the ideal cooking time for a medium-rare fish with a moist centre and slightly crisped outsides. If undercooked fish offends, you give it 4 minutes on the first side and 3 on the second, but beware – you'll have sacrificed some of the texture.

6 Serve 2 pieces of fish (bay leaf side up) on each of 2 warm plates. Scrape off bay leaf bits. Top with the dressing and lots of chopped parsley. Serve immediately.

Total prep time: about 10 minutes.
Total cooking time: 5–7 minutes.
Serves 2. For more, increase fish proportionately and dressing by half.

♣ **SUGGESTED MENU FOR THIS MAIN COURSE**
Starter: Jalapeno Broccoli (page 205)
Accompaniments: Herbed Potatoes (page 215), and steamed green beans
Dessert: Individual Apple Strudel (page 222)

SALMON

The abundance of our excellent and relatively affordable salmon is one of the more compelling reasons to live in North America. There is no trick to cooking salmon. I prefer it undercooked, but it is so full-textured that it works even slightly overcooked. It has a terrific flavour that delights on its own and can be enhanced endlessly. It can be eaten hot or cold, poached or grilled. It is truly a heaven-sent fish. I offer three main-course salmon recipes with which you'll have great success.

Salmon with Shrimp Sauce

This is a spectacular taste sensation that bridges those two favourite ingredients, salmon and shrimp, with a spare but memorable sauce. The recipe was created for Angela Lansbury during the filming of Little Gloria ... Happy At Last.

INGREDIENTS

3½ oz. (100 g) small shrimp, fresh or frozen
1 lemon
few sprigs parsley
¼ cup (50 mL) all-purpose flour
salt and black pepper
2 fresh salmon steaks

2 tbsp. (30 mL) vegetable oil
2 tbsp. (30 mL) white wine
1 tbsp. (15 mL) fresh tarragon leaves OR 1 tsp. (5 mL) dried
1 tsp. (5 mL) capers
2 tbsp. (30 mL) unsalted butter

PREPARATION

1 If using frozen shrimp, defrost them. Bring some water to a boil in a sauce pan. Add the shrimp and cook for 2–3 minutes, just until the water returns to the boil, and the shrimp turn pink and rise to the surface. Drain immediately and run cold water over the shrimp. Peel and reserve.

2 Squeeze the lemon and reserve the juice.

3 Wash, dry and chop the parsley. Reserve, covered with a wet paper towel.

COOKING

4 Spread flour on a plate and season with salt and pepper. Thoroughly dredge the salmon steaks in the flour.

5 Heat vegetable oil in a saute pan over medium-high heat, until it's just about to smoke. Add the dredged salmon steaks and fry, 3 minutes on each side for a total of 6 minutes.

6 While the salmon is frying, make the sauce: In a sauce pan combine the lemon juice, white wine and tarragon. Cook until the liquid has evaporated to about half its volume, and has thickened slightly (about 3 minutes: at this time you should be turning the salmon in the saute pan). Now add the drained capers to the sauce and stir for 15 seconds. Leaving the heat on medium-high, take a small wire whisk in hand and add the butter a little at a time (it'll take 4 or 5 nuggets to add the whole amount), whisking each addition vigorously until it has blended into the sauce. By the time all the butter has been added, the sauce will have the consistency of a thick syrup, and is ready. Turn off the heat. If by chance the sauce has turned out too thick, whisk a teaspoon (5 mL) of water, and then turn off the heat.

7 By now the salmon is cooked. Remove it from the pan and position one steak on each plate. Leaving the heat on, add the shrimps to the saute pan and turn them in the salmon-cooking fat for 30 seconds just to heat them through. Turn off the heat. Scoop up the shrimp and scatter them on and around each salmon steak.

8 Top the salmon and shrimp with sauce. Garnish with the chopped parsley and serve immediately.

Total prep time: 8 minutes.
Total cooking time: 8 minutes.
Serves 2. For 4 servings, double the salmon and shrimp and increase the sauce ingredients by half.

♣ **SUGGESTED MENU**
FOR THIS MAIN COURSE
Starter: Roasted Peppers Antipasto (page 48)
Accompaniments: Herbed Potatoes (page 215) and plain broccoli

Poached Salmon Chinese Style

The aromatic sauce of this recipe is traditionally served with steamed pickerel and other whitefish. It works so well on salmon, and is so very easy to make, that I bravely offer this adaptation; I know the culinary deities of China will forgive me. Had China been a salmon-producing country, its chefs would quite likely have arrived at the same conclusion.

There are two possible ways to cook the salmon for this one: steaming or poaching. I have chosen poaching because it's easier to control and it requires no cumbersome steaming equipment. Please take care that the poaching water is never hotter than a mild, gently wafting steam.

INGREDIENTS

1 lb. (500 g) salmon fillet
1 tbsp. (15 mL) wasabe powder (Japanese horseradish; optional)
1 tbsp. (15 mL) water
1½ in. (3 cm) fresh ginger root

3 green onions
2 limes
¼ cup (50 mL) peanut or other vegetable oil
1 tbsp. (15 mL) soya sauce OR tamari
1 tbsp. (15 mL) sesame oil

PREPARATION

1 Address your chunk of salmon. Run your fingers along its surface and expose any lateral bones that might still be in it. Pull them out, using small pliers if necessary. Wipe fish with a paper towel. Reserve unrefrigerated (room-temperature salmon poaches better).

2 Prepare the horseradish garnish (this is optional if you are averse to having your sinuses cleared): Mix wasabe powder with 1 tbsp.

(15 mL) water in a small bowl. A green paste will emerge. Using a spoon, smooth the paste into an attractive shape. Wipe off any smudges on the bowl and cover it tightly with plastic wrap (this will allow it to develop its full heat). Reserve this to be served at table with the salmon.

3 Peel and chop fresh ginger root into thin oval slices. Wash, trim and chop green onions into 1½ in. (3 cm) pieces, white and

green parts alike. Squeeze limes.
Strain and reserve the juice.

COOKING

4   Use a skillet big enough to hold
the salmon and deep enough to
immerse it in water. Fill half-way
with water and add a little salt
and 1 tbsp. (15 mL) lime juice
(about half your lime juice from
step #3). Heat this water over
medium heat until it's barely
moving and emits a gentle steam
(about 5 minutes). Add the
salmon, making sure the water
covers it and reduce heat to low.
It should take no more than 2–3
minutes for the water to regain
its gentle steam. From that point,
poach the salmon for 10 minutes
(if you want a soft fish with a
moist centre) and up to 15 minutes for well done. (Note: The
water must never actually bubble.
If it does, lower heat some more.)

5   While the salmon poaches, prepare the sauce: Heat the peanut
oil in a sauce pan over high heat
until it's just about to smoke.
Immediately add the sliced ginger
and stir-fry for 1 minute. Add the
chopped green onions and stir-fry
for 1 more minute. Add 1 tbsp.

(15 mL) lime juice and stir-fry
for yet another minute, until the
sizzle has subsided. Take sauce
from the heat and reserve in the
pan.

6   When the salmon has finished
poaching, remove from heat.
Holding the fish down with a
spatula, drain the water from the
skillet. Carefully slip the fish out
of the skillet onto a serving plate.
If any water has come with it, sop
it up with a paper towel and discard.

7   Place the sauce back over high
heat till it sizzles: 1 minute. Take
from the heat and add soya and
sesame oil. Mix well and pour all
over the salmon. Serve immediately, with the wasabe on the
side.

Total prep time:
about 15 minutes.
Total cooking time:
18–20 minutes.
Serves 3–4.

♣ **SUGGESTED MENU**
FOR THIS MAIN COURSE
Starter: Chicken Yakitori
(page 71)
Accompaniments: steamed rice or
refried noodles, a green vegetable
and the wasabe
Dessert: fruit

Burmese Tandoori Salmon

Greg Couillard, a culinary wizard and chef for all ages, created this palate-tingler for Notorious, one of his many Toronto restaurants. It is a fun recipe, starting with the whimsical name (a double oxymoron: Burma — or Myanmar, as it is now called — has no tradition of tandoori, and salmon is about as common there as snow-storms). Couillard's twist on traditional tandoori is that he omits yoghurt, which tends to undercook messily if you're using a grill rather than a tandoori oven. The tandoori paste of this recipe is widely available in Indian shops. The grilling part is best accomplished outdoors, using a flip-grill for painless turning. Beware of broiling this dish inside the house: it has a very pungent smell that will linger for 2 or 3 days!

INGREDIENTS

¾ lb. (375 g) fillet of salmon, skin on

1 lime

2 cloves garlic

few sprigs fresh coriander

3 green onions

2 tbsp. (30 mL) tandoori paste

1 tbsp. (15 mL) vegetable oil

¼ cup (50 mL) canned, unsweetened coconut milk

pinch turmeric

1 green onion

vegetable oil for grilling

1–2 tbsp. (15–30 mL) unsalted butter

PREPARATION

1   Prepare the salmon: Run your fingers along its surface and expose any lateral bones that might still be in it. Pull them out, using small pliers if necessary. Wipe the fish with a paper towel. Using a sharp knife, cut into 2 equal pieces. Cover and refrigerate until the tandoori marinade is made.

2   Make the tandoori marinade: Juice one lime. Finely mince garlic. Wash, dry and chop several sprigs of fresh coriander. Trim and finely chop green onions, white and green parts alike. Using a dish large enough to hold the salmon, combine 1 tbsp. (15 mL) of the lime juice, the garlic, the fresh coriander and the green onions with the tandoori paste and vegetable oil. Mix well

before adding the salmon to the marinade.

3 Turn the salmon in the marinade to moisten all over. Spoon excess marinade over the fish. This marination requires at least 30 minutes. If marinating way in advance, cover the dish and refrigerate till 30 minutes before showtime. If you intend to proceed sooner, reserve the salmon at room temperature.

COOKING

4 While the salmon marinates, start the barbecue, begin the rice and make the sauce: Heat coconut milk in a sauce pan over medium heat. (Make a Thai soup with the rest of the coconut milk.) When the coconut milk begins to steam, add 1 tsp. (5 mL) lime juice and a pinch of turmeric. Stir. Finely chop 1 more green onion and add to the coconut milk. Cook, stirring regularly for 7 minutes or so, until some of the liquid has evaporated and the sauce has thickened somewhat. Reserve off heat. The sauce's final enhancement of butter is added later (in step #6).

5 When the marination is completed and the charcoal ready, gently shake salmon pieces to shed excess marinade. (Discard marinade.) Place flip-grill on the barbecue when it is hot, liberally brush its inner surfaces with vegetable oil. Arrange salmon on the oiled surface and grill for 2–4 minutes per side. The cooking time depends on how you like your salmon. At 2 or 2½ minutes per side you'll get a crisp outside with a rare interior. Obviously, longer grilling (up to a maximum of 4 minutes per side) will result in a firmer interior. Rare means

juicier, and for me that's better. But you be the judge of your own fish.

6   While the salmon grills, return to the sauce: Bring the sauce to a boil over high heat. Lower heat to medium-low and add butter in 1 tsp. (5 mL) chunks. (Use more or less depending on your caloric-derring-do; or omit the butter altogether.) Whisk continuously into the sauce until each addition melts and the butter is finished. Immediately remove from heat.

7   Once the salmon is done, slip it off the grill and onto a plate, one piece per serving, skin side down, flesh side up. Smear some of the coconut-milk sauce alongside. Serve immediately, with the rest of the sauce in a separate bowl.

Total prep time: 45 minutes.
Total cooking time: 5–8 minutes.
Serves 2. For more, increase the salmon and sauce proportionately but the marinade by half.

❖ **SUGGESTED MENU FOR THIS MAIN COURSE**
Starter: a Thai soup — Tom Kha Kai (page 35) or Tom Yum Goong (page 36)
Accompaniments: sauce, rice and a green vegetable
Dessert: sliced mango

Broiled/Grilled Whole Fish

Whole fish, whether oily, dark-fleshed mackerel or lean, delicate porgy or red snapper, always presents challenges to the home cook. First and foremost, the smell lingers for hours after broiling fish in the oven. And even in the warm months when outdoor barbecueing is possible, a second problem remains: that of the head with its forlorn eyes and gaping mouth, and also the tail, fins and assorted bones that stand between you and the mouth-watering flesh.

Then there is the problem of timing. Just when is fish broiled enough? This is entirely a matter of personal preference. As the Japanese and other cultures prove daily, fish is edible even when completely raw. Cooking from 2–3 minutes per side (depending on the thickness) is therefore ample time. Any trace of undercooked flesh at the fish's middle will improve the texture, without in the least compromising your health.

Yes, there are obstacles galore. But the texture and flavour of grilled whole fish make them all worthwhile.

Cooking and turning the fish is much easier when you use one of those interlocking grills that are made for hamburgers. They are cheap, work very well for fish, and can be used on an outdoor barbecue as well as under the broiler of the oven.

The unsightly heads and tails can be removed by the fish vendor. The resurgence of gourmet home cooking has given rise to many fine fish stores where service is personalized. Medium-sized fish (which are the best for broiling/grilling) such as mackerel and snapper can be quickly prepped and trimmed if you ask nicely. All that's needed (after scaling and de-gutting, which is normally done anyway) is a sharp cut lengthwise, down the belly, leaving the skin on the other side intact. The result is a butterflied fish that can be grilled open-faced. This makes for faster cooking and easier serving. (The backbone will stick to one of the fillets, but is easily removed after cooking.)

INGREDIENTS

1 whole fish (mackerel, porgy, snapper)	extra-virgin olive oil lemon wedges parsley

PREPARATION AND COOKING

At home, wipe the fish on both sides with a paper towel. Then (having brushed some oil on both sides, flesh and skin) place the fish, opened to its butterfly position, on the grill. Broiling or grilling, as I noted above, need never take more than 2½ minutes on average, per side.

When ready to serve, transfer fish to a platter, remove the aforementioned backbone, drizzle a little extra-virgin olive oil over all, and serve garnished with lemon quarters and sprigs of parsley.

It's fun to serve some kind of dressing alongside, and ideas on this vary widely. One friend mixes oil, vinegar and crushed almonds with his snapper, and another serves an unadulterated gooseberry jam with her mackerel. Personally, I prefer a sauce that offers an array of Mediterranean tastes. This sauce works with most fish. The whole-grain mustard is essential for strong-flavoured fish like mackerel, but tends to overpower the more delicate taste of porgy or snapper — in which case I omit it.

Lemon-Oil Dressing

For grilled fish.

INGREDIENTS

1 lemon
1 tbsp. (15 mL) whole-grain
   mustard (optional)
¼ red onion

few sprigs parsley
1 tsp. (5 mL) capers
salt and black pepper
¼ cup (50 mL) extra-virgin
   olive oil

PREPARATION AND ASSEMBLY

1 Squeeze the lemon. Strain juice
in a mixing bowl.

2 Add (optional) whole-grain mustard. Combine thoroughly with
the lemon juice.

3 Mince red onion; wash, dry and
finely chop parsley. Add both to
lemon juice, along with drained
capers, salt and freshly cracked
pepper. Mix thoroughly, using a
fork.

4 Add extra-virgin olive oil in a thin
stream while beating steadily. The
result will be a light emulsion
with some oil floating on top.

5 Pour into a sauce boat and serve
alongside broiled or grilled fish.

This quantity serves 3–4.

Spanish Shrimp

This favourite of Spanish tapas bars is a hands-on eating experience that is as stimulating as it is tasty. Strangely enough, despite the oily-spicy sauce, the shrimp themselves taste clean and simple. Having been sauteed in their shells to be peeled at table, they emerge lean and only subtly flavoured. The sauce acts as a dip, allowing each diner the choice of enjoying the succulent shrimp without any sauce at all. Alternatively, if you are a glutton like moi, the peeled shrimp will be liberally dunked in the sauce and, as if that weren't enough, you'll use a piece of bread to sop up the rest. Needless to say, napkins are a must for this recipe, which I have slightly adapted from an original by Luis Suarez of Tapas Bar.

INGREDIENTS

1 lb. (500 g) medium shrimp,
  fresh or frozen
½ green bell pepper
5 cloves garlic
few sprigs fresh parsley

1 lemon
5 tbsp. (65 mL) olive oil
1 tbsp. (15 mL) paprika
pinch cayenne (optional)
salt
pinch oregano

PREPARATION

1 If using frozen shrimp, defrost them. The shrimp for this recipe are fried and presented with their shells on. Remove the thin legs that seem to hide on the underside of the shrimp, from the tail all the way up to the neck. They come off easily, but unfortunately sometimes drag part or all of the shell with them.

If this happens, don't worry: you'll just have one shelled shrimp among all the others. After you've pulled the legs from all the shrimp, wash them in a strainer and lay them on a paper towel to dry.

2 Slice the green bell pepper into ¼ in. x 1 in. (½ cm x 2 cm) strips. Reserve. Roughly chop garlic. Reserve. Wash, dry and chop parsley. Reserve under a wet paper towel. Slice lemon into quarters. Reserve.

COOKING

3 Heat 5 tbsp. (65 mL) olive oil in a saute pan for 1 minute. Add the chopped green pepper and stir-fry for 1 minute until it wilts. Add paprika, a pinch of cayenne, the garlic and some salt. Saute, stirring constantly for no longer than 1 minute. Add the shrimp and fry, stirring and tossing for 2 minutes, by the end of which all the shrimp should be evenly coated with the paprika-reddened oil and turning pink themselves. Add a pinch of oregano. Continue tossing and stirring at high heat for 2 more minutes. By now the shrimp should be done. Test one. It will be firm to the touch and glistening redly. Take from the heat, and transfer to a serving bowl. Garnish liberally with parsley and serve immediately, with lemon quarters and extra salt on the side.

Total prep time:
About 20 minutes.
Total cooking time: 7–8 minutes.
Serves 4 as an appetizer or 2 as a main course. If an appetizer serve with crusty bread. If a main course, start with a soup and accompany the shrimp with a potato salad and greens. For more, increase everything proportionately but the oil by only half.

Shrimp with Feta

An old Greek favourite, this is a lovely, fresh-tasting seafood specialty that can be made for 2 or 200 with equal ease. It is fail-safe because its only fragile ingredient (the shrimp) is cooked at the last minute; and it's easy because it can be assembled in advance, baked in no time and brought to the table piping hot. The Greeks like to bake this in individual earthenware dishes called gouvetsi (and so its name: garides gouvetsi), but any ovenproof dish will do. I recommend that it be cooked all in one dish (as long as it's not piled too high) so that portions can be controlled (small portions for an appetizer, larger portions for a main course).

INGREDIENTS

½ lb. (250 g) small shrimp,
  fresh or frozen
few sprigs parsley
3½ oz. (100 g) mushrooms
1 large or 2 small tomatoes,
  plus 1 tsp. (5 mL) tomato
  paste if tomatoes are out
  of season
1 leek

2 cloves garlic
1 hot chili (optional)
1 tbsp. (15 mL) fresh oregano
  OR 1 tsp. (5 mL) dried
2 tbsp. plus 1 tbsp. (30 mL +
  15 mL) olive oil
salt and black pepper
dash balsamic vinegar
3½ oz. (100 g) feta cheese

PREPARATION

1 If using frozen shrimp, defrost them. Shell the shrimp. You can also devein them (by scraping the coloured matter from their backs), but this is unnecessary for small shrimp. Wash a bowl and line it with a paper towel. Pile the shrimp in it. Reserve in the refrigerator.

2 Wash, dry and chop parsley. Reserve under a wet paper towel. Slice the mushrooms in ¼ in.

(½ cm) slices. Reserve.

3 Prep sauce ingredients: Blanch tomato in boiling water for 30 seconds, then peel, core and seed it. Cut the flesh into small, square pieces. Reserve. (If making this sauce when tomatoes are out of season, smear a little tomato paste on the pieces.) Cut the leek in half and wash it thoroughly. Slice thinly. Reserve. Mince garlic. Reserve. Mince chili. Add to reserved garlic (wash hands right after). If you are using fresh oregano, chop it now.

COOKING

4 Heat 2 tbsp. (30 mL) olive oil in a saute pan over high heat for 30 seconds. Add leeks, salt and pepper. Stir-fry for 2 minutes. Add garlic-chili mixture and stir-fry for 30 seconds. Add tomato pieces, dried oregano (if you're not using fresh) and a dash of balsamic vinegar. Stir-fry until the tomatoes soften (about 2 minutes). Reduce heat to medium and cook 15–20 minutes, stirring occasionally, until the sauce is soft and tasty. Add the chopped fresh oregano from step #3 now, and take pan from heat.

5 While the sauce is cooking, heat remaining tablespoon (15 mL) olive oil in another pan for 30 seconds over high heat. Add sliced mushrooms and stir-fry for 2–3 minutes until mushrooms darken. Take from the heat and reserve until the sauce has finished cooking. Then fold mushrooms into the sauce.

6 Preheat oven to either 425° F (220° C) or 450° F (230° C). (See step #8.)

7 Assemble the dish: Transfer the tomato-mushroom sauce to an ovenproof dish that is large enough to hold it piled no higher than 1 in. (2 cm). Embed all the shrimp into the sauce, distributing them evenly over the surface. Arrange them so that most of their bodies are covered by the sauce. Put the feta cheese into a strainer and run some water over it to remove some of its salt. Make sure that the excess water has run off. Then crumble it coarsely and dot it all over the shrimp (the cheese will not cover the entire surface, but must be distributed evenly).

8 There are two ways to bake this dish: a) Bake it at 425° F (230° C) for 8 minutes and then place it under a hot broiler for 2–3 minutes until the feta topping has charred attractively: or (b) Bake it at 450° F (230° C) for 10 minutes.

9 Carefully transfer the baked shrimp with sauce and feta on top to warm plates. Garnish with chopped parsley and serve immediately.

Total prep time: 20 minutes.
Total cooking time: 35 minutes.
Serves 4 as an appetizer on its
own with crusty bread, and 2
as a main course with bread,
fried zucchini and salad.

Shrimp au Gratin

The combination of moistened bread crumbs and crunchy shellfish is as North American as anything I cook. This recipe is typical family-restaurant fare, reminiscent of lobster and scampi cooked in a similar manner. In fact, this is such a familiar taste and so universally liked that it can save many a dinner party. Children and elders alike will applaud you and you will have the satisfaction of knowing that you've achieved the taste they crave without using a speck of butter.

INGREDIENTS

1 lb. (500 g) medium shrimp, fresh or frozen

3 slices white or brown bread

2 cloves garlic

few sprigs parsley

2 limes

3–4 tbsp. (45–50 mL) grated Romano cheese

¼ cup (50 mL) chicken broth

¼ cup (50 mL) olive oil

½ tsp. (2 mL) each ground black pepper, dried basil, dried oregano and paprika

sprigs of fresh basil, oregano and parsley

PREPARATION

1 If using frozen shrimp, defrost them. Shell and devein shrimp (by scraping the coloured matter from their backs). Wash and reserve on a paper towel.

2 Using a blender, process enough slices of white or brown bread to get 1 cup (250 mL) of bread crumbs.

3 Mince garlic; wash, dry and chop several sprigs of parsley; squeeze 1 lime and strain the juice. Reserve each separately. If using freshly grated Romano cheese, grate it now.

4 Pour chicken broth into a small sauce pan and bring it to a simmer.

5 In another small sauce pan, heat olive oil over medium heat until it's just about to smoke. Take from the stove and add garlic, as well as the ground black pepper, dried basil, dried oregano and paprika. Return the sauce pan to the heat and cook for 30 seconds. Add warm chicken broth and cook, stirring, for 1–2 minutes

until mixture begins to sizzle. Take from the heat and add the lime juice, 2 tbsp. (30 mL) of the grated Romano cheese and 2–3 tbsp. (30–45 mL) of the chopped parsley from step #3. Stir and let cool awhile.

COOKING

6 Preheat oven to either 425° F (220° C) or 450° F (230° C). (See below step #9).

7 Scatter half of the bread crumbs over the bottom of an ovenproof dish that is large enough to hold the shrimp in one layer.

8 Combine sauce and shrimp in a working bowl and fold to mix. Lift out shrimp (by hand is best) and arrange on top of the bread crumbs in the oven dish. (There should be some sauce left over in the bowl.) Scatter the remaining bread crumbs on top of the shrimp. Scatter the remaining grated Romano over the bread crumbs. Finish the assembly by drizzling the remaining sauce evenly here and there over the topping.

9 There are two ways to bake this dish:

(a) Bake it at 425° F (220° C) for 8 minutes and then place it directly under a hot broiler for 2–3 minutes until the topping browns attractively, or (b) Bake it at 450° F (230° C) for 10–12 minutes.

10 While the shrimp bake: Wash, dry and chop some sprigs of fresh basil, oregano and/or parsley. Slice remaining lime in wedges.

11 Carefully transfer the baked shrimp (with browned surface facing up) to warm plates. Garnish each portion lavishly with chopped herbs and a wedge of lime. Serve immediately.

Total prep time: 30 minutes.
Total assembly and cooking time: 20 minutes.
Serves 5–6 as an appetizer on its own with crusty bread and 3–4 as a main course with rice, Summer Zucchini (page 212) and salad. For less, decrease shrimp proportionately but other ingredients only by half.

Jumbo Shrimp Roz Landor

Named after one of the supporting actors of Little Gloria ... Happy at Last, *these shrimp are a quick and luxurious dinner highlight, whose high cost can be defrayed by serving inexpensive side dishes. Peeling the shrimp is a bit of a hassle, but otherwise this one is a cinch.*

INGREDIENTS

12 jumbo shrimp,
   fresh or frozen
2 large cloves garlic
1 lemon

few sprigs parsley
3 tbsp. (45 mL) olive oil
salt and white or black pepper
3 tbsp. (45 mL) white wine

PREPARATION

1 If using frozen shrimp, defrost them. Shell the shrimp. With a thin paring knife make a slit down the back of each and scrape off the dark vein. Wash briefly under cold water and lay on a paper towel to dry.

2 Peel and mince garlic. Reserve.

3 Zest lemon. Add the zest to the reserved garlic. Squeeze the lemon, strain the juice and reserve.

4 Wash, dry and chop the parsley. Reserve, covered with a wet paper towel.

COOKING

5 Heat olive oil with some salt and pepper over high heat until the oil is just about to smoke. Add the shrimp, making sure they're not crowded in the pan. Saute for 2 minutes. Turn them and saute the flip-side for another 2 minutes.

6 Reduce heat to medium, and add the garlic-lemon zest mixture. Stir-fry for 1 minute.

7 Scoop out the shrimp into a bowl, leaving most of the fried garlic and zest in the pan.

8 Increase heat to maximum, and immediately add the lemon juice and white wine to the pan. Heat for 2–3 minutes, scraping the pan with a wooden spoon, until the lemon's acidity and the wine's alcohol have evaporated and the sauce has thickened somewhat. Turn off heat. Scrape the sauce and drippings with a rubber

spatula onto the shrimp and gently toss. Garnish with the chopped parsley. Serve immediately.

Total prep time: about 15 minutes. Total cooking time: 8–9 minutes. Serves 2. For 4, double the amount of shrimp (frying them in 2 batches) and increase the sauce ingredients by half.

❖ **SUGGESTED MENU FOR THIS MAIN COURSE**
Starter: French Vegetable Soup (page 30)
Accompaniment: rice; Zucchini Algis (page 181)
Dessert: strawberries and cream

Shrimp Mick Jagger

This delicate shrimp recipe was part of the Chinese-inspired meal I served Mick Jagger and Jerry Hall way-back-when in their Woodstock hide-out. The original calls for a wok, but a saute pan works just fine. The prep can be done up to an hour in advance; the actual cooking takes next to no time, allowing you ample time to prepare any additional dishes.

Mick used to insist on a pineapple dessert after shrimp and other shellfish. According to him, pineapple has properties that counteract the toxins of shellfish. I have never heard this from anyone else, but I love pineapple, so why not?

INGREDIENTS

½-¾ lb. (250–375 g) small
  shrimp, fresh or frozen
1 in. (2 cm) fresh ginger root
1 small clove garlic
2 green onions
pinch each salt and white sugar

few sprigs of fresh coriander
2 tbsp. (30 mL) peanut or
  other vegetable oil
2 tbsp. (30 mL) Chinese
  rice wine

PREPARATION

1 If using frozen shrimp, defrost them. Shell the shrimp. You can also devein them (by scraping the coloured matter from their backs), but this is unnecessary for small shrimp. Wash and lay them on a paper towel to dry.

2 Mince the fresh ginger and garlic, and chop the green onion into 1 in. (2 cm) pieces. Combine the shrimp, ginger, garlic, green onions, salt and sugar in a bowl. Mix well and let marinate for up to one hour (minimum 10 minutes).

3 Wash, dry and chop some fresh coriander. Reserve under a wet paper towel.

COOKING

4 Heat the peanut oil in a saute pan (or wok) over high heat until it's just about to smoke. Add the shrimp and their marinade and saute for 1–2 minutes, tossing briskly so that both sides of all the shrimp have had contact with the hot oil. The shrimp are done when they turn pink, and feel springy to the touch.

5 Add the rice wine and toss. Lower heat to medium and cook covered, for 1½ minutes.

6 Take pan from the heat. Uncover and toss shrimp. Replace cover and let dish rest for 1 minute. Transfer shrimp to a bowl, garnish with the chopped coriander, and serve immediately.

Total prep time:
about 10 minutes.
Marinating time:
10 minutes minimum.
Total cooking time: 6 minutes.
Serves 2.

❖ **SUGGESTED MENU FOR THIS MAIN COURSE**
Starter: Yam and Pecan Salad (page 62)
Accompaniments: plain rice, refried rapini, bok choy or dandelion greens.
Dessert: Fried Pineapple (page 233)

Lemon Sea Scallops

This zingy recipe, which redefines the normally bland sea scallop, has two critical points. The first is to resist the temptation to overcook the scallops themselves; the second is not to be intimidated by the early, seemingly tricky stages of concocting the sauce. The reward for getting it right is a light but meaningful mantle on plump, juicy morsels of this favourite seafood. Which is exactly what had been requested by Amnon and Marion Medad, for whose Caledon farm-house luncheon this recipe was created.

INGREDIENTS

1 lemon
3 cloves garlic
2 green onions
¼ red pepper
1 small, ripe tomato
few sprigs fresh coriander
1 green onion (to garnish)
¾ lb. (375 g) sea scallops,
   fresh or frozen

½ cup (125 mL) all-purpose
   flour
¼ cup plus 1 tbsp. (50 mL +
   15 mL) olive oil
½ cup (50 mL) white wine
1 tbsp. (15 mL) capers
1 tbsp. (15 mL) unsalted butter
salt and white or black pepper

PREPARATION

1 Zest the lemon and reserve the zest. Then squeeze the lemon, strain the juice, and reserve.

2 Peel and mince garlic; finely chop the green onions. Add both to the reserved lemon zest.

3 Slice red pepper into thin strips. Reserve.

4 Blanch tomato in boiling water for 30 seconds, then peel, core and seed it. Cut the flesh into small, square pieces.

5 Prepare the final garnish: Wash, dry and chop fresh coriander; finely chop the remaining green onion, and add to the coriander. Reserve this mixture, covered with a wet, paper towel.

COOKING

6 Place the scallops in a strainer, and sprinkle the flour over them. Toss together to dredge the scallops.

7 Heat ¼ cup (50 mL) olive oil in a

large saute pan over high heat until it's just about to smoke. Add the dredged scallops and cook for a total of 4 minutes, turning them gently after 2 minutes. They will turn a light beige on both sides. Scoop them out and reserve uncovered. Leave the drippings in the pan.

8   Replace the pan over high heat. Add an additional tablespoon of olive oil, if the pan seems too dry. Add the sliced red pepper, and stir-fry for 1 minute. Add the garlic, lemon zest and green onions, and stir-fry for 1 minute. (The contents of the pan will now appear dry, almost burning: this is normal, and the next addition will remedy it.) Add the lemon juice, and scrape the stuck-on drippings for 1 minute. This will deglaze the pan. Add the tomato pieces and stir for 1 minute. Add the white wine and continue stirring (always on high heat) for 3 minutes. At this point the sauce should be the consistency of heavy cream. If too thin, boil for another minute. If too thick, add a little more wine and reheat for another minute. Add the drained capers, stirring. Add the butter in small chunks, stirring briskly after each addition. Continue cooking and stirring for 1 more minute. Reduce heat to low.

9   Add the scallops and the liquid that has collected under them. Gently fold the sauce over the scallops. Heat for 2 minutes without stirring. Turn off the heat, and resume folding the scallops into the sauce, gently, gently. Taste for seasoning, and add salt and pepper.

10 Transfer the sauce and scallops into a serving bowl. Garnish with the chopped coriander and green onions. Serve immediately.

Total prep time: about 20 minutes. Total cooking time: 15–17 minutes. Serves 2. For 4 servings, double the amount of scallops (frying them in 2 batches) and increase the sauce ingredients only by half.

❖ **SUGGESTED MENU FOR THIS MAIN COURSE**
Starter: Greek Bean Salad (page 46)
Accompaniments: rice; Green Beans with Cashews (page 207)
Dessert: Aristedes' Bougatsa (page 226)

Sea Scallops in Black Bean Sauce

Pungent and flavourful, Chinese fermented black beans work well with sturdy ingredients like chicken, but they also do wonders for fragile things like sea scallops. I used to offer this dish as an occasional treat to the movie crews, and it was so popular that I always wished I had made more. This recipe is cooked in two stages, with the second stage flexible enough to await your pleasure (a rare treat in Chinese cooking). The cashew side course that I recommend is delicious, but can be easily omitted if you're counting calories.

INGREDIENTS

2 cups (500 mL) water
2–3 oz. (75 g) snow peas
3 green onions
½ red or green bell pepper
few sprigs fresh coriander
1 tsp. peanut or other
   vegetable oil
¼ cup (50 mL) raw cashews
1 tsp. plus 1 tbsp. (5 mL +
   15 mL) soya sauce OR tamari
2 cloves garlic
1 in. (2 cm) fresh ginger root

1 tbsp. (15 mL) Chinese salted
   black beans
1 fresh chili (optional)
1 tbsp. (15 mL) peanut or
   other vegetable oil
2 tbsp. (30 mL) Chinese
   rice wine
½ cup (50 mL) chicken broth
½-¾ lb. (250–375 g) sea
   scallops, fresh or frozen
¼ cup (50 mL) cornstarch
2 tbsp. (15 mL) peanut or
   other vegetable oil

PREPARATION

1 Bring water to a boil in a small pot. While water is heating, pull off the hard stems of the snow peas, removing also the little string that runs down one side. When all the peas are thus de-stringed, add them to the boiling water and boil for 90 seconds. Drain immediately and refresh with cold water. Drain again and reserve.

2 Chop green onions in ¼ in. (½ cm) bits and add to the reserved snow peas.

3 Chop red or green bell pepper into 1 in. (2 cm) squares. Reserve.

4 Wash, dry and chop several sprigs

of fresh coriander. Reserve under a wet paper towel.

5 Heat peanut oil in a small saute pan for 10 seconds. Add raw cashews and stir-fry for 2–3 minutes, turning often, until the nuts have browned (be careful: they burn easily). Remove from heat and add 1 tsp. (5 mL) soya sauce. Toss. Transfer cashews to a small serving bowl and reserve.

6 Prep the sauce ingredients: Mince garlic. Peel and finely chop ginger root. Add to garlic. Put black beans into a strainer and run some water over them. Then transfer them to a small bowl and cover with cold water. Mince fresh chili (wash hands right after).

COOKING

7 Heat 1 tbsp. (45 mL) peanut oil in a sauce pan over medium-high heat until it's just about to smoke. Add the garlic-ginger mixture and optional chili. Stir-fry for 30 seconds. Drain black beans and add them. Stir-fry for 30 seconds. Add rice wine; stir-fry for 30 seconds. Immediately add chicken broth. Bring to a boil, then reduce heat to medium. Cook, stirring, for 3–4 minutes, until some liquid evaporates and the sauce thickens somewhat.

Take from heat and cover to let rest. This is the point when you can take a breather. Start your rice, have a sip of wine and when you're ready, proceed (the recipe takes only about 10 minutes from this point).

8 Put scallops in a strainer and sprinkle cornstarch over them. Toss together to dredge the scallops, allowing excess cornstarch to sieve through. (Do this messy job over the sink.)

9 Heat remaining 2 tbsp. (30 mL) peanut oil in a large saute pan (or wok) over high heat until it's just about to smoke. Add the chopped bell pepper and stir-fry for 2 minutes, until the peppers have begun to char. Fish the pepper out of the oil and add to it the reserved snow peas-green onions from step #2.

10 Return the pan and its remaining oil to high heat. Wait 30 seconds for it to heat up. Add the dredged scallops and stir-fry for 2 minutes, turning them gently. Gently fold in the reserved snow peas-green onions and the fried bell pepper. Fry together for 30 seconds. Carefully fold in the black bean sauce (so as not to mash the scallops). Reduce heat to medium and fry, agitating the pan to mix everything. The sauce will thicken during this operation. If it

doesn't, continue cooking and
agitating for another minute, but
no more.

11 Transfer to a presentation bowl.
Garnish liberally with the
chopped, fresh coriander from
step #4 and the fried cashews
from step #5. Serve immediately.

Total prep time: 20 minutes.
Total cooking time: 15 minutes.
Serves 2–3.

♣ **SUGGESTED MENU FOR**
THIS MAIN COURSE
Starter: Don Don Noodles
(page 66)
Accompaniments: rice and a
stir-fried green vegetable
Dessert: a sherbet

Chicken and Veggies Greek Style

This is a cheap and easy recipe that never fails to remind me of home and Mum: my mother serves it to me every time I return to visit her. It is an all-in-one dinner that bakes for 40–50 minutes more or less on its own, allowing the home cook enough leisure to prepare a fancy starter and a nice dessert.

INGREDIENTS

3 medium potatoes
1 yam
1 onion
1 green pepper
1 large tomato
3 chicken legs, with
    thighs attached

1 lemon
2 tbsp. (30 mL) chopped fresh
    basil OR 1 tsp. (5 mL) dried
¼ cup (50 mL) vegetable oil
1 tbsp. (15 mL) paprika
salt and pepper
½ cup (125 mL) water

PREPARATION

1 Add washed potatoes and yam to boiling water in a pot. Bring back to boil, lower heat to medium and cook for 7 minutes.

2 While the potatoes are cooking, preheat the oven to 450° F (230° C). Roughly chop the onion; core and cut green pepper into 8 pieces; slice tomato into 8 wedges. Reserve each.

3 Pat the chicken legs dry and cut two deep slits down the skin side all the way to the bone: one in the thigh, the other in the drumstick.

4 Squeeze the lemon, strain and reserve juice. Chop the basil (if fresh).

5 Pour the vegetable oil into a large oven pan and add the paprika, salt and pepper. Mix with a wooden spoon to colour the oil evenly.

COOKING

6 When the potatoes and yam have cooked for 7 minutes, drain in a colander. Simultaneously put the pan with the spiced oil into the preheated oven and leave for 2 minutes. Cut the potatoes and yams (careful, they're hot) into 1½ in. (3 cm) chunks.

7 Remove pan from the oven, and add the potatoes and yam, turning them in the oil to coat. Make a space in the pan and add the chicken legs, turning them in the oil as well. Make sure the chicken is not crowded. It must finish skin side up. Fit the slices of green pepper into the pan. Scatter the onions over. Add the tomato wedges on top wherever they fall. Add ¼ cup (50 mL) water (reserving the other ¼ cup). Tilt pan to distribute the water. Place in oven and let bake undisturbed for 30 minutes.

8 Remove from oven and working quickly, use a spatula to unstick contents from the pan. Tilt the pan and scoop out drippings to baste chicken and vegetables. Sprinkle half of the reserved lemon juice over chicken and vegetables. Add the other ¼ cup (50 mL) water, and tilt the pan once again to distribute. Sprinkle half of the basil. Return to oven for 15–20 minutes.

9 Just before serving, sprinkle with the rest of the lemon juice and basil.

Total prep time: 10 minutes.
Total baking time: 50 minutes.
Serves 2 or 3. Avoid serving the oily gravy if the sight of grease offends.

❖ **SUGGESTED MENU FOR THIS MAIN COURSE**
Starter: Marinated Mushrooms (page 53)
The chicken and its vegetables are the entire main course.
Dessert: Baklava (page 224)

Chicken Richard Harris

My prime responsibility during the filming of Your Ticket Is No Longer
Valid *was catering to the palate and health of its chief star, Richard Harris.
He had just come off a lengthy bender and couldn't tolerate rich food, but
refused to settle for bland. I created this orangy chicken and saved on the fat
by grilling the chicken (instead of sauteing it) and omitting the cream from
the sauce.*

INGREDIENTS

1 whole (double) chicken
   breast, skinned and boned
   (see below)
1 orange
bunch fresh tarragon OR
   1 tbsp. dried
1 tbsp. (15 mL) Grand Marnier
3½ oz. (100 g) mushrooms

2 green onions
few sprigs parsley
½ cup (125 mL) all-purpose
   flour
3 tbsp. (45 mL) vegetable oil
½ cup (125 mL) warm chicken
   broth OR white wine
2 tbsp. (30 mL) 35% cream
   (optional)

PREPARATION

1 Prepare the chicken breast: Slice
   meat from the bone and remove
   the skin. Skin and bones can now
   be boiled in 2 cups (500 mL)
   water for 40 minutes to provide
   the chicken broth in step #6.
   Lay out the liberated breast
   (known as supremes in French).
   Cut off the long, thin fillet on the
   underside. This is the tenderest
   part of the supreme. It has a
   white tendon that protrudes from
   one end. Grasp the tendon and,
   using the dull side of the knife,
   scrape along it while pulling,
   without injuring the flesh, to remove it and discard. Cut remainder of breast into two equal
   chunks. You'll now have 3 pieces
   from each half or 6 pieces in
   total.

2 Squeeze the orange. Strain juice
   into a bowl. Remove leaves of
   tarragon from stalks (by pulling
   upward to the tip). Chop and add
   to the orange juice (or add dried
   tarragon). Add Grand Marnier.
   Transfer all the chicken to the

orange juice mixture, and let marinate at least 10 minutes (45 minutes maximum).

3 Wipe mushrooms and quarter them. Chop green onions into ½ in. (1 cm) pieces. Reserve mushrooms and green onions separately. Wash, dry and chop parsley. Reserve under a wet paper towel.

COOKING

4 Pour flour onto a deep, flat plate. Remove chicken pieces from the orange juice (reserve the juice) and dredge them in the flour. Heat vegetable oil in a large saute pan over high heat until it's just about to smoke. Working quickly, add chicken pieces to the hot oil. Add chopped mushrooms to the pan, fitting them into the crevices so that everything hits the hot oil. Turn the chicken every minute or so for a total of 4–5 minutes. You don't want to brown it. Test for doneness by pressing it: when both sides of the meat feel spongy it's done. Note that the thin fillet strips cook faster. You can avoid overcooking them by placing them on top of the larger chunks in the latter stages of frying. Also, try to find a moment during these chicken ministrations to toss the mushrooms. At the end of no more than 5 min-

utes, both mushrooms and chicken are done. Scoop them out of the pan onto a side plate and reserve.

5 Immediately add green onions to the pan and stir-fry over high heat for 30 seconds (there will be a lot of stick-ons in the pan: this is normal).

6 Add all the orange juice with its tarragon leaves, along with the warm chicken broth (or white wine). Cook, stirring and scraping the bottom of the pan to deglaze it, for 4–5 minutes, until the sauce thickens and loses its acidity and alcohol. Add the optional dash of cream, stirring to blend just until it starts to bubble (30 seconds). Turn heat down to medium-low: fold the cooked chicken and mushrooms into the sauce. Heat through (less than 1 minute). Turn off heat, sprinkle with parsley and serve immediately.

Total prep time: 15 minutes.
Total cooking time: 12 minutes.
Serves 2. For more, increase chicken proportionately (sauteing in two batches, if necessary) and all other ingredients by half.

❖ **SUGGESTED MENU FOR THIS MAIN COURSE**
Starter: Eggplant with Mint (page 51)

Accompaniment to the chicken: rice or refried potatoes and buttered broccoli.

Dessert: Chocolate Fondue (page 234)

Note: If, like Richard Harris, you need to render this recipe on the lean side, then marinate a whole, deboned and skinned chicken breast and then grill or broil it 3–4 minutes on the first side and 3 minutes on the second. Meanwhile, reduce the marinade in a pan over high heat, down to $\frac{1}{3}$ of its volume (5–6 minutes). Sauce the grilled chicken with the reduced marinade and serve immediately.

Chicken with Cashews

Marinated chicken breast, stir-fried with fresh pepper, leek and cashews in a Chinese-inspired sauce of black beans and garlic: you'll be showered with compliments! The dried chilies are "optional" only for the most timid. This dish needs its heat. And as always with Chinese cooking, prep everything before starting to cook: once under way, this dish waits for nobody.

INGREDIENTS

1 whole (double) chicken breast, skinned and boned

1 leek OR 4 green onions

1½ tsp. (7 mL) soya sauce OR tamari

1 tbsp. (15 mL) Chinese rice wine

1 tsp. (5 mL) cornstarch

1 tbsp. (15 mL) Chinese salted black beans

3 cloves garlic

2 dried red chilies (optional)

½ red or green bell pepper

¼ cup (50 mL) chicken broth

3 tbsp. (45 mL) peanut or other vegetable oil

¼ cup (50 mL) cashew pieces

1 tsp. (5 mL) soya sauce OR tamari

PREPARATION

1 Cut chicken breast into 1 in. (2½ cm) nuggets (slice each half into 3 strips, then cut each strip into 3 pieces). Reserve.

Thoroughly wash, trim and dry leek, and chop into ½ in. (1 cm) rounds. Reserve.

2 Put chicken nuggets in a bowl. Add 1½ tsp. (7 mL) soya, the rice wine and cornstarch. Stir well to coat chicken. Add chopped leek and mix again. Let marinate for 5 to 10 minutes.

3 Meanwhile, put Chinese black beans into strainer. Run cold water through the beans to remove some of the salt. Transfer the washed black beans to a small bowl and cover with cold water. Reserve.

4 Mince garlic. Crumble optional dried chilies into flakes and add to garlic, seeds and all.

5 Chop bell pepper into 1 in. (2½ cm) squares.

6 Heat chicken broth and keep handy.

COOKING

7 Heat vegetable oil in a saute pan or wok over high heat, until it's just about to smoke. Add cashew pieces and stir-fry for 30 seconds until they brown. Scoop them out and reserve. Then add bell pepper squares and stir-fry them for 1 minute until they begin to sear. Scoop them out and reserve.

8 Still over high heat, add garlic and chili flakes to remaining oil in pan and stir-fry for 20–30 seconds (until the garlic is light brown). Drain and add the black beans. Stir-fry for 30 seconds.

9 Add the chicken with all its marinade. Stir-fry for 2 minutes, until the chicken begins to whiten. Add remaining 1 tsp. (5 mL) soya and stir-fry for 10 seconds. Add warm chicken broth, and stir-fry for 1 minute until the sauce is bubbling and has thickened. Stir-fry for 30 seconds more to evaporate some of the liquid.

10 Add reserved cashews and green peppers; stir. Reduce heat to low and let simmer covered for 1–2 minutes. Turn off heat and allow to rest for 1 minute more.

11 Stir, and transfer to a serving bowl. Serve immediately.

Total prep time: 20 minutes.
Total cooking time: 10 minutes.
Serves 2.

❖ **SUGGESTED MENU FOR THIS MAIN COURSE**
Starter: Tom Yum Goong (page 36)
Accompaniments: steamed rice and a stir-fried green vegetable
Dessert: fresh fruit with ice cream

Chicken au Vin

Overcooked fowl in a winy sauce, a.k.a. coq au vin, is second in Gallic stew popularity only to beef bourguignon (which it resembles). It is a hearty dish that totally satisfies meat-eaters, and it is home-cook positive in that it requires little attention: it loves to sit waiting for the rest of the meal to be ready (if anything, resting time improves it). This version was one of my favourite film catering recipes, and a universal hit with my customers. I deviate from the classic coq au vin by using chicken (and therefore changing the very name of the dish), and I make it more palatable to modern diners by replacing the pork and butterfat of the original with oil.

INGREDIENTS

4 chicken legs, with thighs
   attached
4 cloves garlic
1 cup (250 mL) chicken broth
1 tbsp. (15 mL) tomato paste
½ cup (125 mL) all-purpose
   flour
¼ cup (50 mL) vegetable oil
salt and black pepper

3 oz. (85 mL) French brandy
   (or Cognac)
2 cups (500 mL) dry red wine
1 bay leaf
2 tbsp. (30 mL) chopped fresh
   basil OR 1 tsp. (5 mL) dried
pinch oregano
few sprigs parsley
½ lb. (250 g) mushrooms
1 tbsp. (15 mL) olive oil

PREPARATION

1 Separate chicken legs from their thighs, trimming off excess fat and cutting away the cross-bone at the edge of the thigh if possible.

2 Mince garlic and reserve.

3 Heat chicken broth to boiling and dissolve tomato paste in it. Take from heat and reserve.

4 Pour flour onto a plate and dredge the chicken pieces in it.

COOKING

5 Heat vegetable oil in a large saute pan over high heat for 1 minute. Add a little salt and freshly ground pepper and the dredged chicken pieces. Reduce heat to medium-high and fry the chicken 3 minutes on each side (use a frying screen to avoid oil splutters). The chicken will crust on both sides, but its interior will be very much undercooked.

6 Preheat oven to 325° F (160° C). Take pan from the heat and drain away all the fat (an accumulation of chicken fat and the original oil). The safe way to do this is by transfering the chicken pieces to a plate and then draining the fat freely. Then replace the chicken in the pan and return the pan to high heat. Let cook like this for 30 seconds and then drizzle the brandy (or Cognac if you're feeling flush) evenly over the chicken. Use a match to ignite the Cognac, and agitate the pan while the blue flames dance around. When the flames have subsided, immediately take from heat and transfer the chicken pieces to a deep, snug oven proof dish or pot.

7 Return the saute pan to high heat and add the dry red wine, scraping the bottom to release the stick-ons. Add the minced garlic, bay leaf, fresh or dried basil, and a pinch oregano. Add the reserved chicken broth from step #3. Stir and cook for 3–4 minutes until the sauce comes to a rolling boil. Take from heat and pour sauce over the chicken. (It should just about cover the chicken. If not, add a bit more chicken broth and/or wine.)

8 Cover the ovenproof dish (with foil if no lid) and place in the preheated oven. Bake undisturbed for 30 minutes. Take dish from the oven; uncover it and give it a gentle stir. Reduce the oven to 275° F (135° C). Cover the dish again and bake for another 15 minutes. (Thereafter, the dish can wait in the oven with the heat turned off for up to 1 hour).

9 When ready to serve, wash, dry and chop fresh parsley; slice the mushrooms.

10 Heat the olive oil in a saute pan over high heat for 30 seconds and add the mushrooms. Stir-fry for 2–3 minutes, until mushrooms have darkened and wilted. Remove from heat.

11 Remove the chicken from the oven and uncover. There may be quite a bit of fat floating on top of the sauce. Using a spoon, skim off as much of this fat as you can. Then transfer the chicken and all its sauce into a presentation bowl. Scatter the mushrooms decoratively over it, and garnish with the chopped parsley. Serve immediately.

Total prep time: 10 minutes.
Total cooking time: 75 minutes.
Serves 3–4.

❧ **SUGGESTED MENU FOR THIS MAIN COURSE**
Starter: Insalata Caprese (page 49)
Accompaniment:
parsleyed potatoes or noodles
Dessert: fruit

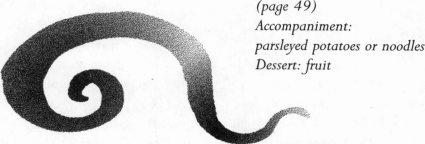

Chicken Livers in Red Wine

Some people love chicken livers and some hate them. If, like me, you belong to the former group, you will enjoy this easy, highly satisfying recipe. The only trick here is to avoid overcooking; the livers must stay pink at their centre. Beyond that, it's clear sailing.

INGREDIENTS

¾ lb. (375 g) fresh chicken
   livers
4 cloves garlic
1 tbsp. (15 mL) fresh rosemary
   OR 1 tsp. (5 mL) dried
few fresh chives OR 3 green
   onions

½ cup (125 mL) all-purpose
   flour
¼ cup (50 mL) olive oil
½-1 tsp. (2–5 mL) black
   peppercorns
½ cup (125 mL) dry red wine
salt

PREPARATION

1 Trim the chicken livers, cutting away any pale parts (only crimson, shiny livers are good), and also the fatty string at one end. Try not to separate the lobes of the livers.

2 Chop garlic into oval slices.

Reserve. Finely chop fresh or dried rosemary. Reserve. Mince several fresh chives (or 3 green onions) and reserve under a wet paper towel.

3 Transfer the chicken livers into a strainer. Sprinkle flour over them. Toss to dredge the livers, letting excess flour sieve away (do this messy job over a sink).

COOKING

4 Heat olive oil and freshly cracked black pepper in a large saute pan over medium-high until it's just about to smoke. Add the dredged chicken livers. Toss so that the livers lie comfortably in one layer in the pan. Immediately add a small pinch of the reserved rosemary and cover the pan with a frying screen. Let cook for almost 2 minutes (by then the splutters should have subsided). Remove the frying screen and turn the livers, tossing and frying them to cook all their surfaces. Total cooking time from the moment the livers are added to the pan will be 4–5 minutes. Cut into a plump one to see how they're doing. If the inside is still bright pink, but no longer oozing juice, then you're ready for the next step (do not overcook).

5 Add the rest of the rosemary and all the garlic and toss-fry briskly for 1 minute.

6 Turn heat to high, and add dry red wine, ⅓ at a time. After each addition, toss-fry for 30 seconds and carefully scrape under the livers to deglaze the delicious stick-ons. When all the wine has been added and the tossing-deglazing is done (a total of less than 2 minutes), you will have a nice, dark syrupy sauce. Take from the heat immediately.

7 Transfer livers to a warm serving plate and garnish liberally with chopped chives (or green onions). Season with a little salt and pour all the sauce from the pan around the livers. Serve immediately.

Total prep time: 15 minutes.
Total cooking time:
about 10 minutes.
Serves 4 as a starter or 2 as a main course. If a starter, serve with crusty bread. If a main course, serve after a soup and accompanied by rice.

Lemon Chicken

It is never wise to forget the very particular tastes of small children. Indeed, they'll make sure you don't forget, by making you miserable until you remember. Here's a quick, easy recipe for home-made chicken fingers that always makes kids happy. If you're hesitant about deep-frying, rest assured that children can tolerate (and even need) some fat in their diets. Anyway, this dish has less fat than an average order of fries from you-know-McWhere. And just in case you decide to serve this item to adults, I include a few optional ingredients to perk things up.

INGREDIENTS

1 whole (double) chicken breast, skinned and boned
1 egg
2 tbsp. (30 mL) milk
3 slices whole-wheat bread
1 tsp. (5 mL) dried basil (optional)

salt and black pepper
1 lemon
few sprigs parsley (optional)
1–2 tbsp. (15–30 mL) unsalted butter
2–3 tbsp. (30–45 mL) chicken broth
½ cup (125 mL) vegetable oil

PREPARATION

1 Slice chicken breast lengthwise into strips ¼ in. (½ cm) wide. (You will get quite a number of them.) Beat the egg with the milk in a large bowl and immerse the chicken strips in it. Reserve.

2 Process 3 slices whole-wheat bread until finely shredded into bread crumbs. Spread them on a flat plate, and add salt and pepper and the optional basil. Mix to distribute seasonings. Reserve.

3 Zest one lemon and reserve (the zest is strictly for adults: children will hate it). Juice the lemon, strain and reserve juice. Wash, dry and chop the optional parsley. Reserve under a wet paper towel.

COOKING

4 In a small sauce pan, combine butter with chicken broth. Add optional zest. Place sauce pan over medium heat until butter

has melted and the mixture has begun to bubble. Take from heat and reserve in the pan.

5 Heat vegetable oil in a large saute pan over high heat till it's just about to smoke. Meanwhile, working quickly, fish the chicken strips out of the egg-milk mixture and transfer them to the plate with the seasoned bread crumbs. Roll the chicken to coat each strip in bread crumbs. When the oil is hot, add the strips to the oil, spacing them to avoid over-lapping. (Be careful to avoid being splattered; tongs work well for this operation.)

While the first side fries (the strips should brown in 90 sec-onds) line a plate with a paper towel. Then, using tongs, turn all the strips to fry their flip-side another 90 seconds.

Remove fried strips and place them on the paper-towel lined plate to shed some of their oil.

6 Meanwhile, place the sauce pan with the butter and broth over high heat. Let it reach a boil and add 1 tsp. (5 mL) of the reserved lemon juice. Let sauce boil for 2 minutes to reduce and also to lose its acidity. If you're serving this to kids, transfer the strips from the paper towel to individ-ual plates and when the sauce is ready, pour it into a small bowl for dipping. If your guests are adults, transfer the strips into a serving bowl and pour the sauce over the chicken. Garnish with chopped parsley. In either case, serve immediately.

Total prep time: 15 minutes.
Total cooking time:
under 10 minutes.
Serves 3–4 children or 2 adults.
For more, increase everything proportionately and fry chicken in 2 batches (keeping the first batch warm in a low oven).

♣ **SUGGESTED MENU FOR THIS MAIN COURSE (FOR ADULTS)**
Starter: Goat Cheese Byzza (page 76)
Accompaniments to the chicken: rice, green vegetable and salad
Dessert: sherbet

Veal with Mushrooms

Once in a while it is fun to indulge in the retro comforts of meat and potatoes. Of course it can't be any-old meat and potatoes. Here's a recipe for tender veal and textured mushrooms in a creamy sauce: the perfect foil for good, old-fashioned mashed potatoes.

INGREDIENTS

1 medium onion

5 oz. (150 g) mushrooms
(fancy or button)

few sprigs parsley

¾ lb. (375 g) veal scallops
(non-Provimi), not pounded

½ cup (125 mL) all-purpose
flour

¼ cup (50 mL) vegetable oil

white pepper

¼ cup (50 mL) white wine

3 tbsp. (45 mL) homo milk

salt

PREPARATION

1   Chop onion into long, thin slices. Wipe mushrooms and slice. Reserve onions and mushrooms separately. Wash, dry, and finely chop a few sprigs of parsley. Reserve under a wet paper towel.

2   Slice unpounded veal scallops in ½ in. (1 cm) strips. Transfer to a colander, and sprinkle flour over the veal. Toss to dredge the strips, allowing excess flour to sieve through. (Do this messy job over a sink.)

COOKING

3   Heat vegetable oil in a saute pan over high heat for 1 minute. Add white pepper and sliced mushrooms and stir-fry for 2 minutes, until the mushrooms have darkened and wilted. Scoop out the mushrooms and reserve.

4   Return the pan and its remaining oil to high heat and add the sliced onion. Fry 1–2 minutes until the onions wilt. Add the dredged veal strips and stir-fry for 4–5 minutes, until all the veal has begun to brown.

5   Add the white wine and stir-fry for 1 minute, scraping the bottom of the pan to deglaze the stick-ons. Cook for another 30 seconds and add the whole milk, stirring continuously (not all

that vigorously: the veal strips should not be broken). Cook for 1 minute. The sauce will be thick and smooth (if too thin, cook for another minute).

6 Reduce heat to medium-low, and fold in the cooked mushrooms. Cook for two minutes, stirring regularly. Transfer to a serving bowl. Season lightly with salt and garnish with chopped parsley. Serve immediately.

Total prep time: 10–15 minutes. Total cooking time: 15 minutes. Serves 2. For more, increase veal and mushrooms proportionately, and all other ingredients by half.

♣ **SUGGESTED MENU FOR THIS MAIN COURSE**
Starter: Baked Goat Cheese Appetizer (page 69)
Accompaniments: mashed potatoes and a green vegetable
Dessert: Individual Apple Strudel (page 222)

Veal Piccata

Arguably the most popular of Italian veal-scallop specialties, piccata combines the delicacy of tender veal with the piquancy of lemon juice, my favourite ingredient. I add a hint of licorice (courtesy of a shot of Sambucca, and fried fennel — finocchio — when it's in season). The best veal these days is free-range, grain-fed, and available only at Italian butcher shops.

INGREDIENTS

¼ bulb fennel OR ¼ red bell
  pepper
1 lemon
3 green onions
1 cup (250 mL) all-purpose
  flour

¾ lb. (375 g) veal scallops
  (non-Provimi), pounded
few sprigs parsley
¼ cup (50 mL) vegetable oil
2 tbsp. (30 mL) Sambucca
3 tbsp. (45 mL) chicken broth
1 tbsp. (15 mL) unsalted butter

PREPARATION

1   Slice fennel into long, thin slices, trimming away and discarding the conical core. Reserve. (If using red bell peppers, slice into strips.)

2   Zest lemon and reserve zest. Then juice the lemon, strain juice and reserve.

3   Chop green onions and add to the reserved zest.

4   Put flour into wide bowl and dredge the pounded veal scallops in it so that they are thoroughly coated with flour.

5   Wash, dry and chop parsley. Reserve under a wet paper towel.

COOKING

6   Heat vegetable oil in a large saute pan over high heat, until it's just about to smoke. Add the sliced fennel and fry, stirring for 2–3 minutes, until the vegetable is wilted but not burned. Scoop the fennel out of the pan and onto a plate. Reserve.

7   Quickly add the dredged veal to the hot oil in the pan (if the oil sizzles too much, reduce heat slightly). Fry veal scallops for 2 minutes and turn them. (Meanwhile, find an unoccupied corner

of the pan and add all the green onions and lemon zest to let them start cooking.) Fry veal scallops for 2 minutes on this second side (by now, after a total of 4 minutes, both sides will have browned). Remove veal from the pan, leaving green onions and zest to continue sauteing. Place veal on a plate, and salt and pepper them lightly. Reserve.

8 Increase heat under pan to maximum. Add lemon juice and Sambucca. Cook for 1 minute, stirring and scraping the stick-ons. Add chicken broth and cook for 2–3 minutes until the sauce has reduced to a syrupy consistency, and has lost its alcohol and acidity.

9 Reduce heat to low and add butter. Swirl into sauce, stirring to blend. The sauce is now ready. Add the veal scallops, turning them once in the sauce. Add the fennel (or bell pepper). Cook for 1 minute over low heat. Transfer to a platter, garnish with parsley and serve immediately.

Total prep time: about 10 minutes. Total cooking time: 15 minutes. Serves 2. For 4, double the amount of fennel and veal (frying scallops in two batches) and increase the sauce ingredients by half.

❖ **SUGGESTED MENU FOR THIS MAIN COURSE**
Starter: Marinated Salmon (page 54)
Accompaniments: rice or pasta, and a green vegetable
Dessert: fruit and cheese

Veal Stew Osso Buco Style

I adapted this recipe from the classic osso buco by choosing a meatier cut than the shank recommended in the original. Shank meat is indeed more textured, but it takes more than 4 lb. (2 kg) of the cumbersome pieces to feed 4 people. This method is more compact, and tastier because I raised the voltage of the sauce.

INGREDIENTS

1 carrot
5 cloves garlic
8 sun-dried tomatoes
1 orange
few sprigs parsley
1¾ lb. (800 g) stewing veal
   (non-Provimi), cut into
   1½ in. (3–4 cm) chunks
½ cup (125 mL) all-purpose
   flour

¼ cup (50 mL) olive oil
1½ oz. (40 mL) Triple Sec OR
   Grand Marnier
½ cup (125 mL) white wine
½ cup (125 mL) chicken broth
2 bay leaves
1 tsp. (5 mL) dried basil
1 tsp. (5 mL) dried oregano
fresh basil

PREPARATION

1 Cut carrot into ½ in. (1 cm) slices and simmer in boiling water for 4 minutes. Drain and reserve.

2 Meanwhile, mince garlic and reserve. Slice sun-dried tomatoes into ½ in. (1 cm) pieces and reserve. Zest orange and reserve the zest. Juice orange (you want ½ cup/125 mL juice), strain and reserve. Wash, dry and chop parsley. Reserve, covered with a wet paper towel.

3 Transfer veal to a colander. Sprinkle flour over the veal. Toss to dredge, allowing the excess flour to sift away. (Do this messy job over a sink.)

COOKING

4 Heat olive oil in a saute pan over high heat until it's just about to smoke. Add half the veal and sear on all sides, turning often, for 2 minutes. Pick out the seared pieces and transfer to a stew pot. Sear the other half of the veal

similarly, and add to the rest in the pot. Sprinkle a shot of orange liqueur (Triple Sec or Grand Marnier) over the meat and toss to mix well.

5 Discard excess oil from the saute pan and return pan to high heat. Add ½ cup (125 mL) orange juice, the white wine and chicken broth. Bring to a boil, scraping the pan so that the stick-ons deglaze. Boil for 1 minute, stirring, and then add to the meat in the pot, using a rubber spatula to get every last drop. Stir the contents of the pot to mix well.

6 Place pot over low heat and add the reserved carrot, orange zest, garlic, sun-dried tomatoes, chopped parsley, bay leaves, dried basil and dried oregano. Mix well. Cover the pot and let simmer for 45 minutes, stirring occasionally. Test the meat. It should be toothsome, and the sauce pleasant. If you want a softer texture, add 2–3 tbsp. (30–45 mL) water and continue simmering for another 15 minutes, at which point let stew rest covered for 15 minutes. Spoon off any oil that has risen to the top and discard.

7 Wash, dry and chop fresh basil. Transfer the veal stew to a serving dish, and garnish with the basil.

Total prep time: about 30 minutes.
Total cooking time: 45 minutes to 1 hour.
Rest time: 15 minutes.
Serves 4–6.

♣ **SUGGESTED MENU FOR THIS MAIN COURSE**
Starter: Mushrooms Provençale (page 213)
Accompaniments: buttered noodles, broccoli
Dessert: fruit

Steak Alfred

Chef Jeff Dueck reinvented steak au poivre for Toronto's Bistro 990, and named it after Alfred Caron, the restaurant's amiable general manager. The optional truffle, alongside all the other pricey ingredients of this seriously meaty specialty, makes it a treat of the highest order for carnivores.

INGREDIENTS

2 trimmed New York steaks,
  1 in. (2½ cm) thick, 6 oz.
  (170 g) each
1 tbsp. (15 mL) freshly cracked
  black peppercorns
¼ red onion
few sprigs fresh thyme or basil
2 tbsp. (30 mL) vegetable oil

½ tsp. (2 mL) whole green or
  black peppercorns
3 oz. (85 mL) Cognac
2 tbsp. (30 mL) 35% or 10%
  cream OR chicken broth
2 tbsp. (30 mL) shaved black or
  white truffle (optional but
  wonderful)
salt

PREPARATION

1 Dredge both sides of steaks in freshly cracked pepper. Lightly press the pepper into the meat to make it stick (the meat should be left out of the fridge for awhile, as it cooks better at room temperature).

2 Finely dice red onion.

3 Wash, dry and chop a couple of sprigs of fresh thyme or basil. Reserve under a wet paper towel.

COOKING

4 Heat vegetable oil in a saute pan over high heat until it's just about to smoke. Add the pepper-dredged steaks and cook for 2½ minutes on the first side. Reduce heat to medium-high, turn the steaks and cook the other side for 2½ minutes (5 minutes total for medium-rare).

5 Remove steaks to a warm plate, leaving the pan on the heat. Add diced red onion and whole green or black peppercorns. Stir-fry for 2–3 minutes until the onion has wilted. Raise the heat to maximum and add Cognac. With any luck (and a little help from a match) the booze will light up in a blue flame. Cook, agitating the pan, until the flames subside. Lower heat to medium and stir the sauce for no more than 30 seconds to deglaze the stick-ons. Add cream (ideally 35%, but 10% will do) or chicken broth (if you're shunning butterfat). Cook at medium heat for 3–4 minutes, until the sauce is smooth and thick.

6 Transfer steaks (and any juice they have emitted) back into the sauce. Spoon sauce over the steaks and agitate pan for no more than 1 minute. Take from the heat and transfer the steaks to 2 warm plates, topping them with equal amounts of the sauce.

Shave equal amounts of truffle over each steak (black truffle if you have used cream, white truffle if you have used chicken broth, to contrast with the colour of finished sauce). Garnish with chopped thyme or basil, season with a little salt and serve immediately.

Total prep time: 5–6 minutes.
Total cooking time:
12–14 minutes.
Serves 2. For more take out a bank loan and increase all ingredients proportionately.

♣ **SUGGESTED MENU FOR THIS MAIN COURSE**
Starter: black caviar and Champagne
Accompaniments: Herbed Potatoes (page 215) Caraway Carrots (page 214) and a vintage Bordeaux
Dessert: something outrageous

Stir-Fried Beef with Broccoli

Aromatic beef, sauce and crunchy broccoli are the attraction of this simple dish. Served over rice, it offers a satisfying alternative to meat and potatoes. This Chinese-inspired recipe has been adapted to work in either a saute pan or a wok, and is foolproof. I've served it for 2 and also for 60 people, and it has yet to fail me.

INGREDIENTS

¾ lb. (375 g) lean steak
1½ in. (3 cm) fresh ginger root
1 tsp. (5 mL) soya OR tamari
1 tbsp. (15 mL) sesame oil
1 tsp. (5 mL) cornstarch
1 tbsp. (15 mL) Chinese
    rice wine
3 green onions

1 branch broccoli
2 cloves garlic
1 dried red chili
3 tbsp. (45 mL) peanut or
    other vegetable oil
1 tsp. (5 mL) soya sauce OR
    tamari
3 tbsp. (45 mL) chicken broth

PREPARATION

1 Trim fat from steak and put in freezer for 10 minutes (this will make it easier to slice). Slice the steak into ¼ in. x 2 in. (½ cm x 5 cm) strips. Transfer to a bowl.

2 Peel ginger root and slice into slivers ¾ in. (2 cm) long. Add to meat and mix. Add 1 tsp. (5 mL) soya, the sesame oil, cornstarch and rice wine to meat. Chop green onions, white and green parts alike, into 1 in. (2½ cm) pieces and add to meat. Mix well.

3 Cut small florets of broccoli from the stalk. No floret should be larger than ¾ in. x 1½ in.

(1½ cm x 3 cm). (Reserve the stalk for another use.) Bring some water to boil in a small pot and add the broccoli. Boil for exactly 90 seconds, drain, and refresh with ice-cold water. Drain florets and reserve. (You can do this step during the 10 minutes that the meat is in the freezer.)

4 Chop garlic finely. Crumble dried chili and combine with the garlic.

COOKING

5 Heat peanut oil in a saute pan or wok over high heat until it's just about to smoke. Add garlic and chili and stir-fry for 30 seconds. Add meat/green onion mixture. Toss and stir to separate the slices and to make sure they all touch the hot oil. Continue to stir-fry for less than 2 minutes, just until all the meat has lost its pinkness.

6 Continuing over the high heat, add the broccoli and stir-fry for 1 minute. Add 1 tsp. (5 mL) more soya and stir. Immediately add chicken broth and stir-fry for 1 minute. A nice, brown sauce will emerge.

7 Cover the pan, reduce heat to simmer and cook for 1 minute.

Turn off heat and let the beef rest for 1 minute. Remove lid, stir and transfer meat and vegetables to a serving dish. Serve immediately.

Total prep time (including 10-minute freezing): 20 minutes. Total cooking time: 7 minutes. Serves 2.

❖ **SUGGESTED MENU FOR THIS MAIN COURSE**
Starter: BlumCorder Soup (page 27)
Accompaniment: steamed rice
Dessert: Chocolate fondue (page 234)

Beef Stew with Chorizo

This stew combines French bourguignon technique with Spanish ingredients like chorizo (widely available in Spanish and Portuguese outlets of major cities) and chick peas. Strictly speaking, it's purely an invention of mine, but once you've tasted it, I'm sure you'll agree it has the savour of a heritage recipe. Because this dish requires about 1½ hours of combined prep and cooking time, it's not a good choice as a quick meal for 2. These quantities will feed 4 to 6 people for an easy and zesty dinner party to beat mid-winter blahs.

INGREDIENTS

4 large cloves garlic
6–7 oz. (200 g) chorizo sausage, hot or sweet
1 cup (250 mL) chicken broth
1½ tbsp. (25 mL) tomato paste
¼ cup (50 mL) olive oil
1½ lb. (750 g) lean stewing beef, in ¾ in. (2 cm) cubes
1 tsp. (5 mL) paprika

pinch dried red chili, crumbled
1 cup (250 mL) dry red wine
black pepper
1 tsp. (5 mL) dried oregano
2 bay leaves
1½–2 cups (375–500 mL) cooked chick peas
few sprigs fresh coriander
¼ red onion

PREPARATION

1 Chop garlic finely. Reserve.
2 Cut chorizo sausage into ½ in. (1 cm) slices.
3 Heat chicken broth and dissolve tomato paste in it.

COOKING

4 Heat most of the olive oil in a saute pan over high heat until it is just about to smoke. (Reserve 1 tsp./15 mL or so for step #5.)

Add half the cubed beef and saute for about 2 minutes, turning often to sear all sides. Transfer seared beef to a stew pot, leaving as much of the oil in the pan as possible. Repeat with the other half of the beef, searing it on all sides for 2 minutes. Transfer this batch to the stew pot as well.

5 Reduce heat to medium and return pan to the fire. Add the remaining oil to the saute pan.

Working quickly, add the sliced chorizo and saute for 2 minutes, turning until the slices have been seared on both sides. Now add the paprika and the optional chili. Fry, stirring for 30 seconds. The paprika must not burn. Immediately add the wine, scraping and stirring. When the wine appears to be warm (1–2 minutes), turn off the heat. Scrape all the contents of the pan onto the seared meat in the pot (use a rubber spatula).

6 Place the pot over medium heat and stir well. Grind some black pepper (salt is unnecessary; the chorizo is salty enough), and add it along with the oregano, the bay leaves, chopped garlic, and the warm chicken-tomato broth from step #3. Cook, stirring, until the stew begins to bubble. Lower heat, cover the pot tightly, and let simmer for about an hour (after half an hour, sneak a peek, taste the sauce and stir the stew once for good luck).

7 Before turning off the heat, add chick peas (if using canned, drain well and refresh with cold water, drain again). Stir gently to mix well, and continue cooking for another 5 minutes until the chick peas heat through.

8 The stew can be eaten at this point, but it's better after resting for at least 15 minutes. (Actually it's at its best after standing in the fridge overnight to develop the flavours. In this case reheat just before serving.)

9 Garnish with chopped fresh coriander and slivered red onion.

Total prep time: 10 minutes.
Total cooking time: 70 minutes.
Rest time: 15 minutes.
Serves 4–6. For smaller or larger batches, decrease or increase the meats proportionately, and the sauce ingredients by half.

❖ **SUGGESTED MENU**
FOR THIS MAIN COURSE
Starter: Roasted Peppers Antipasto (page 48)
Accompaniments: parsley-butter potatoes and a mixed lettuce salad with Vinaigrette Dressing (page 39)
Dessert: in winter, Chocolate Fondue (page 234); in summer, fresh fruit

Grilled/Broiled Lamb Chops

Lamb chops are to Greek carnivores what filet mignon is to North Americans: the red meat beside which all others pale. But there are lamb chops, and then there is the frozen, strangely crimson product of faraway places. Lamb that is worthy of the name is young, fresh, pink and never frozen. It cooks crisp on the outside and intoxicatingly moist on the inside. At least, it does so when cut thick and grilled medium-rare (unlike the Greek preference for thin chops cooked to within an ace of burning). I offer this recipe for properly thick chops, with a rosemary-mustard mantle, invented for Chez Byron, my old restaurant in Montreal.

INGREDIENTS

4 lamb chops, 1 in. (2½ cm) thick, about 5 oz. (150 g) each

1 tbsp. (15 mL) fresh OR 1 tsp. (5 mL) dried rosemary

1 onion

1 tbsp. (15 mL) whole-grain mustard

1 tsp. (5 mL) Dijon mustard

pinch dried thyme

black peppercorns

1 tbsp. (15 mL) olive oil

few sprigs parsley

2 green onions

1 lemon

PREPARATION

1 Trim and discard excess fat from the sides of the lamb chops. Transfer trimmed chops to a dish or bowl.

2 Finely chop fresh or dried rosemary. Transfer to a mixing bowl. Finely dice the onion. Add to rosemary. Add whole-grain mustard, Dijon mustard, dried thyme, coarsely ground black pepper and olive oil to onion-rosemary. Mix well.

3 Smear this thick marinade on the lamb, covering both sides of each chop. Let rest, unrefrigerated, for about half an hour.

4 Meanwhile, start your potatoes; fire up the barbecue; set your patio table (if you're lucky enough to be enjoying this spring time treat on a warm day). Also find time to wash, dry and finely chop parsley and green onions. Combine them, and reserve

under a wet paper towel. Slice a
lemon into quarters.

COOKING

5 Grill or broil the lamb chops,
with as much of the marinade as
will cling to them, for 3–4 minutes on the first side and 2 minutes on the second (for medium-
rare).

6 Transfer to a serving platter and
garnish liberally with chopped
parsley and green onion. Fit the
lemon wedges around the chops
and serve immediately.

*Total prep time (including
marination): 40 minutes.
Total cooking time: 5–6 minutes.
Serves 2.*

❖ **SUGGESTED MENU FOR
THIS MAIN COURSE**
*Starter: Avocado Salad (page 58)
Accompaniments: potatoes and a
Greek Salad (pages 43–44)
Dessert: fruit*

Lamb and Tomato Stew

Saucy and lusty, this easy stew is like a kiss from the Mediterranean. The garlic, tomato, lamb and herbs go together as naturally as scraggy coastlines do with azure coves. This recipe is best when tomatoes are in season and the weather is warm enough to dine al fresco. I've made it in small quantities for my own dinner, and also in enormous batches for film crews. Either way, it has yet to fail.

INGREDIENTS

1 lb. (500 g) tomatoes

2 onions

4 cloves garlic

2 lb. (1 kg) lamb leg or
    shoulder, in 1½ in. (3 cm)
    pieces (bone in, fat trimmed)

½ cup (125 mL) all-purpose
    flour

¼ cup (50 mL) vegetable oil

1 tbsp. (15 mL) olive oil

salt and black pepper

1 tsp. (5 mL) red wine vinegar

1 cup (250 mL) chicken broth
    OR white wine

1 tsp. (5 mL) dried thyme

few sprigs fresh basil and
    parsley

PREPARATION

1   Blanch tomatoes in boiling water for 30 seconds, then peel, core and seed them. Cut the flesh into large chunks. Strain the seeds and discard, reserving the juice.

2   Dice onions, and chop garlic coarsely. Reserve separately.

3   Transfer lamb to a colander. Sprinkle flour over the lamb. Toss lamb to dredge, allowing excess flour to fall away. (Do this messy job over a sink.)

COOKING

4   Heat vegetable oil in a saute pan over high heat until it's just about to smoke. Add half the lamb and sear on all sides, turning often, for 2 minutes. Pick out the seared lamb and transfer to a stew pot. Sear the other half of the lamb similarly and add to the rest in the pot.

5   Having retained all the stick-ons in your saute pan, return pan to

high heat and add the olive oil, diced onions, and salt and pepper. Saute, tossing for 2 minutes until the onions are limp. Add chopped garlic and stir-fry 30 seconds. Add the tomato chunks and juice from step #1, along with the red wine vinegar. Cook over high heat for 4-5 minutes, scraping the bottom of the pan to deglaze the stick-ons, while mashing down the tomato.

6 Add chicken broth (or white wine) and thyme. Stir and bring to a boil (1 minute). Add all the sauce to the meat in the stew pot. Set the stew pot over high heat until the contents begin to bubble (2–3 minutes). Then reduce heat to medium low and cook for 45 minutes, uncovered, stirring every 15 minutes or so to avoid scorching.

7 When the stew is nearly done, wash, dry and chop fresh basil and parsley. Once the stew has finished its 45 minutes, turn off heat, add the chopped herbs and stir well. Cover the pot and let rest at least 15 minutes. (This stew, like any other, is better after several hours of rest, with gentle reheating just before serving.)

Total prep time: About 20 minutes. Total cooking time: 1 hour. Rest time: 15 minutes. Serves 4.

♣ **SUGGESTED MENU FOR THIS MAIN COURSE**
Starter: Greek Winter or Summer Salad (pages 43–44)
Accompaniments: buttered parsley potatoes and a green vegetable
Dessert: fruit

Individual Lamb Moussaka

Baked moussaka pie topped with cheese sauce is a staple of traditional Greek cuisine. It actually derives from this simple Turkish dish that combines a meat sauce with fried eggplant (or even with fried potato), finished either in the oven or in a casserole. I prefer this cheese-less moussaka, probably because I grew up with it during my Istanbul childhood.

INGREDIENTS

2 mini-eggplants, about
   2 in. x 4 in. (5 cm x 10 cm)
1 tbsp. (15 mL) salt
1 medium onion
1 hot green pepper OR
   ½ green bell pepper
3 cloves garlic
1 tomato
1 tsp. (5 mL) olive oil
¼ cup (50 mL) pine nuts

¼ cup (50 mL) vegetable oil
2–3 tbsp. (30–45 mL) olive oil
black pepper
pinch allspice
½ tsp. (5 mL) each dried
   oregano and dried thyme
5 oz. (150 g) lean ground lamb
2 tbsp. (30 mL) currants or
   raisins
few sprigs parsley

PREPARATION

1 Slice the eggplants lengthwise, but don't cut them all the way through. Spread them open, butterfly-like, skin-side down. Salt the surfaces and let stand for 10 minutes.

2 Meanwhile: Dice onion finely. Core green pepper and slice into thin strips (if using hot pepper, wash hands right after). Mince garlic. Slice tomato into wedges. Heat 1 tsp. (5 mL) olive oil in a small pan over medium heat and add pine nuts. Saute them for 1 minute, tossing often. (Be careful: they burn easily.) Reserve.

3 After their 10-minute salting, wash the eggplants under cold running water and pat dry with a paper towel.

4 Heat ¼ cup (50 mL) vegetable oil in a large saute pan over high heat until it's just about to smoke. Add the eggplants cut-side down, and run for cover: they will splutter when they hit the hot oil (or better, use a frying screen to contain the splutter).

Fry for 2 minutes, then turn to fry the skin side (splutter warning still applies). After 2 minutes of frying the skin side, remove eggplant from the oil and drain between paper towels.

5 Discard any excess oil from the pan. Return pan to high heat and add 2–3 tbsp. (30–45 mL) of olive oil. Immediately add black pepper and a pinch of allspice, stir and add the onion. Cook, stirring, for 2 minutes until the onion wilts.

6 Add pepper and garlic from step #2 and stir-fry for 1 minute. Add oregano and thyme and stir-fry for 30 seconds.

7 Add lamb and stir-fry for 2 minutes, until the meat has lost its redness. Add currants and stir-fry for 1 minute.

8 Reduce heat to medium-low, stir once more and let cook for 3–4 minutes. Taste. It should be delicious. Stir, and turn off heat. Cover and let rest 5 minutes.

COOKING

9 Preheat oven to 425° F (220° C). Spread the fried eggplant skin-side down in an oven tray. Sprinkle the pine nuts evenly over the flesh side. Top with the lamb mixture. Spread the tomato slices so that they cover the stuffing decoratively. (The recipe can now wait in this state for up to 1 hour.)

10 Bake the stuffed eggplant in the preheated oven for 20-25 minutes, until the tomato has baked down and everything looks shiny. Meanwhile, wash, dry and chop some parsley.

11 Transfer onto dinner plates (use a spatula: this dish is soft and slippery). Garnish with chopped parsley and serve.

Total prep time: 35 minutes.
Total baking time:
less than 30 minutes.
Serves 2.

❖ **SUGGESTED MENU FOR THIS MAIN COURSE**
Starter: Greek Winter or Summer Salad (pages 43–44)
Accompaniments: crusty bread and steamed buttered green beans
Dessert: Baklava (page 224)
(Note: See page 191 for a vegetarian version of this moussaka.)

Hazelnut Pork Chops

This nutty, flavourful recipe has always gotten kudos. Guests may praise the subtle but meaningful chutney and the double hazelnut deployment, but I'm not fooled: what people really like about this dish is the breading and frying. Unhealthy or not, we are all seduced by the oily, crunchy appeal of fried food. So be it. (Note: Hazelnuts (a.k.a. filberts) are available wherever nuts are sold, and always at health-food stores. Use the raw, skin-on variety.)

INGREDIENTS

2 pears (or apples)
1 tsp. (5 mL) unsalted butter
1 tsp. (5 mL) whole-grain
   mustard
2 tbsp. (30 mL) chicken broth
   OR white wine
few sprigs parsley
½ cup (125 mL) hazelnuts OR
   ½ cup (125 mL) hazelnut
   flour

1 egg
¼ cup (50 mL) milk
½ cup (125 mL) all-purpose
   flour
4 pork chops, ½ in. (1 cm)
   thick, about 3½ oz.
   (100 g) each
¼ cup (50 mL) vegetable oil
2 tbsp. (30 mL) Frangelico
freshly cracked black
   peppercorns

PREPARATION

1 Peel, core and cut pears (or apples) into long, thin slices. Melt butter in a small saute pan over medium heat. Add pear slices and cook, tossing gently for 3 minutes (the fruit will turn light brown). Add whole-grain mustard and gently toss-fry for 1 minute. Add chicken broth or white wine and cook, stirring, for 2 minutes. Turn off heat and leave in the pan.

2 Wash, dry and chop parsley. Reserve under a wet paper towel. If making your own hazelnut flour, process ½ cup (125 mL) skin-on, raw hazelnuts in a blender at high speed for 2–3 minutes, until flour-like in consistency.

3 Have ready 3 wide bowls. Crack an egg into the first and add milk. Beat to mix. Pour all-purpose flour into the second bowl. Pour

½ cup (125 mL) hazelnut flour into the third bowl. Dunk the pork chops one by one into the egg-milk bowl, making sure they get thoroughly wet. Holding each chop by its edge, dredge in flour, covering both sides. Return chops to the egg-milk bowl, and immerse them as best you can.

COOKING

4 Heat vegetable oil in a large saute pan over medium-high heat until it's just about to smoke. While the oil is heating, position the bowl with the hazelnut flour near the stove, and the bowl with the dredged pork chops in the egg-milk mixture right next to it.

5 Holding each pork chop by its edge, dredge one by one in the hazelnut flour (both sides) and add to the hot oil. Reduce heat to medium and fry the first side for 2–3 minutes, until properly browned on the bottom (do not burn). Using tongs, carefully turn the pork chops (avoiding oil splutters). Line a platter with paper towels. Cook the flip-side of the chops for 2–3 minutes over medium heat. (The underside must be browned.) Turn off heat, and transfer chops to the paper-towel lined platter to

absorb excess grease. Season lightly with salt.

6 Immediately turn on the heat under the small pan with the pear-mustard chutney to high. Cook for 1 minute to heat through. Add Frangelico, and cook just until the alcohol has evaporated (1–2 minutes).

7 Spoon chutney evenly across 2 dinner plates. Place chops on the chutney; garnish with parsley and freshly cracked black peppercorns. Serve immediately.

Total prep time: 8–10 minutes. Total cooking time: 10 minutes. Serves 2. For more increase all ingredients proportionately (fry the pork chops in 2 batches if necessary, and keep them warm in a low oven).

♣ **SUGGESTED MENU FOR THIS MAIN COURSE**
Starter: Italian Squid Salad (page 56)
Accompaniments: rice or potatoes and a green salad with Vinaigrette Dressing (page 39)
Dessert: something light

Hoisin Pork

Sweet, nutty hoisin sauce, which most of us know in its raw state from Peking duck, is very pleasant when cooked into a sauce. This mild but tasty stir-fry teams it with green onions — its favourite partner — and other aromatics to dress up thin strips of pork. Hoisin is sold bottled at Chinese markets, as are all the other ingredients of this recipe. To make things easy I've adjusted this dish to work in a saute pan, though a wok is always helpful in Chinese-inspired cooking.

INGREDIENTS

¾ lb. (375 g) lean, boned pork (either from chops or tenderloin)
3–4 green onions
2 tbsp. (30 mL) Chinese rice wine
1 tbsp. (15 mL) sesame oil
1 tsp. (5 mL) cornstarch

1 in. (2½ cm) fresh ginger root
5 tsp. (25 mL) peanut or other vegetable oil
1 tbsp. (15 mL) hoisin sauce
2 tbsp. (30 mL) water
1 tbsp. (15 mL) soya sauce OR tamari
toasted sesame seeds

PREPARATION

1 Cut lean pork into strips ¼ in. x ½ in. x 1 ¾ in. (½ cm x 1 cm x 4 cm — kind of like fat matches). Transfer to a working bowl.

2 Trim 3 green onions and slice lengthwise cutting the white part in half. Line up the six halves and cut into 1¾ in. (4 cm) pieces. Combine these thin slivers with the pork strips in the bowl. (While you're at it take 1 more green onion, trim, and chop it finely. Reserve under a wet paper towel for the garnish.)

3 Sprinkle rice wine, sesame oil and cornstarch over the pork-green onion mixture. Mix well and let marinate for a few minutes.

4 Meanwhile, peel and finely mince the fresh ginger root.

COOKING

5 Heat peanut oil in a saute pan or wok over high heat until it's just about to smoke. Add minced ginger and stir-fry for 30 seconds until it floats in the oil. Add hoisin sauce; stir-fry with the ginger for 30 more seconds.

6 Add the meat and its marinade and fry, stirring and turning regularly (but not constantly) for 3–4 minutes until the meat darkens. Taste a sliver; it should be succulent.

7 In a small bowl mix water with soya. Add to the pan. Stir-fry briskly for 1 minute. A rich, brown gravy will emerge, and everything will glisten.

8 Take from the heat and transfer to a serving bowl. Garnish with the finely chopped green onion from step #2 and a generous sprinkling of toasted sesames. Serve immediately.

Total prep time:
under 20 minutes.
Total cooking time: 10 minutes.
Serves 2–3. For more increase
everything proportionately, but the
oil by only half.

♣ **SUGGESTED MENU FOR THIS MAIN COURSE**
Starter: Asian Seafood Salad
(page 64)
Accompaniments: steamed rice,
green beans
Dessert: fruit

Ribs Oriental

There are many variations on barbecued ribs out there, and all of them are basted in some form of ketchup. Here's a ketchup-less version that had them smacking their lips on the set of National Park, *deep in the Laurentians. For summer parties, batches of these ribs can be grilled on the barbecue (baste them often). In winter, they can be baked in the oven to recapture that summery feeling.*

INGREDIENTS

1½ lb. (750 g) pork back ribs, trimmed and cut into 2-rib portions

chopped fresh coriander and toasted sesame seeds to garnish

MARINADE

¼ cup (50 mL) soya sauce OR tamari

¼ cup (50 mL) orange juice

3 tbsp. (45 mL) maple syrup OR 2 tbsp. (30 mL) honey

2 tbsp. (30 mL) peanut or other vegetable oil

1 tbsp. (15 mL) Chinese rice wine

1 tbsp. (15 mL) aji mirin

1 tsp. (5 mL) sesame oil

3 large cloves garlic, minced

½ tsp. (2 mL) wasabe powder

½ tsp. (2 mL) crumbled dried red chili (optional)

PREPARATION

1   Place ribs in a large pot of water and bring to a boil. Skim the surface once with a slotted spoon. Lower heat to medium-high and cook, uncovered, for 15–20 minutes (till a knife pierces the meat easily).

2   Preheat oven to 450° F (230° C) Meanwhile, mix the marinade in a large bowl: Combine soya, orange juice, maple syrup, peanut oil, rice wine, aji mirin, sesame oil, minced garlic, wasabe powder and the optional chilies. Whisk for 1 minute.

3   Drain the cooked ribs and, if you have the patience, peel off the membrane from the back (grab an edge with a paring knife and scrape and pull until the skin

comes off). Line an oven pan with aluminum foil (to facilitate clean-up later). Then dunk each piece into the marinade, coating it thoroughly, and place in the foil-lined pan. Do not overlap. Spoon a little additional marinade over each piece.

COOKING

4 Place ribs in preheated oven and bake uncovered and undisturbed for 20 minutes.

5 Remove pan from oven and quickly turn the pieces, basting them with additional marinade. Return to oven for another 15 minutes.

6 Remove pan from oven. Reduce oven temperature to 325° F (160° C). Baste again with the remaining marinade and return to oven for a further 10–15 minutes (and no more).

7 Serve on a platter, garnished with chopped coriander and sprinkling of sesames. (Make sure bits of foil have not stuck to the bottom of the ribs.)

Total prep time: 20 minutes.
Total baking time:
45–50 minutes.
Serves 2.

❧ **SUGGESTED MENU FOR THIS MAIN COURSE**
Starter: Avocado Salad (page 58)
Accompaniments: rice or corn bread, and Summer Zucchini (page 212)
Dessert: fruit

Zucchini Algis

Photographer Algis Kemezys, my long-time sous-chef and partner, invented this simple yet satisfying dish as a vegetarian main course for Chez Byron, our Montreal restaurant. It also works wonderfully as a summer appetizer, or side dish to accompany a meat-based meal.

INGREDIENTS

½ lb (250 g) zucchini
1 onion
5–6 oz. (150 g) mushrooms,
   button or fancy

1 tomato
2 large cloves garlic
few sprigs fresh basil or dill
¼ cup (50 mL) olive oil
salt and black pepper

PREPARATION

1 Slice zucchini on the bias so that they make long oval slices, approximately 1½ in. x ¼ in. (3 cm x ½ cm).

2 Cut onion in half lengthwise and peel off the skin. Lay each half down on its flat side and cut lengthwise slices that are ¼ in. (½ cm) thick. You will finish with long, elegant strips.

3 Wipe mushrooms and slice ½ in. (1 cm) thick.

4 Blanch tomato in boiling water for 30 seconds, then peel, core and seed it. Chop flesh into small dice. Strain the seeds and discard them, reserving the juice.

5 Finely mince the garlic.

6 Wash, dry and chop the basil or dill. Reserve under a wet paper towel.

COOKING

7 Heat olive oil in a large saute pan over high heat until just about to smoke. Add zucchini and onions, salt and pepper. Saute, tossing for 4 minutes until the zucchini begin to sear and the onions wilt.

8 Add the mushrooms and continue to saute over high heat, folding the ingredients gently (to sear mushrooms yet not injure the zucchini, 2–3 minutes).

9 Lower heat to medium-high; add tomato and garlic. Cook,

tossing for 2–3 minutes, until the tomatoes melt and sauce forms.

10 Raise heat to maximum. Immediately add tomato juice from step #4 and stir gently for 1–2 minutes. The sauce should be spare yet luscious and everything perfectly cooked. Remove from heat and transfer to a serving dish. Garnish with chopped basil or dill, and serve immediately.

Total prep time:
about 10 minutes.
Total cooking time: 10 minutes.
Serves 2 as a main course (over rice) or 4 as an appetizer or a side course.

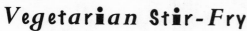

Vegetarian Stir-Fry

A light and colourful stir-fry of vegetables with tofu, this makes a balanced, nutritious vegetarian meal. With its contrasting textures of crunchy vegetables and silken tofu, subtly flavoured with Chinese rice wine, ginger and soya it goes well with Stir-Fried Rice Noodles (page 108).

INGREDIENTS

½ lb (250g) tofu
¼ lb. (125 g) broccoli florets
1 onion
½ red (or green) bell pepper
20 canned or fresh water
   chestnuts
2–3 oz. (75 g) snow peas
2 green onions
1½ in. (3 cm) fresh ginger root

½ cup (125 mL) all-purpose
   flour
1 tbsp. plus 2 tbsp. (15 mL +
   30 mL) peanut or other
   vegetable oil
2 tbsp. (30 mL) Chinese
   rice wine
1 tbsp. (15 mL) soya sauce OR
   tamari
3½ oz. (100 g) bean sprouts
2 tbsp. (30 mL) water

PREPARATION

1 Cut tofu into 1 in. (2 cm) cubes. Reserve.

2 Chop off the entire stalk of a bunch of broccoli right up to the florets. Reserve stalk for another use. Separate remaining branches into individual florets and reserve. You should have about ¼ lb. (125 g) of florets.

3 Peel and cut onion into ¼ in. (½ cm) slices. Slice bell pepper into 1 cm strips. Reserve onion and pepper together.

4 Drain 20 canned water chestnuts and refresh with cold water (or peel 20 fresh water chestnuts and wash with cold water). Reserve.

5 Stem and string snow peas. Finely chop 2 green onions, white and green parts alike. Reserve snow peas and green onions together.

6 Peel ginger root and chop finely.

COOKING

7 Bring some water to boil in a small pan. Immerse the broccoli florets, turn heat to high and cook for 2 minutes exactly. Drain immediately, and refresh gently with ice-cold water to retain colour. Reserve.

8   Pour flour onto a plate. Gently (so as not to break them) dredge the tofu cubes in the flour. Heat 1 tbsp. (15 mL) peanut oil in a saute pan over high heat until it's just about to smoke. Add the dredged tofu and fry for 2 minutes, agitating the pan to prevent sticking. Gently turn tofu with a spatula and fry the second side for 2 minutes. The tofu will have a light yellow crust and will have absorbed all the oil. Remove from heat, and reserve in the pan.

9   Heat remaining 2 tbsp. (30 mL) peanut oil in a large saute pan or wok over high heat until it's just about to smoke. Add the chopped ginger and stir-fry for 30 seconds. Add the onion-pepper mixture and stir-fry for 2–3 minutes, until the vegetables wilt. Add the blanched broccoli and the drained water chestnuts. Stir-fry for 2–3 minutes to sear. Add

snow peas and green onions and stir-fry for 1 minute. Add Chinese rice wine and soya. Stir-fry for 1 minute.

10   Add bean sprouts and the fried tofu. Gently fold into the rest of the stir-fry and agitate pan to distribute sauce and ingredients, trying not to break up the tofu unduly (2 minutes, total). Add 2 tbsp. (30 mL) water and gently fold once again, agitating pan for 1 minute. Remove from heat.

11   Cover pan and let the stir-fry rest for 1–2 minutes. Transfer to a serving dish and serve immediately.

Total prep time: 15 minutes.
Total cooking time: 25 minutes.
Serves 2–3.

❖   **SUGGESTED MENU FOR THIS MAIN COURSE**
Starter: BlumCorder Soup (page 27)
Accompaniments: Stir-Fried Rice Noodles (page 108)
Dessert: sherbet

Judi's Enchiladas

This vegetarian Tex-Mex palate-rouser is yet another memento of my long and fondly remembered collaboration with Judi Roe, the superchef of south-western Quebec. The cheese can be omitted if you are allergic to dairy, or if you prefer a vegan supper. The only unusual requirement for this otherwise unfussy recipe is fresh tortillas, which fortunately are getting easier to find as our multicultural palate creates a demand. (If you can't find fresh, frozen tortillas are always available, and will serve once properly defrosted.) Ideally, the sauce is made with home-made vegetable broth and home-made tomato juice. But I've seen Judi use health-food store-bought broth and canned tomato juice, and I've experimented with straight V8 vegetable juice. Both shortcuts work well.

INGREDIENTS

½ lb. (250 g) potatoes
1 onion
2 cloves garlic
1 tomato
3 tbsp. (45 mL) vegetable oil
1 tbsp. (15 mL) chili powder
salt
1 cup (250 mL) vegetable broth
1 cup (250 mL) tomato juice

1 tsp. (5 mL) cornstarch
1 tbsp. (15 mL) water
1 19 oz. (540 mL) can Romano beans OR 2 cups (550 mL) home-cooked Romano beans
5–6 oz. (150 g) Monterey Jack or medium Cheddar
12 tortillas
few sprigs fresh coriander

PREPARATION

1   Bring about 6 cups (1½ L) salted water to boil in a small pot. Add whole, unpeeled potatoes and bring back to boil. Reduce heat to medium and cook potatoes for 30–40 minutes until very tender when pierced with a fork.

2   Meanwhile, make the sauce: Dice onion finely. Reserve. Mince garlic. Reserve. Blanch tomato in boiling water for 30 seconds and then peel, core and seed. Cut the flesh into small cubes. Reserve. Heat vegetable oil in a sauce pan over high heat. Add chili powder and a pinch of salt. Stir-fry for

1 minute until the oil is vibrantly coloured, but before the spice turns black. Add the diced onion; stir-fry for 2 minutes until limp. Add the garlic and stir-fry for 1 minute. Add vegetable broth and tomato juice and stir over high heat until the mixture bubbles. Reduce to medium-low, and cook 4–5 minutes. Dissolve cornstarch in water and add to sauce, stirring briskly. Continue cooking and stirring for 2-3 minutes. The sauce will thicken slightly to the consistency of thin syrup. Stir in the cubed tomato. Remove sauce from heat and let rest while you return to the potatoes.

3   Make the stuffing: Drain cooked potatoes under cold water. When they are cool enough to handle, slip off their skins (use a paring knife, if necessary). Cut peeled potatoes into ½ in. (1 cm) cubes and transfer to a working bowl. Add red Romano beans. (If using canned, drain and run water over them to remove all canning residue. Drain again before using.) Shred cheese and add to the potatoes and beans. Fold ingredients together thoroughly but gently, to avoid breaking the beans.

ASSEMBLY AND BAKING

4   Preheat oven to 350° F (180° C). Choose a rectangular ovenproof dish that will snugly hold 12 stuffed tortillas. Oil pan lightly.

5   Grasping a tortilla firmly by one edge, dunk it into the sauce to coat it. Transfer the dunked tortilla to the oven dish. Pile 2 tbsp. (30 mL) of the stuffing down the middle and roll it up like a cigar. Push the rolled enchiladas to one corner of the pan and proceed with the rest until they're all stuffed and neatly arranged.

6   Pour remaining sauce evenly over the enchiladas. Bake for 15–20 minutes (any longer will dry them out). While they're baking, wash, dry and chop some fresh coriander.

7   Using a long spatula, transfer 3–4 enchiladas to each plate (carefully; they're very soft). Garnish with coriander (and if you insist, a dollop of sour cream, although I disapprove). Serve immediately.

Total prep time: 45 minutes.
Total assembly and baking time: 35 minutes.
Serves 3–4.

❖ **SUGGESTED MENU FOR THIS MAIN COURSE**
Starter: Avocado Salad (page 58) or Avocado Soup (page 25)
Accompaniments: rice, green salad and Salsa Cynthia (next recipe)
Dessert: ice cream or sherbet

Salsa Cynthia

This is a basic hot sauce that is perfect as a dip for nachos and as a sauce for Mexican-style tortilla dishes like enchiladas. I dedicate this recipe to Penguin Canada's head honcho, Cynthia Good, who likes things hot.

INGREDIENTS

1 lb. (500 g) ripe tomatoes
1 red (or white) onion
2 cloves garlic
3½ oz. (100 g) Jalapeno peppers

salt
2 tbsp. (30 mL) vegetable oil
1 lime
few sprigs fresh coriander

PREPARATION

1 Blanch tomatoes in boiling water for 30 seconds and then peel, core and seed. Transfer remaining flesh to the bowl of a food processor (not a blender). Strain seeds, and add whatever tomato juice results to the bowl.

2 Peel onion and cut into eighths. Add to the processor. Peel and smash garlic. Add to the processor. Remove the stems of the Jalapenos; cut peppers into halves. Scoop out and discard the core and most of the seeds. (Retain as many as you can tolerate: the more seeds, the hotter your sauce. Or discard all the seeds and still have a mildly hot sauce.) Chop the peppers roughly, and add to the processor along with any retained seeds. (Wash your hands with soap right after cleaning the chilies.)

3 Add salt and process salsa ingre-dients with a couple of "pulses," then on high speed for 1 minute, until everything is minced yet not liquefied. Transfer to a sauce pan and add oil. Place over medium heat for 6–8 minutes, until mildly bubbling and foaming pinkly. Remove from the heat and let salsa cool 10 minutes or longer.

4 While the sauce rests, squeeze one lime, strain juice and reserve. Wash, dry and chop some sprigs of fresh coriander; reserve under a wet paper towel. When you're ready to serve the sauce, add lime juice and coriander and stir well.

Total prep time: 30 minutes. Rest time: 10 minutes minimum This recipe yields about 2 cups (500 mL). Leftovers improve in the fridge for 3–4 days. Stir thoroughly before each use.

Veggie Cassoulet

Cassoulet is a wintry, 'round-the-hearth,' family sort of dish. This is indisputably true when it is enjoyed in the original, with its many, fatty meats and juices permeating the practically candied beans. That classic version requires a strong constitution (and a well-ventilated room) to digest. I invented this lighter variation that calls for no meat at all and can be eaten in any season. Whatever the weather, any cassoulet needs an occasion. My recipe is simplified, but even so it's too much work for a small dinner of just 2 or 3. I've therefore suggested quantities that will serve a dinner party of 6–7 people.

INGREDIENTS

1 19 oz. (540 mL) white
   kidney beans
1 10 oz. can (540 mL) red
   Romano beans OR 3–4 cups
   (750–1000 mL) home-cooked
   red and white beans

TOPPING
few sprigs parsley
4 bricks pressed tofu
3 cups (750 mL) bread crumbs
1 clove garlic
½ tsp. (2 mL) ground allspice
3 tbsp. (45 mL) French brandy
salt
2 eggs
3 tbsp. (45 mL) olive oil

SAUCE
½ lb. (250 g) leeks
1 lb. (500 g) ripe tomatoes
6–7 sun-dried tomatoes
1 red bell pepper
1 small carrot
6 cloves garlic
½ lb. (250 g) button
   mushrooms
5 tbsp. (75 mL) olive oil
salt and black pepper
1 tsp. (5 mL) dried oregano
1 tsp. (5 mL) dried basil
1 tbsp. (15 mL) balsamic
   vinegar

PREPARATION

1 Of the 3 main stages of preparation and assembly required here, it's best to start with the one that will be needed last, to get it out of the way: the topping. Wash, dry and chop several sprigs of parsley. Reserve under a wet paper towel. Transfer pressed tofu into a bowl. (Note: Regular tofu contains too much water for this recipe; pressed tofu, which is off-white in colour, is generally sold alongside the regular. Don't confuse it with fried tofu, which is yellow.) Crush tofu using a potato masher (don't use a processor for this job; you want the tofu crushed, not pureed).

Add bread crumbs and 4–5 tbsp. (50–60 mL) of the chopped parsley. Use the potato masher again, mashing for 2–3 minutes, till the mixture is homogenized (it'll be quite firm).

Mince garlic through a garlic press directly onto the mixture, and blend well. Add allspice, brandy and a little salt. Beat eggs in a small bowl and add to the mixture. Mash thoroughly again for 2–3 minutes. Reserve this topping.

2 Now the sauce: Trim leeks and slice lengthwise. Wash thoroughly of grit, especially where the green and white parts meet. Dry leeks and chop into ¼ in. (½ cm) bits, green and white parts alike. Reserve. Wash, stem and cut tomatoes into eighths (mercifully, the tomatoes don't need to be skinned or seeded for this dish). Roughly chop sun-dried tomatoes

and add to the fresh tomatoes. Reserve in a bowl. Wash, core and seed bell pepper. Cut into long strips of ¼ in. (½ cm) wide. Reserve. Wash and slice a small carrot in half lengthwise. Aligning the 2 halves cut-side down, chop crosswise into thin half-moon slices. Reserve. Peel and finely chop garlic. Reserve. Wipe mushrooms and slice thinly. Reserve.

Heat olive oil in a large saute pan over high heat for 1 minute. Add salt and freshly ground pepper and the chopped leek, bell pepper and carrot. Stir-fry for 3–4 minutes, turning often until leeks and peppers wilt. Now add fresh and sun-dried tomatoes, garlic, oregano, basil and balsamic vinegar. Stir-fry over high heat, mashing down the tomatoes, for 4–5 minutes until a sauce begins to emerge. Mash down once again and stir. Lower heat to medium. Let the sauce cook for 15–20 minutes, stirring occasionally.

3 Meanwhile, deal with your beans. If using canned, drain (both kinds together), and refresh with running water to remove all canning residue. Reserve in the strainer to drain all water.

4 When the sauce seems about ready, add the chopped mushrooms to it and fold in. Let cook for another 3–4 minutes to soften the mushrooms.

ASSEMBLY AND BAKING

5 Preheat oven to 400° F (200° C). Choose an ovenproof baking dish that will comfortably hold all these ingredients and that is attractive enough to present at table. Transfer the drained beans into the dish and spread them evenly. Pour the sauce over the beans. Fold one into the other until everything is evenly distributed. Now take spoonfuls of the tofu topping and cover the entire surface of the beans. You should have a pie-like filling 1¾ in. (4 cm) deep that is completely covered by about ½ in. (1 cm) of topping. Drizzle 3 tbsp. (45 mL) olive oil evenly over the topping. You can omit this oil, but you will have a dryer topping if you do.

The dish now needs an hour of baking. It can be prepared in advance to this point, and baked whenever you wish. If you refrigerate it, bring it back to room temperature before baking.

6 Bake the cassoulet, uncovered and undisturbed in the preheated oven for 30 minutes. Take it out of the oven. Reduce oven temperature to 350° F (180° C). The topping will have crusted. Using a spoon, crush it here and there to allow a lower layer of topping to come to the surface (it also will crust and give more texture).

7 Return the cassoulet to the lowered oven, and bake for another 30 minutes. Take it out of the oven and let sit for 10 minutes, while you chop some more parsley. Garnish cassoulet with parsley and serve from its baking dish, crusty topping side-up.

Total prep and assembly time: 1 hour minimum.
Total baking time: 1 hour.
Serves 6–7. For less, decrease all ingredients proportionately.

❖ **SUGGESTED MENU FOR THIS MAIN COURSE**
Starter: a leafy salad with Vinaigrette Dressing (page 39)
Accompaniments: Stir-Fried Red Cabbage (page 203) and crusty bread
Dessert: sherbet

Individual Vegetarian Moussaka

The original Turkish name for this dish is Imam Bayildi, which means, "the imam fainted." The legend goes that an iman so enjoyed this meal that, being frugal, he asked his wife how much olive oil she had used to make it. When she told him, he was so shocked that he fainted. I have reduced the amount of oil for this version, but any way you look at it, this or any other successful eggplant dish is an oily pleasure.

INGREDIENTS

2 mini-eggplants, about 2 in. x
    4 in. (5 cm x 10 cm)

1 tsp. (15 mL) salt

1 medium onion

1 hot green pepper OR ½ green
    bell pepper

3 cloves garlic

1 tomato

1 tsp. plus 2–3 tbsp. (5 mL +
    30 mL–40 mL) olive oil

¼ cup (50 mL) pine nuts

¼ cup (50 mL) vegetable oil

black pepper

pinch cinnamon

1 tsp. (5 mL) dried oregano

2 tbsp. (30 mL) currants or
    raisins

few sprigs parsley

PREPARATION

1   Slice the eggplants lengthwise, but don't cut all the way through. Fan them open, butterfly-style, skin-side down. Salt the cut surfaces, and let stand for 10 minutes.

2   Meanwhile: Dice onion finely. Core and slice green pepper into thin strips (if using hot, wash hands right after). Mince garlic. Slice tomato into thin wedges. Reserve each ingredient.

3   Heat 1 tsp. (5 mL) olive oil in a small pan over medium heat, and add pine nuts. Saute them for 1 minute, tossing often. Be careful; they burn easily. Reserve.

4   After their 10-minute salting,

wash the eggplants under cold running water, being careful not to separate them. Pat them dry with a paper towel.

5 Heat the ¼ cup (50 mL) vegetable oil in a large saute pan over high heat until just about to smoke. Add the eggplants, cut-side down, and run for cover: they will splutter when they hit the hot oil (it's safer to use a frying screen). Fry for 2 minutes, then turn to fry the skin side (same splutter caution). After 2 minutes of frying this side, remove eggplants from the oil and drain between paper towels.

6 Discard excess oil from the pan. Return pan to high heat and add 2–3 tbsp. (30–45 mL) olive oil (3 is better than 2). Immediately add black pepper and a pinch of cinnamon, then the diced onion. Cook, stirring, for 2 minutes, until the onion wilts. Add the strips of green pepper and stir-fry for 1 minute. Reduce heat to medium and add the minced garlic, oregano and currants. Stir and cook for 1–2 minutes, then remove from heat.

COOKING

7 Preheat oven to 425° F (220° C). Spread the fried eggplants skin-side down in an oven tray.

Sprinkle the toasted pine nuts evenly over the flesh side. Top evenly with the onion mixture. Spread the tomato slices decoratively over the stuffing. (The recipe can now wait in this state for up to an hour.)

8 Bake the stuffed eggplants in the preheated oven for 20–25 minutes until the tomatoes have baked down and everything looks shiny. Meanwhile, wash, dry and chop some parsley.

9 Transfer onto dinner plates (use a spatula: this dish is very soft and slippery). Garnish with chopped parsley and serve.

Total prep time: less than 30 minutes.
Total baking time: less than 30 minutes.
Serves 2 as a main course or 4 as an appetizer.

❖ **SUGGESTED MENU FOR THIS MAIN COURSE**
Starter: Greek Winter Salad (page 43) or Greek Summer Salad (page 44)
Accompaniments: crusty bread and steamed buttered green beans
Dessert: Aristides' Bougasta (page 226)

Cauliflower Pea Curry

Kamala McCarthy, who has already lived enough for 3 people, now divides her time between India and Quebec's Eastern Townships. I visited her once on a perfect July day as she garnered the daily harvest from her husband Kabir's loaded vegetable garden. We then retired to her sunny kitchen where she whipped up this lively vegetable curry in less than an hour. Although a relatively simple concoction, it calls for 18 ingredients, several of which (garam masala, mustard seed, cumin seed, ghee) you will probably have to purchase from an East Indian specialty store. The spices keep well and have uses in many non-Indian dishes. Ghee — clarified butter can be made at home by cooking butter very slowly over low heat and skimming off the whey as it rises to the surface.

INGREDIENTS

1½ lb. (750 g) ripe tomatoes
2 medium onions
5 cloves garlic
2 in. (5 cm) ginger root
2 hot green chilies
1 head cauliflower
few sprigs each fresh mint and
    coriander
1 tbsp. (15 mL) turmeric
1 tbsp. (15 mL) ground
    coriander seed
¼ cup (50 mL) clarified butter
    (ghee)

1 tsp. each black mustard seed,
    whole cumin seed and whole
    fennel seed
1 tbsp. (15 mL) salt or to taste
¾ cup (175 mL) frozen peas
1 tsp. (5 mL) garam masala
½ cup (125 mL) plain yoghurt

RAITA

1 ripe mango (or green apple
    or peach)
1 cup (250 mL) plain yoghurt
1 tsp. (5 mL) garam masala
few drops vegetable oil

PREPARATION

1 Clarify butter, if making your own.

2 Blanch tomatoes in boiling water for 30 seconds, then peel, core and seed them. Cut flesh into chunks. Strain seeds and discard, reserving the tomato juice.

3 Peel and quarter onions. Peel

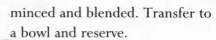

minced and blended. Transfer to a bowl and reserve.

7 In the same processor (don't bother to wash it), pulp the tomatoes and tomato juice from step #2. Transfer to a bowl and reserve.

COOKING

8 Heat clarified butter in a stew pot (or better, in a cast-iron Indian wok) over high heat for 90 seconds. Immediately add the mustard, cumin and fennel seeds. Stir-fry for 2 minutes, until the mustard seed turns grey and the other seeds are beginning to pop. Immediately add the reserved bowl of processed onion-garlic-spice mixture. Still at high heat, stir-fry for up to 5 minutes longer, until the mixture begins to darken slightly. Add processed tomato and cook for 5 more minutes, stirring. Add salt (more or less to taste). You'll now have a rich, red sauce, happily bubbling.

9 Fold the cauliflower into the sauce. Reduce heat to just above medium and cook, stirring occasionally, for 20 minutes.

10 Meanwhile, start your rice, and also make the raita that you'll serve alongside the curry: Peel a ripe mango (or apple or peach)

garlic and cut each clove into quarters. Peel ginger root and dice into ½ in. (1 cm) cubes. Cut the stems off chilies and discard. Chop chilies into ½ in. (1 cm) bits (wash hands right after).

4 Trim away stalk portion of a head of cauliflower to within 1½ in. (3 cm) of the florets. Reserve stalk for another use. Separate the florets into small, neat pieces.

5 Wash, dry and chop several sprigs of fresh mint and fresh coriander. Reserve each under a wet paper towel.

6 Put the following ingredients in a food processor: onions, garlic, ginger root, turmeric, ground coriander seeds and chilies. Process at high speed until all ingredients are thoroughly and dice flesh into ½ in. (1 cm) cubes (retaining whatever juices flow out during the dicing process). Add 1 cup (250 mL) yoghurt to the fruit and its juices, and mix well. Sprinkle 1 tsp. (5 mL) garam masala on the raita, along with a few drops of vegetable oil if desired. Let rest, uncovered and unrefrigerated, until ready to use.

11 At the end of its 20 minutes of cooking, test the cauliflower. It should be soft and flavourful. Lower heat to medium, and add the frozen peas directly from the freezer. Add chopped mint and 1 tsp. (5 mL) garam masala. Fold together gently, and cook for 3–4 minutes until the peas have warmed through.

12 Add ½ cup (125 mL) yoghurt; stir gently to blend. Cook for 1–2 minutes, give it a final stir, then take the curry from the heat.

13 Let rest for a few minutes, uncovered. Then transfer curry to a serving bowl, sprinkle a little more garam masala on it, and garnish generously with chopped fresh coriander. Serve accompanied by the raita from step #10, to be ladled at table.

Total prep time: 10–15 minutes.
Total cooking time: 40 minutes.
Serves 4–6.

❖ **SUGGESTED MENU FOR THIS MAIN COURSE**
Starter: Avocado Salad (page 58)
Accompaniments to the curry: raita, rice, and Spinach Dal (page 196)
Dessert: Baked Ricotta Meenakshi (page 228)

Spinach Dal

This flavourful, soothing and very nutritious Indian lentil (dal) recipe shows the flip-side of Kamala McCarthy spicy cooking. She serves it over rice with a vegetable curry (like the cauliflower pea recipe) for a balanced meal. Kamala prefers to use chana dal, which requires an hour of soaking, and an hour and a half of cooking. Instead, I've chosen, masoor dal, the tiny red lentil that needs next to no soaking and cooks quickly. Admittedly, I lose the nuttier texture of the chana, but I gain the creamy, rich consistency of the smaller lentil, as well as its vibrant colour. All the spices can be purchased in East Indian grocery stores, as can the clarified butter (ghee). Ghee can be made at home by heating butter over low heat very gradually (without boiling it) and skimming off whey as it rises to the surface.

INGREDIENTS

3½ cups (875 mL) masoor dal
   (lentils)
1 tsp. (5 mL) whole cloves
3 bay leaves
1 tbsp. (15 mL) turmeric
2 onions
5 cloves garlic
2 in. (5 cm) fresh ginger root
1 lb. (500 g) bunch spinach

2 tbsp. plus ¼ cup (30 mL +
   50 mL) clarified butter (ghee)
1 tbsp. (15 mL) salt
1 tsp. (5 mL) black mustard
   seed
1 tsp. (5 mL) whole cumin seed
1 tbsp. plus 1 tsp. (15 mL +
   5 mL) garam masala
few sprigs fresh coriander

PREPARATION

1 Clarify butter if making own.
2 Place masoor dal in a large strainer and rinse under running water. Drain and transfer to a large pot with about 8 cups (2 L) water. Bring to a boil, then turn off heat. Add cloves, bay leaves and turmeric; stir. Let soak for 10–15 minutes. The dal will quickly swell and soak up much of the water.
3 Finely chop the onions. Reserve. Mince garlic; peel ginger root and mince. Combine ginger with garlic and reserve.
4 Thoroughly wash and dry spinach. Cut out the stalks and discard. Slice leaves finely and reserve.

COOKING

5 Place the pot with the lentils, spices and water over high heat and cook for 5–7 minutes, stirring occasionally, until the contents begin to bubble. Reduce heat to medium and cook, stirring occasionally, for 15-20 minutes, until the dal is tender. (If for some reason the dal becomes dry, add more water).

6 Meanwhile, heat 2 tbsp. (30 mL) of clarified butter in a saute pan over high heat for 30 seconds. Add the chopped onion and stir-fry for 2 minutes. Add the garlic-ginger mixture and stir-fry for another 2 minutes. Remove from heat and wait for the dal to finish cooking its 15–20 minutes. Then add the contents of the saute pan to the cooked dal. Continue cooking the dal with its new addition for another 5 minutes, stirring occasionally.

7 Add spinach and 1 tbsp. (15 mL) salt (any less would make the dal bland). Stir well, and continue cooking for 10 minutes.

8 In the last 5 minutes of step #7, heat ¼ cup (50 mL) clarified butter in a small sauce pan over high heat for 1 minute. Add the mustard and cumin seeds. Stir-fry for 3–4 minutes until the seeds begin to pop and the mustard begins to turn grey. Add this bubbling mixture to the simmering dal. The hot fat will hit the wet lentils with a distinct sizzle (this is called a "chaunk"). Stir, and add 1 tbsp. (15 mL) garam masala. Mix again, reduce heat to medium-low, and continue cooking for 5 more minutes, stirring occasionally.

9 Take pot from the heat and let rest, uncovered, for 15 minutes. Transfer to a serving bowl, sprinkle with 1 tsp. of garam masala, and garnish with chopped fresh coriander. Serve by ladling individual portions.

Total prep time: 10–15 minutes.
Total cooking time: 45 minutes.
Minimum rest time: 15 minutes.
Serves 4–6 with leftovers that are wonderful the next day, either heated as is, or made into a soup by combining 1 cup (250 mL) of dal per 1 cup (250 mL) of vegetable broth.

❖ **SUGGESTED MENU FOR THIS MAIN COURSE**
Starter: Avocado Salad (page 58)
Accompaniments: rice, any curry and a raita
Dessert: Baked Ricotta Meenakshi (page 228)

Side Vegetables

Vegetables should need no introduction. Neither should anyone need to be convinced of the health advantages of vegetables. Vitamins, minerals, fibre, colour, freshness: happiness. And taste too, if one can overcome both old and new ideas about cooking vegetables. Happily, we rarely encounter anymore the old, "boil 'em and butter 'em" philosophy.

The modern way (briefly steaming vegetables and offering them puritanically unadorned) might be healthy, but it is too stark: The resulting hypercrunchy texture makes them twice the penance they used to be.

The answer lies somewhere in the middle and originated — where else? — in France. The French boil vegetables vigorously in ample water for 5–6 minutes and then drain them, refresh them in ice-cold water, drain them again and reheat them in a little fat (oil or butter) just before serving. This method yields lively texture (neither too crunchy nor too soft), vibrant colour, full-bodied flavour and a rich taste that makes them palatable even to the meat-and-potato lovers who still thrive among us despite the health movements, food cults and nutritional hype of the last quarter-century.

Rapini with Balsamic Vinegar

Some of the healthiest vegetables are also the most difficult to make attractive. I'm talking about bitter greens like dandelions and rapini (a.k.a. broccoli rabe), the mere mention of which brings sweat to the collective brow of the North American dining public. The main reason for this aversion is that most people treat the bitters as if they were spinach, steaming them slightly and serving them either plain or buttered as a side vegetable. Done that way they taste like poison.

We must travel to Italy to find the treatment that will make them enjoyable. The Italians use their unrivalled condiments and cheeses to create just the kind of culinary sorcery needed to make bitter greens pleasurable: olive oil, balsamic vinegar and Parmesan cheese lend flavours and qualities that work with the bitterness and make it interesting.

These enhancements are particularly effective with dandelions and rapini. Dandelions are trimmed, washed, immersed in shallow water and boiled for 4 minutes, then drained and sauced, to be served immediately. Rapini require more of a production and therefore merit this detailed recipe.

INGREDIENTS

1 bunch rapini
1 tsp. (5 mL) salt
few sprigs fresh basil or parsley
3 tbsp. (45 mL) balsamic
   vinegar

2 tbsp. (30 mL) extra-virgin
   olive oil
black pepper
Parmesan or Pecorino cheese
1 tbsp. (15 mL) olive oil

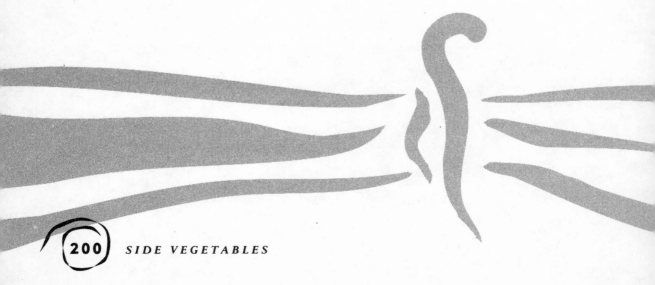

PREPARATION

1 Wash the rapini and drain but do not dry. Trim and discard the last 1½ in. (3–4 cm) of the stalks. Cut off the top 2½ in. (6–7 cm) – the part that has the flowers and tender leaves – and reserve. Cut the remaining stalks into 1½ in. (3 cm) slices and reserve.

2 Heat about 1½ in. (3 cm) water in a large pot and bring it to the boil. Add salt. Add the chopped stalks and let boil for 4-5 minutes. Add the reserved tops, cover the pot and continue cooking for 3 more minutes. Drain immediately and refresh with some cold water. Let stand in the colander to drain.

3 Wash, dry and chop some fresh basil or parsley. Transfer to a bowl and add balsamic vinegar, extra-virgin olive oil, and freshly ground black pepper. Whisk with a fork until a light emulsion forms. Reserve.

4 Using a grater or a paring knife, finely shave 2–4 tbsp. (30–50 mL) fine Parmesan or Pecorino (the quantity is up to you, but I say the more the better). Reserve.

COOKING

5 When ready to serve, heat 1 tbsp. (15 mL) olive oil in a large saute pan over high heat for 1 minute. Add the drained rapini and toss-fry 2–3 minutes, turning constantly, till all the pieces have touched the hot oil and are warmed through. Transfer to a large, flat platter and drizzle as evenly as possible with the sauce. Top with the shaved Parmesan. Serve immediately, making sure that each person gets some of the sauce from the bottom of the platter, as well as some cheese.

Total prep time: about 20 minutes. Total cooking time: 6–7 minutes. Serves 4–6. For less, decrease ingredients proportionately, but you'll still need 1 tbsp. (15 mL) of oil for the final sauteing of the rapini.

Garlic Beets

These marinated beets live in the fridge for up to a week, providing a healthy and ever-more-flavourful side course at a moment's notice. The onion and garlic are cut thick so that they can be avoided by those on a heavy date.

INGREDIENTS

4 young beets
4 cloves garlic
¼ red onion
salt and black pepper

2 tbsp. (30 mL) red wine
   vinegar
3 tbsp. (45 mL) extra-virgin
   olive oil
few sprigs fresh coriander or
   parsley

PREPARATION

1 Trim greens and stalks from the beet roots. (Reserve greens for another use – they're good quick-boiled as a side dish.) Do not peel the beets, but wash them to rub off any earth. Bring water to boil in a small pot. Immerse beets in the boiling water. They should be covered by 1½ in. (3–4 cm) of water. Reduce heat to medium and cook uncovered, for 50 minutes, until a skewer or thin knife pierces them easily. As the water evaporates below beet level during cooking, replace it with more hot water.

2 Peel garlic and slice coarsely. Slice red onion. Add to the garlic and reserve together.

ASSEMBLY

3 When the beets have cooked, remove from heat and fish them out of their pot (reserve the bright-red cooking liquid). Let the beets cool for a few minutes and then take them in hand. The dull-looking skin will slip off with hardly any resistance to reveal the luscious redness underneath. Using a knife, trim the two ends and any small blemishes.

4 Slice peeled beets into rounds ¼ in. (½ cm) thick. Transfer slices to a working bowl. (Your hands and cutting board will be stained a purplish-red. This is normal.) Add salt, freshly ground

pepper, the onion-garlic mixture and red wine vinegar. Fold to mix (without breaking the beet slices).

Add extra-virgin olive oil and 3 tbsp. (45 mL) of the beets cooking liquid. (You can discard the rest of the water, or feed it to a plant.)

Mix well, cover and let rest at least 20 minutes.

5 Wash, dry and chop fresh corian-

der or parsley, or some of each. Transfer beets to a serving bowl, folding in the marinade a few times. Garnish with the herb(s) and serve.

Cooking time: almost 1 hour.
Prep and assembly time:
10 minutes.
Rest time: 20 minutes.
Serves 4–6.

Stir-Fried Red Cabbage

Slightly tart red cabbage adds welcome colour and texture to most main courses, be they meat-centred or vegetarian. The fennel seeds and fresh dill in this recipe add character without drawing attention away from the humble cabbage.

INGREDIENTS

1 lb. red cabbage
1 tbsp. plus 1 tbsp. (15 mL + 15 mL) cider vinegar
1 green bell pepper

few sprigs fresh dill
2 tbsp. (30 mL) vegetable oil
salt and black pepper
1 tsp. (5 mL) whole fennel seeds

PREPARATION

1 Wash and thinly shred red cabbage. Transfer to a small pot. Cover cabbage with cold water, add a little salt and 1 tbsp. (15 mL) cider vinegar, and mix.

Place pot over high heat for 7–8 minutes until the water is steaming and just about to bubble. Taste a shred of cabbage. It should be soft, yet still crunchy.

Drain immediately and run a little cold water over the cabbage to refresh.

2 While the cabbage is cooking, wash, seed and slice green pepper into thin strips. Reserve. Wash, dry and chop several sprigs of fresh dill. Reserve under a wet paper towel.

COOKING

3 Heat vegetable oil in a large saute pan over high heat for 30 seconds. Add salt, freshly ground black pepper and fennel seeds. Stir-fry for 1 minute till the fennel begins to pop and darkens slightly. Add chopped green pepper and stir-fry for less than a minute, until the pepper wilts.

4 Add the drained red cabbage and (still over high heat) stir-fry for 3–4 minutes until all the cabbage is shiny and has heated through. Add 1 tbsp. (15 mL) cider vinegar and stir-fry 1 minute longer.

5 Take pan from heat. Mix in half the reserved, chopped dill. Transfer cabbage to a serving dish, and garnish with remaining chopped dill. Serve immediately.

Total prep time: 12 minutes.
Total cooking time:
less than 10 minutes.
Serves 4. Any leftovers can be enjoyed the next day – either reheated, or cold as a side salad.

Jalapeno Broccoli

The stubby, lush green chilies that take their name from the Mexican city of Jalapa (in the state of Vera Cruz) have become as common in our markets as they are in their home country. Here is a recipe that uses their sweet heat to dress up therapeutic broccoli and actually make it fun to eat. This is a salad-like concoction that works well alongside broiled meat or fish.

INGREDIENTS

1 head broccoli

1 tbsp. (15 mL) balsamic
   vinegar

1–2 fresh Jalapeno peppers

1 tbsp. (15 mL) olive oil

¼ cup (50 mL) pine nuts

2 tbsp. (30 mL) extra-virgin
   olive oil

salt

PREPARATION AND ASSEMBLY

1 Prepare broccoli: Trim and discard last 2–3 in. (5–7 cm) of stalk. Cut off rest of stalk to within 1½ in. (3 cm) of the florets, and peel it. Discard the peel, and cut the peeled core into 1½ in. (3 cm) slices. Put broccoli slices into a pot with enough water, add salt and turn heat to high. While the water reaches a boil, return to the florets. Separate into elegant pieces of 2–3 in. (5–7 cm) long and about 1½ in. (3 cm) wide. As soon as the water boils, add the florets, submerging them. Boil for exactly 3 minutes and immediately drain in a colander, refresh with ice-cold water (to retain the green colour). Arrange broccoli, both florets and stalks, on a salad platter, and drizzle evenly with balsamic vinegar.

2 Trim the stem from 1 Jalapeno pepper (2 peppers, if you like heat). Slice the pepper in half, scoop out and discard most of the seeds (or leave some seeds in for more heat). Thinly slice the flesh of the pepper. Reserve, along with the desired amount of seeds. (Wash hands with soap right after.)

3 Heat 1 tbsp. (15 mL) olive oil in a small saute pan over medium heat for 30 seconds. Add pine nuts and fry, stirring continuously for 1–2 minutes until the nuts

turn a light brown (be careful: they burn easily). Scoop the pine nuts out of the pan and sprinkle them evenly over the broccoli. Try to leave some oil in the pan.

4   Return pan to medium heat and add the chopped Jalapenos. Stir-fry for 1 minute. Turning off heat, scoop out peppers and all the oil and sprinkle evenly over the broccoli.

5   Drizzle 2 tbsp. (30 mL) of extra-virgin olive oil all over the broc-coli. This dish can be served immediately, or it can wait up to an hour uncovered and unrefrigerated.

Total prep time: 15 minutes.
Serves 4–6 as an appetizer, salad, or side vegetable.

Green Beans with Cashews

INGREDIENTS

1 lb. (500 g) fresh green beans
¼ red onion
few sprigs parsley

2 tbsp. (30 mL) olive oil
⅓ cup (75 mL) raw cashew
   pieces
salt and black pepper

PREPARATION

1 Trim the woody ends from the green beans and immerse in boiling water. Boil for 5 minutes at high heat. Drain, and immediately refresh in a bowl of ice water for 1 minute. Drain and reserve.

2 While the beans cool: Slice red onion into thin slivers. Chop the parsley.

Prep time: 7 minutes.
Cooking time: about 5 minutes.
Serves 2—4, and if left over it's great the next day at room temperature.

COOKING

3 Heat olive oil in a saute pan over high heat. Add onion slivers, the cashews, salt and pepper. Stir-fry for 2—3 minutes until the onions and cashews become a little charred.

4 Add the cooled green beans and stir-fry over high heat for 2—3 minutes longer, until the beans feel hot to the touch.

5 Transfer to a bowl and garnish with chopped parsley. Serve immediately.

Green Beans and Tomato

These slow-simmered green beans belong to that group of oily, overcooked vegetables the Greeks call "lathera" (literally, "cooked in oil"). They may seem a bit retro after the current trend toward super-crunchy, sparsely sauced vegetables, but they offer their own reward. Mushy and saucy, these are the beans I grew up with in my mother's Greek kitchen, and it took years (plus several revelations) to convince me that a crunchy green bean could be not only edible but also digestible.

INGREDIENTS

1 lb. (500 g) fresh green beans
2 onions
1 sweet or hot banana pepper
4 cloves garlic
few sprigs parsley

2 tomatoes
¼ cup (50 mL) olive oil
salt and black pepper
1 tsp. (5 mL) sugar
1 tbsp. (15 mL) tomato paste
½ cup (125 mL) warm water

PREPARATION

1 Trim the woody ends from the green beans. Leave beans whole, unless they're unusually long, in which case cut them in half.

2 Slice onions in ¼ in. (½ cm) thick. Core, seed and slice pepper (if using hot, wash hands right after). Chop garlic into match-head sized pieces. Wash, dry and chop parsley coarsely. Slice toma-toes into wedges (retaining the skin and seeds: this is a heritage recipe that ignores niceties). Reserve all the ingredients separately.

COOKING

3 Heat olive oil in a stew pot over high heat until it's just about to smoke. Add salt, pepper and the onions. Cook, stirring for 2 min-utes until onions wilt. Add banana pepper and stir-fry for 1 minute. Add garlic and sugar, and contin-ue stirring for 30 seconds. Add the tomato wedges, stir once and let cook for 1–2 minutes, while you dissolve tomato paste in the warm water. Add this to the pot, along with the chopped parsley.

Cook, stirring, for 1 minute, until the contents are bubbling.

4   Add green beans and stir well. The contents will reach a bubble very quickly. Stir again, move to a back burner, set the heat on low and let simmer for 30 minutes, stirring very occasionally.

5   Taste a bean to see if you can stand it much softer. If you decide to cook on (this will improve the taste), check the liquid. It should be at least 1½ in. (3 cm) high with some beans peeking above it. If it has reduced much lower than that, add ¼ cup (50 mL) more water, stir well, and return to simmer for another 15 minutes. (If you decide to stop cooking after half an hour, don't worry, I'll look the other way.)

6   Whether cooked for 30 or 45 minutes, the beans must rest covered for 15 minutes before serving. This does wonders for their flavour. And if there are any left over, an overnight rest in the fridge, with an hour at room temperature before serving, will make them delightful the next day. Connoisseurs cook them one day, and let them rest till the next. But then again, they have the time.

Total prep time: 15 minutes.
Total cooking time:
35–50 minutes.
Minimum rest time: 15 minutes.
Serves 4–6 as a side vegetable or 2–3 as a vegetarian main course over rice with a side salad.

Fried Zucchini with Tzatziki Sauce

This is a big fave in Greece, where it is always served with a side of Tzatziki (yoghurt-cucumber sauce: recipe below). It can act as an appetizer or a side vegetable, and is a relatively benign fried item in that it doesn't absorb much oil — at least, not nearly so much as eggplant.

INGREDIENTS

2 medium zucchini
1 cup (250 mL) all-purpose
    flour
salt and black pepper
¼ cup (50 mL) vegetable oil

TZATZIKI SAUCE

1 cup (250 mL) plain yoghurt
3 in. (7½ cm) chunk of
    cucumber
2 cloves garlic
salt
1 tsp. (5 mL) extra-virgin
    olive oil
pinch cayenne or paprika

PREPARATION

1 Make the Tzatziki Sauce: Put yoghurt in a working bowl. Using a grater over another bowl, shred cucumber (peeled or unpeeled). The shreds will end up sitting in the cucumber juice that results from the grating. Transfer shreds and juice to a strainer and let drain. Gently press the shreds (with a spoon or fingers) to remove as much liquid as possible. Add drained cucumber to the yoghurt. Peel and mince garlic in a garlic press. Add to the yoghurt. Add salt. Mix well. Transfer sauce to a serving bowl and drizzle 1 tsp. (5 mL) extra-virgin olive oil over the tzatziki. Do not mix in: let it float on top (Greeks love the sight of olive oil floating on a sauce). Sprinkle a pinch of cayenne (if you like it spicy) or paprika over tzatziki. Reserve, uncovered and unrefrigerated, until the zucchini are ready.

2 Trim stems from zucchini. Slice lengthwise, a bit less than ¼ in. (½ cm) thick to obtain long, thin, elegant slices. Pour flour onto a plate. Mix in some salt and pepper. Place this plate near the stove and have zucchini close by.

COOKING

3 Heat vegetable oil in a large saute pan over medium-high heat until it's just about to smoke. Working quickly, dredge zucchini slices in the seasoned flour and add to the oil, avoiding overlapping. (Depending on the number of slices and the size of your pan, you might have some leftover zucchini that you'll have to fry in a second batch once the first is ready.) Fry the first side for 1–2 minutes until golden (do not burn). Turn (using tongs) and fry the second side similarly. Line a plate with a paper towel. As the slices are ready, transfer them from the hot pan to the paper towel to absorb excess oil. (Fry your second batch, if necessary.)

4 Transfer drained zucchini slices to a serving plate, and serve with Tzatziki Sauce from step #1 on the side as a sauce or dip. (If you eschew dairy products, serve zucchini with a wedge of lime or lemon for sprinkling at table.)

Total prep time: 15–20 minutes.
Total cooking time: 6 minutes.
Serves 2–3 as an appetizer, and 3–4 as a side vegetable.

Summer Zucchini

This is an ideal recipe for lush, juicy summer zucchini (the kind that all our friends with vegetable patches never seem to give us enough of). I use the young of both yellow and green, giving the dish additional colour with red bell peppers (another summer specialty).

INGREDIENTS

1 red bell pepper
3 green onions
½ lemon
few sprigs fresh basil and
  parsley

4 young zucchini, 6 in. (15 cm)
  maximum (2 green and 2
  yellow, for colour)
3 tbsp. (45 mL) olive oil
salt and black pepper

PREPARATION

1 Core and seed pepper and slice into long strips ½ in. (1 cm) wide. Chop green onions into ¼ in. (½ cm) bits, white and green parts alike. Squeeze ½ lemon and strain juice. Wash, dry and chop a few sprigs of fresh basil and parsley. Reserve all these ingredients separately.

2 Slice zucchinis into ¾ in. (1½ cm) rounds, discarding hard stem at bottom end.

COOKING

3 Heat olive oil in a saute pan over high heat for 1 minute. Add salt and pepper, the zucchini and the red pepper strips. Stir-fry for 5–7 minutes until the zucchini have browned on both sides and the red pepper has wilted.

4 Add green onions. Stir-fry for 30 seconds longer and remove from heat. Transfer to a serving dish and drizzle 1 tbsp. (15 mL) lemon juice evenly over the zucchini. Garnish with chopped parsley and basil, and serve immediately.

Total prep time:
about 10 minutes.
Total cooking time: 7–8 minutes.
Serves 3–4 as a vegetable side dish.

Mushrooms Provençale

These quick-to-fry mushrooms are wholesome as a side course, and satisfy wonderfully as an appetizer on their own. The only thing to watch for here is to maintain very high heat while searing them (so that they retain their moisture) but without burning them. If properly made, they'll be succulent even when cold and therefore can be enjoyed at a buffet lunch or dinner.

INGREDIENTS

½ lb. (250 g) button mushrooms
2 cloves garlic
½ lemon

few sprigs parsley
2 tbsp. (30 mL) olive oil
salt and black pepper

PREPARATION

1 Wipe mushrooms and trim ½ in. (1 cm) from the stems to give a clean edge. Reserve.

2 Peel and mince garlic. Reserve. Squeeze half a lemon, strain and reserve juice. You should have at least 1 tbsp. (15 mL). Wash, dry and chop a few sprigs of parsley. Reserve under a wet paper towel.

COOKING

3 Heat olive oil in a large saute pan over high heat until it's just about to smoke. Add freshly ground black pepper and the mushrooms. Toss-fry for 2–3 minutes, turning the mushrooms often to sear them on all sides, but take care to avoid burning them.

When the mushrooms have browned somewhat, add the minced garlic and toss-fry briskly for 1–2 minutes.

4 Remove from heat and add a little salt. Drizzle of lemon juice (a total of 1 tbsp./15 mL) over all. Toss well to mix, then transfer mushrooms and pan drippings to a serving bowl or dish. Garnish with chopped parsley. Serve immediately for a hot meal, or serve later for a buffet (naturally, they are at their absolute best piping hot).

Total prep time: 10 minutes.
Total cooking time: 5–6 minutes.
Serves 2–3 as an appetizer, or 3–4 as a side vegetable.

Caraway Carrots

INGREDIENTS

1 lb. (500 g) carrots
½ lemon
few chives or 1–2 green onions
2 tbsp. (30 mL) butter
1 tbsp. (15 mL) cold water

1 tbsp. (15 mL) whole caraway seed
1 tbsp. (15 mL) honey, maple syrup or brown sugar
½ tsp. (2 mL) cornstarch

PREPARATION

1 Slice carrots on the bias, to obtain oval slices approximately ½ in. x 2 in. (1 cm x 4 cm).

2 Add carrot slices to boiling water (enough to cover). Return to boil, reduce heat to medium-high and cook for 5–8 minutes (depending on desired tenderness). Drain over a bowl and reserve carrot water separately.

3 Squeeze ½ a lemon; strain and reserve the juice. Chop chives or green onions and reserve under a wet paper towel.

COOKING

4 Heat butter in a deep sauce pan over medium heat for 1–2 minutes until bubbling. Add caraway seeds and stir-fry for 1–2 minutes until they begin to pop.

5 Add ½ cup (125 mL) of the carrot water to the pan with the caraway and butter. Add sweet-ener of your choice, and cook, stirring occasionally, until the sauce is near boiling (2–3 minutes). The recipe can wait at this point. When ready to serve, bring the sauce back to a near-boil and proceed:

6 Dissolve cornstarch in the cold water. Add to the bubbling sauce, reduce heat and cook, stirring, until the sauce bubbles and thickens to the consistency of a thin syrup (2–3 minutes).

7 Fold carrots into the sauce. Cook over low heat for 2–3 minutes longer, stirring occasionally. Add the lemon juice, stir and remove from heat. Transfer to a serving dish and garnish with chives or green onion. Serve immediately.

Total prep time:
about 15 minutes.
Total cooking time: 9 minutes.
Serves 3–4 as a vegetable side dish.

Herbed Potatoes

INGREDIENTS

¾ lb. (375 g) new potatoes
1 lemon
2 cloves garlic
3 tbsp. (45 mL) olive oil
salt and black peppercorns

few sprigs of the herb of your
choice (parsley, tarragon,
chives, rosemary, thyme,
oregano)

PREPARATION

1 Put washed new potatoes and some salt into a pot of boiling water (to cover). Bring back to boil and cook over high heat for 5 minutes.

2 While the potatoes cook: Zest the lemon and reserve. Squeeze the lemon; strain and reserve juice. Chop garlic, and add to reserved zest. Chop the herb of your choice (choose one) and reserve separately.

3 Drain the cooked potatoes, and cut each in half (careful, they're hot).

COOKING

4 Heat the olive oil in a saute pan over high heat until it's just about to smoke. Meanwhile, grind some fresh black pepper into the oil. Now add the potatoes without crowding. Let them fry for 3–4 minutes.

5 Turn the potatoes. Fry on their flip-side for another 3–4 minutes. (By now they should be slightly brown on both sides. If not, then continue frying for another 2–3 minutes.)

6 Reduce heat to moderately-low. Add the garlic-lemon zest and stir-fry (trying not to break the potatoes) for 1–2 minutes.

7 Add the chopped herb and continue stir-frying for 1 minute.

8 Sprinkle the lemon juice all over the potatoes. Raise heat, tossing for 1 minute, until the lemon has finished sizzling, and the acidity is gone.

9 These potatoes are at their best if served immediately. However, if a delay is necessary, they can be made in 2 stages. In this case, stop after step #5 and let the potatoes cool, uncovered, for up to half an hour. When ready to continue, return the pan to high heat, bring to a sizzle (1–2 minutes of toss-frying), and then proceed with steps #6–8.

Prep time: 8 minutes.
Total cooking time:
12–14 minutes.
Serves 2–3.

French Potato Salad

Here's a version of the old picnic staple that uses no mayonnaise and will therefore better survive the rigours of a warm day. It is also wonderful to eat freshly made, while still lukewarm.

INGREDIENTS

2 lb. (1 kg) new potatoes
2 tbsp. (30 mL) red wine
    vinegar
3 tbsp. (45 mL) dry red wine

3 tbsp. (45 mL) French whole-
    grain mustard
1 small onion
few sprigs parsley
¼ cup (50 mL) extra-virgin
    olive oil

PREPARATION AND ASSEMBLY

1 Wash whole new potatoes and boil in plenty of well-salted water until a knife or skewer pierces one easily. Drain and transfer to a cutting board. Holding the hot potatoes with cloth towel or oven mitt, slice into rounds ¼ in. (½ cm) thick. Transfer slices to a large working bowl.

2 Working quickly, combine in a small bowl the red wine vinegar, dry red wine, French whole grain mustard, and a good amount of freshly ground black pepper. Whisk these ingredients and immediately drizzle over the still-steaming potatoes. Fold-mix gently to dress all without breaking any more than necessary.

3 Slice onion into thin slivers. Scatter on the potatoes. Wash, dry and chop several sprigs of parsley. Reserve half and scatter the rest on the potatoes. Drizzle extra-virgin olive oil over all, fold-mix gently to distribute dressing.

4 Transfer potato salad to a serving bowl and garnish with the reserved parsley. Serve immediately or if intended for a picnic, make it in the morning and use it the same day without refrigerating.

Total prep, cooking and assembly time: about 45 minutes.
Serves 6–8.

Desserts

Baked Apple

A conscientious dessert that is also schedule-friendly, in that it can be prepared in advance and then baked in exactly half an hour while you're enjoying dinner.

INGREDIENTS

1 tbsp. (15 mL) dessicated
  coconut
1 tbsp. (15 mL) sliced almonds
½ in. (1 cm) fresh ginger root
1 tbsp. (15 mL) brown sugar
pinch cinnamon

1 tsp. (5 mL) Frangelico or
  Amaretto liqueur
2 Delicious apples
  (golden or red)
1 tsp. (5 mL) unsalted butter
2 scoops vanilla ice cream
  (optional)

PREPARATION

1 Simmer coconut in ½ cup (125 mL) water for 4 minutes until the coconut has lost most of its crunch. Remove from heat and reserve in its pan.

2 Preheat oven to 350° F (180° C). Roughly chop sliced almonds to obtain fine crumbs. Transfer to a working bowl. Peel and mince ginger root; add to the almonds along with brown sugar and a pinch of cinnamon. Mix with a fork. Drain coconut shreds and add to the bowl. Sprinkle Frangelico (or Amaretto) over all and mix well.

3 Core the unpeeled apple, trying not to pierce the other end. Use a paring knife to enlarge the hole.
Scrape out all seeds and fibrous seed pods carefully. Divide the stuffing between the 2 apples. Top each with ½ tsp. (2 mL) unsalted butter. Transfer stuffed apples to a baking dish.

The recipe can now wait — proceed whenever you're ready.

BAKING

4 Bake in the preheated oven for exactly 30 minutes. The apples will feel soft to the touch, the peel will be unbroken, and the top of the stuffing will have browned nicely. Carefully transfer one apple per plate, using a sturdy spatula. Serve

immediately. For effect, cut each apple in half at table with a serrated knife to reveal the stuffing and the steaming apple flesh. Top with a scoop of vanilla ice cream (if you can brave the cholesterol) and watch it melt lacily, bathing the foaming apple with soothing richness.

Total prep time: 20 minutes.
Total baking time: 30 minutes.
Serves 2.

Apple Betty

This is a simple dessert that can be whipped up quickly and arrive at the table steaming with nostalgic aromas reminiscent of bygone and (what we imagine to have been) better times. The butter can be reduced by half, but the gain to your health will be the palate's loss.

INGREDIENTS

½ lemon
3 apples (sweet or tart)
1 tsp. (5 mL) cinnamon
1 tbsp. (15 mL) cornstarch
2 tbsp. (30 mL) brown sugar
¼ cup (50 mL) walnut pieces
1 tbsp. (15 mL) currants
1 tbsp. (15 mL) unsalted butter

18% cream (optional)

TOPPING
1 cup (250 mL) graham cracker crumbs
¼ cup (50 mL) melted unsalted butter
1 tbsp. (15 mL) brown sugar

PREPARATION

1 Squeeze half a lemon to obtain 1 tbsp. (15 mL) lemon juice. Transfer juice to a large working bowl. Peel and core the apples and slice the flesh into ½ in. (1 cm) slices. Add slices to the bowl as you work, turning each in the lemon juice to prevent discolouration. (It is best to peel and slice one apple at a time

before proceeding with the next; peeled apples discolour very quickly.) Sprinkle cinnamon, cornstarch and brown sugar over the apples. Fold to distribute evenly, without breaking slices. Add walnut pieces and currants to the apples and fold again to mix. Let rest a few minutes.

2 Prepare the topping: In a separate bowl, combine the graham cracker crumbs (either ready-bought or processed by you from whole graham crackers), melted (not boiled) butter and brown sugar. Mix together with a fork to obtain a mealy, paste-like texture.

ASSEMBLY AND BAKING

3 Preheat oven to 350° F (180° C). Choose a compact ovenproof dish that is attractive enough to bring to table. Grease the dish with 1 tbsp. (50 mL) unsalted butter and transfer the apple mixture into it, spreading evenly. Top apple layer with the graham cracker topping, spreading evenly and pressing some of it into the apples.

4 Bake in the preheated oven for 35–40 minutes. Take it out and test it. A knife should pierce the apples with no resistance, and the topping should be attractively

brown. If not yet done to your taste, bake for another 5 minutes.

5 Remove from the oven and rush it to the table. Spoon it out carefully into dessert plates or bowls, topping-side up. Pass some cream in a creamer for each person to add (or not) as desired.

Total prep time: 15 minutes.
Total assembly and baking time: 50 minutes.
Serves 5–6.

Individual Apple Strudel

Filo dough works so well for strudel, one would swear it was invented for it. I've enriched this basic recipe with pecans, which lend a sun-belt warmth that is particularly welcome when this dessert is served in winter.

INGREDIENTS

¼ cup (50 mL) pecan halves
½ orange
3 apples
2 tbsp. (30 mL) cornstarch
2–3 tbsp. (30–45 mL) brown
    sugar (more or less, depend-
    ing on tartness of apples)

1 tsp. (5 mL) cinnamon
½ tsp. (2 mL) nutmeg
⅓ cup (75 mL) golden raisins
½ cup (100 mL) unsalted butter
12 sheets of filo dough

PREPARATION

1 Make the filling: Spread pecans on an oven tray without crowding them. Brown in an oven (or toaster oven) for 6–9 minutes at 350° F (180° C). (Watch them carefully after 6 minutes: they burn easily past a certain point.) Remove from oven and cool.

2 Meanwhile: Squeeze half an orange to obtain 2–3 tbsp. (30–40 mL) orange juice. Strain juice and transfer to a working bowl. Peel, core and seed apples. Slice thinly, adding slices to the orange juice as you go. Turn slices in the juice to prevent dis-colouration.

3 Add cornstarch to the apples and

turn to coat evenly. Add brown sugar, cinnamon and nutmeg to the apples. Turn to distribute these ingredients. Separate raisins and sprinkle over the apples. Add browned pecans and turn again.

ASSEMBLY

4 Melt butter (without boiling) in a small sauce pan. Choose an oven pan and using a pastry brush, lightly grease the bottom of the pan with some of the butter.

5 Preheat oven to 350° F (180° C). Give the apples a good stir to reincorporate any juice that might have separated. Now follow Basic Method for Filo Pies, steps #4–5 (pages 85–86). To continue: Wipe off working surface with a paper towel and continue until you have rolled all 6 pies. The pies in the oven pan should be spaced so that they don't touch each other.

BAKING

8 Place the pies in the preheated oven and bake for 15–20 minutes until the filo has turned golden. Remove from the oven and let cool for 10 minutes or so before serving.

It's also possible to bake the strudels in advance. In this case leave them to cool, uncovered, until you are ready for dessert, then warm them in a 300° F (150° C) oven for 10 minutes, and serve. (If cooked way in advance and refrigerated – or if left over and refrigerated – then let strudels come to room temperature before proceeding with the 10 minute warm-up.)

Total prep time: 15 minutes.
Pie assembly time: 30 minutes.
Total baking time: 20 minutes.
Cooling-off time: 10 minutes.
Serves 6.

Baklava

Here's one version of the gooey Levantine dessert that doesn't drip with sugar and that somehow stays crunchy without the 6 hour slow-bake method usual in the Middle East.

INGREDIENTS

¾ cup (175 mL) walnut pieces
½ cup (125 mL) sugar
1 tsp. (5 mL) cinnamon
¼ cup (50 mL) unsalted butter

10 sheets filo dough
¼ cup (50 mL) best-quality honey
¼ cup (50 mL) water

PREPARATION

1 Prepare the filling: Put walnut pieces, sugar and cinnamon into the bowl of a food processor. Pulse several times until the contents are thoroughly mixed and the nuts have been more or less ground (it's fine to have a few larger crunchy bits). Transfer to a bowl and reserve.

2 Preheat oven to 350° F (180° C). Meanwhile, melt butter in a small pan until just liquid and before it begins to bubble. Choose a rectangular pan that is about ⅔ the dimensions of your sheets of filo.

3 Using a pastry brush, lightly grease the bottom of the pan with some melted butter. Lay out a sheet of filo in the pan, crunching it here and there to make it fit (this helps the filo to finish airy and crusty). Using the pastry brush, dab little bits of butter all over the filo, lightly moistening its entire surface. Continue similarly with 4 more sheets of filo, dabbing butter on each as you go, building the bottom crust of the baklava.

4 Now spread the filling evenly over the entire surface of the filo.

5 Lay 5 more sheets of filo dough, as in step #3, dabbing melted butter on each sheet before adding the next. When you arrive at the last filo, lay it as flat as possible, tucking the ends into the sides of the baklava. On this last filo, *brush* butter liberally instead of dabbing it, so that the entire surface is moistened. (The ¼ cup/50 mL butter recommended should be more than enough to last the total of 10 filos. But if you dabbed too freely in the middle and then ran out before the end, just melt some more butter.)

BAKING AND FINISHING

6 Bake the baklava in the preheated oven for 30–40 minutes. Take it out and check at 30 minutes. It should be golden on top and nicely crusted on the bottom (poke with a spatula to check the bottom: the baklava shrinks a little during baking and pulls in, which makes checking easier). If not done, return to the oven for another 5–10 minutes, but no more.

7 Towards the end of the baklava's baking, combine honey with water in a sauce pan. Heat the mixture to boiling. It'll become a thin syrup. Remove from heat and reserve in the pan to cool slightly.

8 When the baklava is done, remove from the oven. Immediately pour the warm syrup evenly over the baklava. It'll sizzle and most of it will be absorbed very quickly.

Let the baklava cool for 20 minutes to an hour. Then cut into serving portions right in its baking pan (it's extremely tricky to transfer an uncut baklava out of its pan). Make a "Union Jack" cut (two diagonals and a cross), using a heavy chef's knife or a pizza cutter to produce 8 triangular portions (cut with authority: it's crunchy and may threaten to shrivel, but in fact cuts quite cleanly).

Total prep time:
about 35 minutes.
Total baking time: 40 minutes.
Minimum rest time: 20 minutes.
Serves 8 or more if you cut the pieces in half once again. Leftovers are stored at room temperature and are good the next day.

Aristedes' Bougatsa

The Canadian-Greek superchef Aristedes has invented to date close to 800 dishes for the menus of his 40 restaurants in Canada and the U.S. Though I've loved (and gushed over, in my NOW Magazine food column) a great number of them, the one I always crave is this simple custard pie, a contemporary embellishment of a traditional Greek dessert. Here it is as related to me by Aristides' long-time lieutenant and sous-chef, Kenny Brudner.

INGREDIENTS

1 orange
2 cups (500 mL) homo milk
½ cup (125 mL) sugar
½ tsp. (2 mL) vanilla essence
⅛ tsp. (½ mL) rosewater

3 tbsp. plus 4 tbsp. (45 mL + 60 mL) unsalted butter
½ cup (125 mL) semolina
sliced fruit (1 mango OR 8 berries OR 1 pear)
8 sheets filo dough
sprinkling of cinnamon

PREPARATION

1 Zest the orange and reserve the zest. (Then squeeze the orange and drink the juice: zested citrus fruits dehydrate quickly if not used promptly.)

2 In a small pot, heat the milk over low heat till hot, yet not scalding. Add sugar, the orange zest, vanilla essence and rosewater. Lower heat to simmer. Let the flavoured milk cook for 5 minutes, watching it carefully: it mustn't boil.

3 While the milk cooks, melt 3 tbsp. (45 mL) unsalted butter in a saute pan over medium heat. Add semolina and stir until all of it has been moistened by the butter. You'll have a thick, coarse paste. Cook for 2 minutes, stirring continuously to prevent sticking. Remove from heat.

4 With whisk in hand and milk still on the simmer, add semolina paste to the milk ¼ at a time, whisking vigorously after each addition. When all the semolina paste has been added, continue whisking and simmering for 3–4 minutes. The custard will thicken and become quite stiff. Remove from heat and cool completely. Cover, and leave it alone.

ASSEMBLY

5 Melt (but do not boil) 4 tbsp. (60 mL) unsalted butter in a small sauce pan. Choose a compact oven pan and, using a pastry brush, lightly grease the bottom of the pan with melted butter. Slice your favourite fruit in ½ in. (1 cm) slices and reserve (mango, berries or pear all work well).

6 Preheat oven to 350° F (180° C). Uncover the custard and give it one good stir to mix in the film that has formed over the surface.

Now follow Basic Method for Filo Pies, steps # 4–5 (pages 85–86). To continue: Wipe off working surface with a paper towel and continue until you have rolled all four pies. The pies in the oven pan should be spaced so that they don't touch each other.

BAKING

7 Place the pies in the preheated oven and bake for 15–20 minutes until the filo has turned golden. Remove from the oven and let cool for 10 or so minutes. Sprinkle some cinnamon over the pies, and serve lukewarm. It's possible to bake the bougatsas in advance and leave them out, uncovered, until you are ready for dessert. Then warm them up in a 300° F (150° C) oven for 10 minutes or so. Sprinkle with cinnamon and serve. If cooked way in advance and refrigerated (or if left over and refrigerated), then let pies come to room temperature before proceeding with the 10 minute warm-up.

Custard-making time: 15 minutes.
Custard-cooling time: 45 minutes.
Pie assembly time: 30 minutes.
Total baking time: 20 minutes.
Cooling-off time: 10 minutes.
Serves 4.

Baked Ricotta Meenakshi

Meenakshi, chef and all-around famous person of Taos, New Mexico, invented this extremely simple dessert as the closing parenthesis to her popular Indian meals. It approximates the taste and texture of authentic Indian sweets such as rasmalai, but with half the sugar and much less fat. Cardamon is readily available in either pod or ground form. If using the pod, peel off the husk to reveal the dark seeds inside. These can be ground in a mortar or a coffee grinder.

INGREDIENTS

1 lb. (500 g) ricotta cheese
¾ cup (175 mL) icing sugar
1 tbsp. (15 mL) ground
cardamon

1 tbsp. (15 mL) vegetable
shortening
¼ cup (50 mL) 35% cream
¼ cup (50 mL) shelled, skinned
pistachio nuts

PREPARATION

1 Preheat oven to 325° F (160° C). Put the ricotta in a working bowl. Sift icing sugar onto the cheese through a wire strainer. Sprinkle ground cardamon seeds on top. Using a wooden spoon, beat the mixture thoroughly.

2 Generously grease the bottom of a small, square baking pan with the vegetable shortening. Pour ricotta mixture into the pan and smooth (the filling should be at most 1½ in./3 cm high in pan).

BAKING

3 Bake for 1 hour. The ricotta is ready when it has turned light brown and shrunk to half its original height. It will feel firm to the touch. Take out of the oven and let cool for at least half an hour.

4 When ready to serve, cut into 2 in. (5 cm) squares. Using a spatula, lift the pieces and arrange on a presentation plate. Pour heavy cream evenly over the ricotta squares. Crush pistachios and sprinkle decoratively over all.

Total prep time: 10 minutes.
Total baking time: 1 hour.
Rest time: at least 30 minutes.
Serves 4–6.

Wrenn's Ricotta Pie

Cooking for the same movie crew for a stretch of many weeks while stuck in an exotic location (like the wilds of Newfoundland) and running out of new desserts is no laughing matter. An emergency phone call to Wrenn Goodrum in New York produced this lovely, no-bake cheesecake, reminiscent of Italian cannoli, without any of the fuss. It's not exactly diet material, but then again what proper dessert is?

INGREDIENTS

1 cup (250 mL) graham cracker crumbs

¼ cup (50 mL) unsalted butter, melted

1 tbsp. (15 mL) sugar

1 tbsp. (15 mL) unsalted butter

¾ cup (175 mL) slivered almonds

1 lb. (500 g) ricotta cheese

¼ cup (50 mL) sugar

½ cup (125 mL) bittersweet chocolate chips

1 tbsp. (15 mL) Amaretto liqueur

½ cup (125 mL) 35% cream

Note: The 2 almond requirements of this recipe can be satisfied by 200 g raw slivered almonds.

PREPARATION

1 Preheat oven to 350° F (180° C). In a bowl, combine graham cracker crumbs (either ready-bought or processed by you from whole graham crackers), melted butter and 1 tbsp. (15 mL) sugar. Mix together with a fork until you've obtained a mealy, paste-like texture.

2 Choose a round ovenproof dish about 12 in. (30 cm) in diameter and about 2 in. (5 cm) deep. Grease the pan with 1 tbsp.

(15 mL) unsalted butter. Transfer the graham cracker crust to the dish and distribute, pressing down to cover the entire bottom (it's not necessary to cover the sides).

3 Place the raw slivered almonds in an oven pan and spread them in a single layer. Bake both items (the crust in the dish, and the almonds in the pan) in the pre-heated oven for 10–12 minutes. Take them out of the oven and let them cool to room temperature. (This will mean a wait of 45 minutes or more.)

4 When the almond slivers have cooled, divide them in half. Reserve one half for the final garnish. Process the other half in a food processor to the consistency of coarse meal. Reserve.

5 In a working bowl, combine ricotta cheese with ¼ cup (50 mL) sugar. Blend thoroughly. Then add the processed almonds, chocolate chips and Amaretto. Beat well until you have a smooth, soft mixture speckled with ground almonds and chocolate chips.

6 Whip the cream until stiff. Fold gently but thoroughly into the cheese mixture.

7 Spoon the cheese-cream mixture evenly onto the cooled, baked crust. Garnish with reserved almond slivers from step #4, studding them over the entire surface. Cover with food wrap and refrigerate for at least 2 hours (3–4 are even better). When the cheese stiffens the dessert is ready.

Total crust time: 18–20 minutes.
Total cooling time: 45 minutes.
Filling and topping time:
30 minutes.
Chilling time: at least 2 hours.
Serves 8–12.

Tiremisu

Tiremisu means, literally, "pick-me-up." This is a soft, trifle-like dessert with a sodden crust and a super-rich topping. It has become such a favourite that restaurants charge handsomely for it, even though it's simple to make and rather basic in its expense. Mascarpone is an Italian cream cheese, whose 50% butter fat content is a real assault on one's health consciousness (if not, in actuality, one's health). You can replace it with ricotta or even creamed cottage cheese, but it won't taste the same. Lady fingers are light, airy spongecakes, golden-yellow with a light glaze on one side. The best ones are imported from Italy or France and are widely available.

INGREDIENTS

7 oz. (200 g) Mascarpone cheese

2 cups (500 mL) strong coffee, preferably espresso

1 lemon

2 eggs

3 tbsp. (45 mL) sugar

pinch cinnamon

24 imported lady-finger biscuits

1½ tbsp. (22 mL) best-quality unsweetened cocoa

1 package (300 g) frozen raspberries

PREPARATION AND ASSEMBLY

1 Remove Mascarpone cheese from the fridge. Let come to room temperature and soften.

2 Meanwhile, make some strong coffee, preferably espresso. You will need 2 cups (500 mL). Pour coffee into a wide bowl to cool.

3 Zest 1 lemon and reserve the zest. (Then juice the lemon for another use; zested citrus fruits dehydrate quickly if not used promptly.)

4 Separate eggs. Reserve yolks in a working bowl. Put whites into the bowl of a mixer.

5 Add sugar to the egg yolks. Using a wire whisk, beat mixture until it's foamy and canary-yellow, and comes off the whisk in ribbons. Add the softened Mascarpone, lemon zest and a pinch of cinnamon. Whisk until the mixture is homogeneous and smooth. Reserve.

6 Choose a rectangular presentation dish large enough to hold all the biscuits in one layer, and about 2 in. (5 cm) deep. Dunk one lady finger at a time in the coffee to drench completely, then quickly (before it disintegrates) place in the dish. Continue aligning dunked biscuits, until the whole surface of the dish is covered with this coffee-sodden "crust."

7 Beat egg whites in the mixer at high speed until stiff (4–5 minutes). Transfer onto the cheese mixture in the working bowl. Fold these ingredients together, using a spatula in a circular motion, until the whites are completely incorporated (do not beat: this would deflate the whites).

8 Smooth this icing evenly over the biscuit crust. Put cocoa into a shaker (or use a very fine strainer) and sprinkle a good layer over the icing (the surface should be completely dusted with cocoa). Cover with food wrap and refrigerate at least 2 hours to become firm and develop flavour.

9 Meanwhile, prepare the garnish: Defrost frozen raspberries. When quite soft, process or blend them (with 1 tbsp./15 mL sugar, if you insist) to create a sauce, or "coulis." Stir to homogenize, and reserve until ready to use.

10 To serve, smear 2 tbsp. (30 mL) of the raspberry sauce on each dessert plate. Then carefully place scoops of Tiremisu on top of the sauce. You should finish the portions that have crust on the bottom and icing on top.

Total time: 45 minutes.
Chilling time: 2 hours.
Serves 8–10.

Fried Pineapple

Here's one for those days when time is of the essence, but not at the expense of forgoing dessert altogether. Assuming that your larder is already equipped with such dessert staples as sugar, unsalted butter, raw cashews and bittersweet chocolate, all you need from the store is a ripe pineapple, and then 10 quick minutes of easy tasks.

INGREDIENTS

1 oz. (28 g) bittersweet
   chocolate (one square)
½ ripe pineapple

2 tbsp. (30 mL) sugar
2 tbsp. (30 mL) unsalted butter
¼ cup (50 mL) whole raw
   cashews

PREPARATION

1 Grate the chocolate and reserve.

2 Cut a pineapple in two crosswise. Wrap half and reserve in the fridge for another use. Peel the other half and cut into rounds ½ in. (1 cm) thick. Spread sugar on a plate; dredge the pineapple slices in the sugar.

COOKING

3 Heat butter in a saute pan over high heat until it bubbles (don't let it burn).

4 Add the sugar-dredged pineapple to the pan. Fry over high heat for 2 minutes. Sprinkle cashews in the spaces around the edge of the pan. Make sure they all hit the hot fat. Turn the pineapple and fry the flip-side for 2–3 minutes, taking a bit of time also to turn the cashews as they brown. At the end of this time, the sugar will begin to caramelize, and the cashews will have browned. Remove pan from heat.

5 Lay out 4 dessert plates. Transfer one slice of fried pineapple per plate and sprinkle 1 tsp. (5 mL) or so of the grated chocolate on each slice. Spoon cashews evenly on or around each slice of pineapple. Using a rubber spatula, scrape whatever juices remain in the pan onto the pineapple. Serve immediately.

Total prep time: 6–7 minutes.
Total cooking time: 5–6 minutes.

Serves 4. Note: The old trick for choosing a ripe pineapple was to pull one of its top leaves to see if it comes off easily. It doesn't hurt also to squeeze the pineapple and see if it's soft — a much better indication of its ripeness.

Chocolate Fondue

This one is for lovers. The two of you can invoke St. Valentine any day of the year with a pot of melted chocolate, some fruit, biscuits and a lot of affection.

INGREDIENTS

3½ oz. (100 g) fine chocolate, preferably bittersweet

2 tbsp. (30 mL) Frangelico liqueur

1 tbsp. (15 mL) water

asssorted imported biscuits (wafers, piroulines, petits-beurres, shortbreads)

assorted fruit slices (plum, peach, banana, mango, starfruit)

PREPARATION

1 Melting chocolate is one occasion when I don't mind using a microwave oven (cooking bacon is another). If you don't have a microwave pour 3–4 cups (750–1000 mL) water into a pot and place over medium heat until the water heats up.

Then place a smaller pot inside the first one, making sure that the bottom of the smaller pot is just above water level. (This is a makeshift bain-marie, or double boiler. If you're lucky enough to possess the genuine article, then use it.) When the water of the bottom pot comes to the boil, reduce heat to simmer, so that only a steady steam rises. Place chocolate (broken into pieces), Frangelico and water into the top part of the double boiler. Cover, and let melt for 10–15 minutes.

2 While the chocolate melts,

choose your prettiest serving platter. Decorate the edges with assorted biscuits, slices of fruit and two dainty forks. Leave a space in the middle for the chocolate.

3 Check the chocolate after 10 minutes. Test by poking it with a fork: if it goes right through with no resistance, the chocolate is ready. If not, continue cooking for up to 5 minutes more. When the chocolate is extremely soft (miraculously, it still retains its shape), remove the double boiler from the heat. Using a fork or a small whisk, beat the chocolate for 1–2 minutes to incorporate the liquids into it. This will yield a thick and runny sauce, hopefully without lumps.

SERVING

4 Transfer the chocolate to a beautiful bowl (crystal is best) and position bowl in the centre of your serving platter. Now you and your mate are free to cuddle up and dip fruit and biscuits into the chocolate while whispering sweet nothings into each other's ear.

Total time: 15–20 minutes. Serves 2. For orgies, increase quantity accordingly.

Tom and Gerry's
New Orleans Bread Pudding

Tom Hanes, gentleman chef from the Old South and proud owner of the erstwhile (but fondly remembered) Tom and Gerry's Louisiana Eatery in Toronto, gave me this recipe for the famous Creole dessert based on humble, leftover bread. I knew it in Quebec as pudding du chômeur ("pudding of the unemployed"): yet another Acadian connection between the two French-speaking centres of North America.

INGREDIENTS

4 thick slices dry bread
1 tsp. plus 1 tsp. (5 mL + 5 mL) unsalted butter
¼ cup (50 mL) pecan halves
3 oz. (90 mL) currants
4 eggs
1½ cups (375 mL) sugar
1 tsp. (5 mL) ground nutmeg
¼ tsp. (1 mL) cinnamon
¼ cup (50 mL) unsalted butter
2 cups (500 mL) cold homo milk
1 tsp. (5 mL) vanila essence

2 tbsp. (30 mL) bourbon whiskey

LEMON-BOURBON SAUCE
1½ lemons
½ cup plus ¼ cup (125 mL + 50 mL) water
1 cup (250 mL) sugar
2 tbsp. (30 mL) bourbon whiskey
1 tsp. (5 mL) vanilla essence
2 tbsp. (30 mL) cornstarch

PREPARATION

1 Cut 4 thick 1 in. (2 cm) slices of white bread and let them dry out for 24 hours (or use leftover dry bread). Cut the dry bread into ½ in. (1 cm) cubes. (This quantity should make 4 packed cups of bread cubes.)

2 Choose a deep ovenproof dish (a souffle dish works well) and grease its entire surface, bottom and sides, with 1 tsp. (5 mL) unsalted butter. Transfer the bread cubes to the dish.

3 Melt another 1 tsp. (5 mL) unsalted butter in a saute pan over high heat. Add pecan halves and toss-fry them for 2–3 minutes until shiny and brown (do not burn them). Add this to the bread cubes; then add the currants. Mix well.

4 Crack eggs into the bowl of a mixer and start the beaters. Begin adding sugar in a steady, thin stream. Once it's all in, beat 3–4 minutes at high speed until thick, foamy and canary-yellow. Add nutmeg and cinnamon. Continue beating for 1 minute longer. Reserve in the mixer.

5 Melt butter in a small pot over medium heat. Remove from heat and add milk, vanilla and bourbon. Mix, then add to the eggs in a quick stream while beating at

medium speed. Add this mixture to the bread cubes in the dish. Fold to submerge the bread (some of which will bob to the surface). Cover the dish and let rest for 20-30 minutes, to allow the bread to absorb the liquids.

6 Meanwhile, preheat the oven to 350° F (180° C). To make the sauce: Zest 1½ lemons and reserve zest. Squeeze the lemons and transfer strained juice to a small pot. Add ½ cup (125 mL) water and sugar. Stir, then place over high heat until mixture comes to the boil. Stir to dissolve the sugar.

7 In a small bowl combine ¼ cup (50 mL) water, bourbon and vanilla. Add cornstarch and stir to dissolve. When the lemon syrup in the pot has reached the boil, reduce heat to low and add the dissolved cornstarch mixture. Cook over low heat, stirring gently yet continuously, for 4–5 minutes, until the sauce has thickened and there are shiny bubbles. Stir in reserved lemon zest. Cover and let cool.

BAKING

8 Uncover the pudding in the ovenproof dish. Most of the liquid will have been absorbed. Give the pudding another fold (without mashing the wet bread) and place it in the preheated oven. Bake for 40 minutes, then increase the temperature to 425° F (220° C) and bake an additional 10 minutes to brown the top. (These times are accurate for a gas oven. Electric ovens tend to brown the top prematurely and you must watch for this. If the top begins to brown before the first 40 minutes are up, cover the pudding loosely with tin foil. Then uncover, and proceed with the increased temperature for the last 10 minutes as above.) Remove from oven. (Pudding should now be puffed up and browned.) Let cool for 20–30 minutes, during which time it will deflate a bit.

9 Ideally, this pudding should be enjoyed after its initial cooling, while it's still lukewarm. If you must let it wait, then warm it in a 250° F (115° C) oven for 10 minutes before serving. The pudding can be served directly from its dish by scooping it out like a souffle, or it can be unmolded: Run a knife around the edge to unstick the sides and immerse the bottom of the dish in a bowl of warm water for 30 seconds. Wipe the bottom and, holding a presentation plate over it, invert it and tap it once. The pudding should fall right onto the plate. Portion it out onto dessert plates. Streak some of the lemon-bourbon sauce on top and serve. Offer leftover sauce at table.

Initial pudding assembly:
20 minutes.
Absorption and sauce making:
20–30 minutes.
Baking: 50 minutes.
Cooling off time: 20–30 minutes.
Serves 6–8.

Ingredient Index